APPLIED ECONOMICS Made Simple

The Made Simple series
has been created
primarily for self-education
but can equally well
be used as
an aid to group study.
However complex the subject,
the reader is taken
step by step,
clearly and methodically,
through the course. Each volume
has been prepared by experts,
using throughout the
Made Simple technique of teaching.
Consequently the gaining
of knowledge now becomes
an experience to be enjoyed.

Bal. of payments p. 98

In the same series

Accounting
Acting and Stagecraft
Additional Mathematics
Advertising
Anthropology
Applied Economics
Applied Mathematics
Applied Mechanics
Art Appreciation
Art of Speaking
Art of Writing
Biology
Book-keeping
British Constitution
Calculus
Chemistry
Childcare
Commerce
Commercial Law
Company Administration
Computer Programming
Cookery
Cost and Management Accounting
Data Processing
Dressmaking
Economic History
Economics
Electricity
Electronic Computers
Electronics
English
French
Geology
German
Human Anatomy
Italian
Journalism
Latin
Law
Management
Marketing
Mathematics
New Mathematics
Office Practice
Organic Chemistry
Philosophy
Photography
Physics
Pottery
Psychology
Rapid Reading
Russian
Salesmanship
Soft Furnishing
Spanish
Statistics
Transport and Distribution
Typing

APPLIED ECONOMICS Made Simple

Derek T. Lobley, B.A. (Econ.)

Made Simple Books
W. H. ALLEN London
A Howard & Wyndham Company

Made and printed in Great Britain
by Richard Clay (The Chaucer Press), Ltd, Bungay, Suffolk
for the publishers W. H. Allen & Co., Ltd.
44 Hill Street, London, W1X 8LB

First edition, February 1972
Second (revised) edition, October 1974
Third (revised) edition, April 1976

ISBN 0 491 01812 6 Paperbound

Foreword

Applied Economics is the name given to the study of economic policy. The subject constitutes an important part of courses leading to the Higher National Certificate and Higher National Diploma in Business Studies, and of CNAA degree courses as well as the final examinations of many professional bodies. This book has been written with students on such courses especially in mind, particularly HNC students studying on a part-time basis. They should find that the book covers the bulk of their first year's work in Applied Economics, while pointing clear signposts to the further areas of study to be undertaken in subsequent years. At the same time it is hoped that it will be of use to students at other stages of their study of economics—those studying at Advanced Level and those in the first year of University courses. The book is also designed to appeal to the intelligent layman who wants to be able to relate important matters of current affairs, such as the level of unemployment, the impact of strikes, and the balance of payments to certain basic principles. For this reason the subject-matter is treated descriptively and analytically.

The scope of the subject of Applied Economics is so wide that some selection is inevitable. I have included the topics that are usually found in the first year HNC and HND courses and which arouse the greatest interest among students. But no single book can meet the student's requirements. Accordingly a brief bibliography is attached to each chapter, and the student is advised to keep abreast of current economic matters by regularly referring to *The Economist*; the *Financial Times*; the *Bank of England Quarterly Bulletin* and the quarterly Bank Reviews published by the Clearing Banks.

A large number of tables and diagrams are included in the text. It is recommended that the student studies these closely as the information they convey is not necessarily fully repeated in the text. The student may acquire the current figures by reference to the Annual Abstract of Statistics, the Blue Book of National Income and Expenditure, Financial Statistics, the Monthly Digest of Statistics and other Government publications.

In writing this book I have received the assistance of a large number of people. In particular I should like to thank the Controller of H.M. Stationery Office for allowing me to draw heavily on many Government publications, which are individually acknowledged; the publishers of *Barclays Bank Review* and the Central Electricity Generating Board for allowing me to reproduce diagrams; the Bank of England for tables from the Quarterly Bulletin; and the IMF and IBRD group for a large amount of information contained in Chapters Eight and Ten: their publication, *Finance and Development*, is an invaluable commentary on the activities of these institutions.

Finally, I must acknowledge my indebtedness to three individuals: to my colleague Mr. Geoffrey Whitehead for his encouragement and criticism during the preparation of the manuscript; to Mr. Leslie Allan for his perceptive reading of the typescript; and to my wife who prepared the typescript and to whom this book is dedicated.

DEREK LOBLEY

Table of Contents

CHAPTER ONE

THE AIMS OF ECONOMIC POLICY

(1) Introduction

If the aim of economic activity is the production of goods and services for the satisfaction of human wants, the broad aim of economic policy may be regarded as ensuring that as many as possible of those wants are satisfied. But the object of economic policy is not simply to ensure the maximization of production. There are, for example, many different kinds of wants to be met, and one of the problems to be solved by economic policy-makers is the correct balance between the various claims on resources. It will be convenient to consider the aims of economic activity in two broad categories—**macro-economic objectives** concerned with the economy as a whole, and **micro-economic objectives** concerned with various sectors of the economy. In practice, of course, such a distinction is an artificial one: it is not possible to pursue macro-economic aims without at the same time furthering or jeopardizing micro-economic aims. But this broad division does help us to realize the difficulties facing the Government in its economic policy.

(2) Macro-economic Aims

Full Employment. The maintenance of full employment is regarded by Western Governments as one of their major obligations, and the achievement of full employment is felt by many commentators to be an end in itself. But while there are powerful sociological and humanitarian arguments for securing full employment, its achievement may be regarded principally as a means to an end. Although at times of extremely high unemployment the Government has been forced to employ labour on less than top priority public works schemes, the real reason for aiming for full employment is to secure the production of goods and services desired by consumers on the one hand and entrepreneurs on the other. In practice it is impossible to achieve literally full employment (see Chapter Three) and, because of the pressures that its achievement would generate, Governments are normally satisfied with something just under 100 per cent full employment. In 1944 the Government felt that 3 per cent unemployed would constitute full employment. It is conventional to measure unemployment in terms of the amount of labour unemployed, but it is frequently not only the output of labour that is foregone but also the output of the machinery that the labour would be using. Sometimes, of course, labour will be unemployed *because* machinery is doing its work and in this case it is the Government's task to create an economic climate in which new jobs are open to absorb the newly redundant labour.

Economic Growth. The principal economic reason for aiming for full employment is to produce more goods and services, and it is the production of more goods and services each year that gives a rough indication of the extent of economic growth. It is a basic tenet of economic thinking that man's wants are insatiable. Once he has satisfied the needs of subsistence he raises his sights and continues to do so every time a new level is reached: in California the two-car family is poverty-stricken; already in Britain schools are designed with pupils' car parks rather than bicycle sheds; push-bikes, like wash-boards, are in danger of being relegated to museums, coloured television is ousting the black-and-white version, and automatic dishwashers are replacing the human variety. All this and much more besides (the reader can probably think of a thousand examples) occurs in the name of economic growth, or in order to improve the standard of living. These two aims are to a certain extent in conflict since a high current standard of living means that resources are not put aside to encourage growth (see page 19). The main underlying concern of post-war British Governments has been to secure an adequate rate of economic growth, though for long periods this has given precedence to the solution of Balance of Payments problems. The blinkered pursuit of growth suggests to many that modern industrial societies have their priorities wrong; that once a reasonable level of material welfare has been achieved more attention should be focused on the costs of economic growth and on improving the 'quality of life' and to this end a Royal Commission on the Environment has been established.

However, for the present, the emphasis is placed on the rate of growth and without an adequate rate the provision of much urgently needed **social capital** becomes very difficult. (Social capital includes the whole range of amenities provided by Central and Local Governments—schools, hospitals, roads, swimming-pools, and so on.)

The aims of economic growth and full employment are compatible in some respects: if there are 750,000 unemployed, some growth will be generated if they can be brought into productive work. In the long run economic growth may necessitate some temporary unemployment as labour-saving methods are adopted, but this is a feature of growth that has been observed for the last two hundred years and the labour is normally quickly reabsorbed. Experience suggests that the faster the rate of growth the higher the level of employment. A further aim of economic policy does not fit so tidily into the pattern.

Price Stability. While the significance of an adequate rate of economic growth may elude many people, the desirability of steady prices is apparent to everyone. Public reaction to the long period of low economic growth in the United Kingdom since 1950 has been minimal; reaction to high unemployment is somewhat sharper but is reduced by various social security payments; but reaction to rising prices is much clearer and prolonged. The problems caused by inflation are discussed in Chapter Four, but we must note here that attempts by the British Government to achieve full employment in the 1950's and 1960's invariably led to rising prices. Because rising prices and a high level of demand produce an adverse Balance of Payments the Government then had to create unemployment in order to achieve reasonable stability of prices. Experience showed that once unemployment was around 2 per cent the severe inflationary pressure would be under control. Since 1971, however, prices have gone on rising even though unemployment has been as high as 4 or 5 per cent: this is one of the unresolved problems of economic policy.

Nor does the achievement of stable prices seem to fit in very well with the achievement of an acceptable rate of economic growth. This is mainly because, for reasons discussed later (see page 20), growth in the United Kingdom comes in fits and starts associated with the stop-go policies of successive Governments. Industry finds it difficult to plan on a long-term basis because even the medium-term prospects for the economy are not clear. Consequently, when the Government decides to expand the economy and to generate growth (which cannot be achieved merely by waving a magic wand) many industries respond merely by taking on more labour to utilize existing plant. Such measures quickly lead to the conflict between employment and price stability discussed above. If the Government's expansionary policy is to be successful it is essential that the means of generating growth are laid down before the period of expansion begins. This only brings us to another conflict: during a deflationary period businessmen will not take a very bright view of the future and will consequently be reluctant to invest in new machinery which may not be used to its full capacity; but after a period in recession businessmen will expect the level of activity to begin to increase and to the extent that they begin to invest in anticipation of the upturn the expectations become self-realizing: investment, the seed of economic growth, rises. Because of the other pressures on resources at this time it becomes almost impossible to control prices and the brakes are applied again: growth like full employment yields precedence to price stability.

It is not usually the desire for stable prices that dictates policy in this way. Inflation must be controlled for the sake of securing a reasonable surplus on the Balance of Payments—the fourth aim of economic policy.

A Balance of Payments Surplus. If we lived in a closed economy, with no international trade at all, the combined aim of full employment, reasonable growth, and price stability would make a difficult target. In the very open economy in which we actually operate the combination of these three with a Balance of Payments surplus has presented a problem beyond solution so far as United Kingdom Governments have been concerned. In fact each of the first three aims conspires to sabotage the achievement of the fourth: the attempt to secure faster economic growth leads to falling unemployment and rising prices which leads to an external deficit. The removal of the external deficit then assumes priority and until a surplus is achieved the three domestic aims are forgotten.

The priority accorded to the Balance of Payments stems from the international economic framework. This is fully explained in Chapters Seven and Eight and here it is sufficient to note that of the two elements comprising international prices, one, the exchange rate of one currency against all others is virtually frozen for long periods at a time: devaluation is frowned upon by the international monetary authorities. Any adjustment to relative international prices must therefore be achieved via the other component—domestic costs or prices. The object of increasing unemployment is to reduce price inflation to secure a Balance of Payments surplus to preserve the exchange rate—the totem-pole of international economics.

In the case of the United Kingdom the fact that other countries keep their reserves (their means of payment) in the form of sterling provides an extra disincentive to devaluation, since a reduction in the exchange value of sterling automatically reduces those countries' reserves.

Here, then, we have the major constraint on an expansionary economic policy. Nothing can be done without considering its effect on the Balance of Payments. Perhaps the greatest irony is that Balance of Payments problems as we know them are of man's own making: by allowing exchange rates to fluctuate freely surplus and deficits could be eliminated, though the costs of free rates in other respects may be too high (see page 134).

So far we have examined what may be described as the major aims of macro-economic policy. There are at least two further aims which add to the complexity of the Government's problems.

The Distribution of Income. The Government must concern itself not only with increasing the size of the national income but also with its distribution. Table 1 shows the differences in personal income and Table 2 estimated differences in personal wealth. Policies of Governments of left and right have both incorporated schemes to reduce the inequality.

Progressive taxation of income and capital combined with a wider variety of welfare payments constitute the main policies. Desirable as it probably is

Table 1. Distribution of Personal Income (1971–2)

Lower limit of range of income	Number of incomes (000's)	Income before tax (£ millions)
All incomes	20,970	35,599
Income before tax		
420	699	323
500	891	491
600	1,041	677
700	1,019	765
800	2,183	1,963
1,000	4,961	6,201
1,500	4,492	7,828
2,000	4,106	9,807
3,000	1,187	4,337
5,000	323	2,124
10,000	58	757
20,000	10	325

Source: Annual Abstract of Statistics.

Table 2. Estimated Wealth of Individuals in Great Britain (1973)

£	Number of cases (000's)	£'000 millions
Not over 10,000	13,879	46·2
10,000–15,000	1,500	18·6
15,000–20,000	503	8·9
20,000–25,000	303	7·3
25,000–50,000	522	18·9
50,000–100,000	210	13·7
100,000–200,000	70	9·0
200,000	30	15·8
	17,017	138·4

Source: Annual Abstract of Statistics.

to aim for greater equality, it cannot be achieved without jeopardizing some of the major aims: taxing the rich for example may divert funds from investment in the private sector thus inhibiting growth; and it may reduce the supply of executive labour; excessive welfare payments will generate inflation, and may reduce the supply of manual labour. Similar problems are involved in considering the balance between the public sector and the private sector.

The Balance Between Sectors. The **private sector** embraces all those activities undertaken by private individuals either on their own behalf or on behalf of a private institution. The **public sector** includes all the activities conducted by the Central Government, Local Authorities, or such bodies as Public Corporations acting on behalf of the Government. One of the objects of economic policy is to achieve a proper balance between the two sectors. The difficulty is to decide what is the proper balance or indeed whether there should be any balance—one solution would be to abolish the private sector altogether. Since this is a remote possibility the Government must take action to influence the allocation of resources between sectors: labour and capital cannot be used for building cars as well as building hospitals and schools. The allocation that is achieved will affect the major aims outlined above, and will also have an important influence on the micro-economic aims of Government. One of the paradoxes of economic policy is that while the public sector is most easily expanded and contracted, it is in many ways providing the most important services, and as a result credit squeezes have to be aimed at the private sector.

(3) Micro-economic Aims

The borderline between micro- and macro-economics is an indistinct one. Many topics have a foot in each camp: taxation, for example, is used primarily as a means of influencing the general level of economic activity, but it necessarily has micro-economic effects. The Government may decide that an increase in taxation is necessary to reduce the overall pressure of demand. The effects of that increase in taxation will depend on whether purchase tax or income tax is raised; and in the case of a rise in purchase tax, on the commodities that are chosen to bear the extra tax.

In many other areas the borderline is blurred, but it is convenient to isolate two of many micro-economic aims.

Regional Development. If economic growth is to be adequate, and the level of employment satisfactory it is important that all resources should be properly used. Even if the overall level of unemployment is at a level of 1½ per cent the Government cannot be happy if there are areas where it reaches 4 per cent; if the overall rate of growth is 3 per cent per annum it is inadequate if some regions are not growing at all. Because macro-economic policies are not designed to deal with problems of this kind, successive Governments have found it necessary to introduce policies specially designed to ensure the proper use of resources throughout the country.

Competition. Although the conditions of perfect competition exist only in the textbook, post-war Governments have been anxious to ensure that obstacles to competition are removed, in the belief that this will facilitate the best uses of resources.

The ostensible desire for competition has to be modified in the light of certain social and political objections: if wages were left simply to the forces of supply and demand, unwarrantable hardship might be inflicted on those in declining industries; completely free trade would force most British farmers out of business; a private market in education would lead to the severe underuse of important talents, and so on.

The pursuit of these and other aims necessitates Government intervention in the economy, if only as a kind of referee. But it is not sufficient to accept that the Government needs to interfere without trying to decide on the amount of intervention that is necessary.

The broad alternatives available are:

(*a*) not to intervene at all or,
(*b*) to adopt a middle course and intervene only in certain areas or,
(*c*) to abolish free markets entirely;

(4) The Free Economy

No one has proclaimed the virtue of the free economy more eloquently than Adam Smith in the *Wealth of Nations*, and while it is a rather weighty volume the reader is strongly advised to read at least the opening chapters of it.

In a completely free, capitalist economy the allocation of resources depends upon the profit motive. Where profits are good and entrepreneurs or shareholders get a good return on the capital they have invested new capital will be attracted and the industry will expand. Where demand for a product is low and profits consequently inadequate, new capital will not be forthcoming, existing equipment will not be renewed, and the industry will decline.

In such a system consumers' spending power may be compared to economic votes: by buying particular commodities they vote for the continued existence of the industries producing those commodities; by withholding expenditure they vote for the decline of particular industries. Even if the Government intervenes to delay the decline of such industries economic forces are likely to prevail eventually—but even without Government interference it may take many years for the industry to disappear.

Not only shareholders and their capital are subject to market forces in a completely free economy: the wages paid for different kinds of labour will depend on the demand for that labour relative to supply: those without the skills or other attributes that happen to be in demand will suffer from cuts in wages, only those in possession of skills in short supply would enjoy wage increases.

The underlying assumption of such a system is that in pursuing his own best interest the individual will inevitably contribute to the common good. We shall see throughout this book that there is often a conflict between individual and community interests and the State has to intervene to protect the community against the individual. The reader should note that this does not really amount to a criticism of a free economy since the State is frequently interfering to prevent monopolists exploiting their position—whether they are monopolists in the form of shareholders or in the form of trade unions. We may conclude that an economy free of State intervention is an impossibility since it is at the mercy of great concentrations of power.

(5) The Mixed Economy

The Decline of Free Trade. The free economy does not and cannot exist outside the textbook. Economic laws of supply and demand and profit cannot exist in a vacuum. Political, sociological, ethical, and geographical factors need to be assessed before the Government can take economic policy decisions. If this were not so, economics would be a far more exact science than it is, and economists would probably be subject to far less abuse for matters which are well outside their main field of interest. The example of the nationalized industries illustrates the point. On economic grounds there could be no case for the railways operating on the scale that they were in 1960. The bulk of the system would have been closed down by private enterprise. But the Government decided that there were good social and political reasons for the system to remain intact—even though the majority of users were not prepared to pay the economic cost of the services they were using.

In many other fields the Government has found it necessary to intervene to prevent the operation of economic forces, and to protect individual groups of the population against abuse.

The whole history of the nineteenth century is full of examples of the Government intervening to wean the economy away from *laissez-faire* principles—except in the field of free trade where it was not only in accord with the principles of Adam Smith but also in the interest of the United Kingdom to remove all obstacles. In the domestic economy the Factory Acts, Education Acts, Railway Acts, and Trade Union legislation all indicate areas in which a free market was not considered to provide the best solution. And the mass of legislation of any of the post-war years is an indication of the extent of the erosion of market forces: if the Government does not plan the economy then big business will.

But to what extent is it legitimate to say that the Government does plan the economy?

British Economic Planning. All economies are planned to some extent. Governments, we have seen, have a variety of economic aims and they must plan to achieve them, however obliquely. The very use of fiscal or monetary policy presupposes certain targets and to this extent some planning normally exists. In this case the plan is usually the control of the level of demand.

Normally the planning is rather more positive than this. In the United Kingdom planning was at its most rigid during and immediately after the war, when a great array of direct controls was established to ensure the most appropriate use of scarce resources, and to safeguard the Balance of Payments.

The planning of the 1960's has derived from the low rate of economic growth achieved in Britain compared with our main competitors (see Chapter Two). It was to improve this particular aspect of economic performance that the **National Economic Development Council** was established in 1961. There were already in existence a number of advisory bodies, but the NEDC, with a permanent secretariat in the form of the National Economic Development Office was envisaged as a rather more powerful body, specifically designed to identify the reasons for the poor growth rate and to point the way to a better performance. The initial basis of the work of the NEDC was an industrial survey seeking information on the likely output of industry by 1966 on the assumption of a 4 per cent growth rate. The trouble was that no one really expected the economy to grow at 4 per cent, a rate well in excess of the rates actually achieved in previous years. In effect the survey published in 1963, *Growth of the United Kingdom Economy to 1966*, was a projection of the best that could be achieved if everything went right. In practice everything did not go right: the Balance of Payments collapsed in 1964 and any hope of a 4 per cent growth rate collapsed with it. In any case the NEDC was soon to adopt a secondary role in economic planning.

An important development under the NEDC was the establishment of a number of Economic Development Committees for particular industries. These committees with members from both sides of the industries and from the Government have the task of investigating performance in the industry and making recommendations as to its future development.

In 1964 the NEDC was superseded as the main planning authority by the Department of Economic Affairs, which, led by the then Mr. George Brown, set about the construction of the National Plan.

Like the NEDC plan the National Plan was based on a wide industrial inquiry 'to elicit the facts not simply about the past but about future intentions, potentialities, and problems'. All plans must have a target and the National Plan sought a growth rate of 3·8 per cent per annum—less optimistic than the NEDC but still substantially higher than anything recently achieved.

The National Plan is now of largely historical interest for its objectives were really impossible from the outset. It acknowledged that its accomplishment depended on the successful removal of the Balance of Payments problem. Devaluation being ruled out this initial requirement could not be met and the remaining objectives collapsed as well. But planning of a kind continues—successive Governments have tried with mixed success to plan the growth of incomes; to secure economic growth; to encourage the development of the regions, even setting up Regional Economic Planning Councils (see Chapter Thirteen).

However such planning is indicative, and at best marginal. It tries to indicate what is wanted but does not supersede the market. Most decisions are left to the market: British planning tries merely to influence the market, not replace it. In other countries planning is much more positive: decisions are made not through the market but by the appropriate planning committee. In this case the Civil Servant or politician is assumed to know better than the consumer how resources should be used. But between these two sorts of planning lie many compromises, with Government intervention varying from country to country according to individual needs, usually being greater in the underdeveloped countries than in the industrialized ones (see Chapter Ten).

(6) The Scope of the Book

This book is an examination of the major aims of economic policy and the effectiveness of Government policies in achieving those aims. The topics mentioned in this chapter and summarized below are examined in greater detail in the chapters that follow. Each topic has its own historical background, its present situation, and its likely future development. For the most part problems are considered in the context of United Kingdom experience, but where appropriate international comparisons are included. It is assumed that the student has studied basic economic principles and is ready to examine the problems of society in the light of those principles.

(7) Summary of Chapter One

(1) The aim of economic activity is the production of goods and services for the satisfaction of human wants.

(2) The purpose of economic policy is to facilitate the production of goods and services, while exercising a general supervision over conflicting claims on the resources of the economy.

(3) The aims may be divided into macro-economic aims which include the achievement of full employment, an adequate rate of economic growth, price stability, and a Balance of Payments surplus; and micro-economic aims such as the control of industrial location and monopoly.

(4) The framework within which economic activity takes place varies from country to country.

(5) At one extreme there is the completely free economy in which all decisions are made through the action of market forces.

(6) In practice Governments are forced to intervene in the market to prevent the exploitation of minority groups and to secure what they consider an appropriate allocation of resources.

(7) In the United Kingdom the two most noteworthy attempts at planning were those of the National Economic Development Council and the Department of Economic Affairs.

(8) These represented a form of indicative planning and were most noteworthy for their optimism. In other countries, especially the underdeveloped countries, more positive planning occurs.

(8) Suggested Further Reading

BRITTAN, S., *Steering the Economy*, Secker & Warburg, London, 1969.
CAVES, R. E. *et al*, *Britain's Economic Prospects*, Brookings Institution, New York, 1968.
LIPTON, M., *Assessing Economic Performance*, Staples Press, London, 1968.
WHITEHEAD, G., *Economics Made Simple*, W. H. Allen, London, 1970.

Exercises Set 1

1. What difficulties face the Government in determining its economic priorities?
2. Using the appropriate tables in the *Annual Abstract of Statistics*, comment on the recent performance of the United Kingdom economy under the headings: (*a*) employment; (*b*) price stability; (*c*) Balance of Payments.
3. How do you account for the increasing extent to which post-war Governments have found it necessary to intervene in the economy?
4. Distinguish between micro-economic and macro-economic problems.
5. What are the main aims of economic policy? To what extent are they incompatible?
6. To what extent is the United Kingdom a planned economy?
7. Trace the course of economic planning in Britain since 1945, commenting on the difficulties that have had to be overcome.
8. What would be the likely effects of leaving all economic decisions to market forces?
9. What are the principal dangers of an increasing proportion of economic activity being undertaken by the public sector?
10. Write a report on the present condition of the economy, recommending the changes in policy you believe necessary.

CHAPTER TWO

ECONOMIC GROWTH

(1) Introduction

Economic activity is concerned with the production of goods and services for human satisfaction. In order that consumption of those goods and services might increase each year the economy must grow.

For the best part of two hundred years from about 1750 economies were left to grow by themselves, and although this long period was characterized by a series of remarkably regular trade cycles, during which consumption and standards of living sometimes fell, it needs to be remembered much more for the great leap in wealth and income that occurred, especially since the beginning of this century.

The period since the Second World War has seen great attention paid to the process of economic growth; the forces that engender expansion; the changes that it involves; the benefits that accrue; and the disamenities that are created as an economy grows have all been brought under the economic microscope in recent years. While some aspects and requirements of growth may be the same in both advanced and backward economies the latter have special problems that do not exist for the industrialized regions and for this reason they are dealt with separately in Chapter Ten.

(2) Growth of What?

This is far from being a rhetorical question. Economists (and much less their critics) are by no means unanimous as to what constitutes economic growth. The commonest measure is that of national income and for some purposes it may be sufficient to conclude that if the national income has grown by x per cent there has been economic growth of x per cent. The difficulty immediately arises of deciding which national income is significant—Gross National Product at market price or at factor cost. (The measurement of these concepts is discussed on page 12.) Once this problem has been determined there are further obstacles to agreement.

The Standard of Living. Many feel that the Gross National Product itself is too crude a measure to use, and argue that it is the composition of that Product that is important: they are more interested in the level of consumption in relation to national income and might feel that even if the Gross National Product grew considerably there had been no worthwhile economic growth unless consumption (as opposed to exports or investment) had grown. (People who give priority to consumption are really interested in the current standard of living which is discussed on page 11.)

National Income per head. While many accept that the level of the Gross National Product or consumption can give a broad indication of the way the economy is developing most prefer to relate these quantities to the size of population, and to find a figure for the Gross National Product per head or consumption per head. This seems a more satisfactory approach but there are still difficulties: it has been pointed out elsewhere that some heads are bigger than others!*

* M. Lipton, *Assessing Economic Performance.*

Distribution of National Income. Moreover, like most averages the concept of national income per head disguises more than it reveals: it says nothing of the commodity structure of the national income, makes no allowance for the age structure of the population (though this latter can be achieved via rather complex statistical techniques), and makes no allowance for changes in quality. Since one of the purposes of growth is presumably to increase 'welfare' in some way, it would be helpful to know something of the distribution of the national income between rich and poor. There may be little point in generating great increases in income if the benefits go mainly to the rich who already have a very low marginal utility of income. Indeed if the object of economic growth is to achieve the greatest increase in the standard of living of the community it would be desirable at least in the short run for all the increase to go to the poor.

The Problem of Time. Further, there is the problem of time: is it this year's welfare that we should try to maximize? If so we should advocate heavy taxation of the rich and redistribution of income to encourage consumption. Or is it welfare in some future year that we should be concerned with? If so we ought perhaps to put more emphasis on encouraging investment, and reduce today's standards of living in order to improve tomorrow's. It is one of the major problems confronting Governments to strike a compromise between these two aims: a high standard of living this year necessitates a high level of consumption this year; but if resources are devoted to consumption, they cannot be used for the investment required to generate next year's production. It is one of the criticisms of post-war British economic policy that it has allowed too much consumption and achieved too little investment. However, let us suppose that we accept that the concept of national income per head gives an indication of the level of economic growth. Are there any further qualifications that should be made?

(3) Disutilities or Disamenities

It is rightly said that economic activity is concerned with the creation and distribution of utilities. The difficulty is that with our sights firmly fixed on this purpose and on the achievement of greater and better performance we tend to forget the mess that is left in the wake of progress. Frequently we read of rivers polluted by sewage and industrial effluent; of water contaminated by poisons carelessly dumped; of workers whose health has been ruined by contact with dangerous processes and substances. This is the result of industrialization; of the headlong rush for greater output. But this is not all. Tons of cement dust, sulphur, and other industrial effluent are deposited via the atmosphere on towns and villages windward of industrial areas, causing ill health, inconvenience, and not a little cost to ratepayers and local authorities. The motor manufacturers may proudly boast of a record output of 1,000,000 cars per year but as far as the community as a whole is concerned the traffic congestion, atmospheric pollution, and danger to life and limb may well be regarded as retrograde features of economic growth. The decline in the strength of community life in the United Kingdom in all but the remotest areas, the increasing pressures of the industrial life, the developing social problems such as drug-addiction, student violence and unrest, while not all directly and entirely ascribable to the desire for growth are yet illustrative of the disutilities that the emphasis on material economic growth may generate.

In micro-economic policy cost-benefit techniques (see page 204) can take some account of disutilities, but this is more difficult in macro-economics and we have to be satisfied with a mental note that even a 1 per cent growth of the Gross National Product creates some further disamenities, which detract from the standard of living. Nevertheless we still come back to the position that an increase in the Gross National Product per head is accepted as an indication of an increase in the standard of living and that for most purposes, especially in the short run, it is a reliable indicator. We conclude this discussion by noting one or two further modifications of this general point:

(*a*) We must make allowance for inflation. Thus, measured in current prices Britain's national income increased 130 per cent between 1963 and 1973, but in terms of 1970 prices the growth was only 30 per cent. Thus the bulk of the growth was attributable to rising prices. Moreover the distortions produced by inflation (see page 40) may have especially severe effects on the poor and their standard of living.

(*b*) Because the type of goods produced changes over a period of years there are dangers in comparing the national income over too long a period. Frozen foods, colour television, and jet aircraft were not available in 1938; and this makes valid comparisons between 1938 and 1976 difficult.

(*c*) As already mentioned the distribution between rich and poor and between consumption and investment are important. Moreover the standard of living depends partly on the redistributive effects of fiscal policy: a 50 per cent income tax on those earning over £10,000 to finance an increase in old-age pensions will probably increase the general standard of living while not necessarily affecting the size of the Gross National Product in the year in which it occurs.

(*d*) A whole range of non-economic factors needs to be borne in mind—for example a rise in national income per head accompanied by the loss of religious, political, or economic freedom may be regarded by many as leading to a lower standard of living.

(4) The Measurement of National Income

If we accept that the growth of national income or national income per head is what we mean by economic growth we must be clear exactly what is meant by that term. Figure 1 illustrates the working of a very simple economy of two sectors. The household sector has two functions, first to supply factors of production to the firms in exchange for wages, rent, interest, and profit, and second to spend their earnings on the goods they have helped to produce as owners of factors of production.

If we wish to measure the value of the Gross National Product we may do so in three ways: first we may count incomes at point 1 as people receive them, and although in practice there may be time-lags in the receipt of some incomes such as rent and dividends the total incomes received will be equal to the value of the goods produced—no more and no less. Alternatively, we could count the value of the output of all firms as it is produced at point 2, and finally we could count the expenditure of the households on the goods produced at points 3. In each case the result should be the same.

For example, if a car is made for £2,000 (no expenditure taxes) wages and salaries might amount to £900, rent of property to £400, and interest charges £400, leaving £300 for eventual distribution to shareholders. Thus the income derived from production of the car amounts to exactly £2,000. The person who buys the car spends £2,000 and the value of the car is £2,000.

In practice there are certain complications. Table 3 gives the figures for the Gross National Product for 1973. The following points are important.

Income Method. In the personal sector are included only those incomes received in exchange for goods and services provided in the relevant year. Thus wages, rent, profit, and most interest payments are included, but receipts such as retirement pensions, students' grants, interest on Government securities (which constitutes the National Debt), and receipts from private sales of

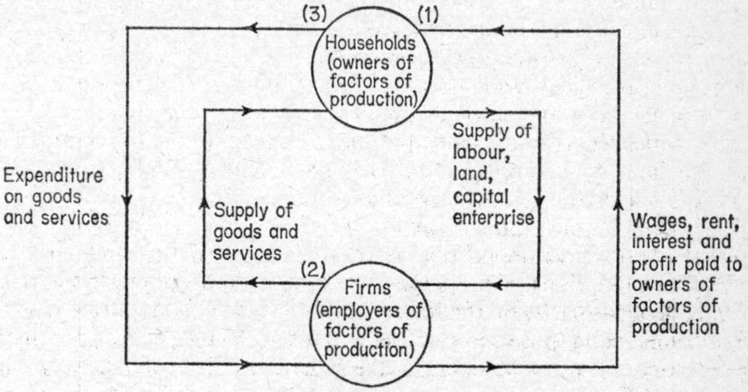

Fig. 1. The circular flow of income

second-hand goods need to be rigorously excluded so that the size of the Gross National Product is not exaggerated. Such payments are regarded as *transfer payments* or incomes which are received although no economic service is rendered in exchange at the time.

The undistributed profits of firms are included since they represent that part of annual production which does not immediately become personal income but which is nevertheless part of the Gross National Product. Similarly the surplus of Government enterprise must be included, just as the profits of private enterprise are included either as personal income or as undistributed profits. If these items were ignored the size of the Gross National Product would vary according to the freedom of the dividend policy of firms and to the size of the public sector. Finally, it should be noted that this method and the next gives us *Gross National Product at factor cost*—that is it measures the full cost of producing the goods and services that make up the national income, but ignores the effect of indirect taxes and subsidies.

Output Method. The main difficulty here is to avoid double counting. Therefore it is the net output of each enterprise that is included. Sometimes this is referred to as the *value added* method since we count the value added to raw materials and components by the labour and capital of each firm. The adjustment for property income from abroad is necessary to reconcile the figure obtained by this method with that obtained from the income method:

Table 3. United Kingdom National Income (1973)

(A) Expenditure Method	£ millions	(B) Income Method	£ millions	(C) Output Method	£ millions
Consumers' expenditure	44,855	Income from employment	42,890	Extractive industries	2,744
Public Authorities current expenditure on goods and services	13,270	Income from self-employment	6,244	Manufacturing	19,103
Gross domestic fixed capital formation	13,871	Gross trading profit of companies	8,476	Construction	4,429
Value of physical increase in stocks	574	Gross trading surplus of public Corporations and other public enterprises	2,194	Gas, Electricity, and Water	1,939
Total Domestic Expenditure at Market Prices	72,570	Rent	4,894	Transport and Communication	5,460
Exports and property income from abroad	21,542	*Total Domestic Income before Depreciation and Stock Appreciation*	64,698	Distributive trades	6,122
Less imports and property income paid abroad	−22,291	Less Stock Appreciation	−3,111	Insurance, Banking, and Finance	5,774
Less taxes on expenditure	−10,006	Residual error	589	Ownership of Dwellings	3,668
Subsidies	1,456	*Gross Domestic Product at Factor Cost*	62,176	Public administration and Defence	4,266
Gross National Product at Factor Cost	63,271	Net property income from abroad	1,095	Public Health and Education	3,726
		Gross National Product at Factor Cost	63,271	Other Services	6,908
				Adjustment for Financial Services	−2,552
				Residual error	589
				Gross Domestic Product at Factor Cost	62,176
				Net property income from abroad	1,095
				Gross National Product at Factor Cost	63,271

Source: National Income and Expenditure 1973

some of the personal incomes (and perhaps some corporate and Government incomes) will have accrued from securities or real estate held in other countries. Although the property is located overseas its product is regarded as part of the United Kingdom national income and must be added in when computing by the output method. Similar treatment is accorded to dividends paid to foreign holders of shares in United Kingdom industry, or rents paid to overseas owners of property.

The deduction for stock appreciation is necessary because goods may go into stock at perhaps £5 each in June and remain in stock until the end of the year, when owing to a general rise in prices they are worth £5·50 on the market. The 50p represents no actual production and so like transfer payments it must be excluded from the value of the Gross National Product.

Expenditure Method. Once again the difficulty is that of double counting. If we count the expenditure of a motor company on tyres and then count an individual's expenditure on the motor-car embodying those tyres their value will have been included twice. We therefore count final domestic expenditure. As this expenditure will be partly on imports (which were not produced in the United Kingdom) we must deduct their value and add in the value of exports which Britain did produce but did not purchase. At the same time we make the same adjustment for property income as we did under the output method. This method indicates *Gross National Product at market prices* and to convert it to factor cost we must deduct taxes on expenditure and add subsidies (e.g. the market price of cigarettes is perhaps 30p but 20p of this is tax, leaving just 10p as the factor cost).

Thus all three methods lead us to the Gross National Product, a measurement of the total value of goods produced before allowing for depreciation. It is worth noting, however, two other measures of national income in fairly common use:

(i) *The Net National Product* is equal to the GNP less a depreciation allowance for capital resources used up during the process of production.

(ii) *The Gross Domestic Product* is the value of the output not of all the factors owned by United Kingdom residents but of all the factors located within the United Kingdom. The difference between the two will, of course, be greatest in those countries which allow a high level of foreign investment.

(5) The British Performance

Estimates of the national income of the United Kingdom are published annually in the 'Blue Book' of National Income and Expenditure, and this includes a wealth of information on the performance of the economy. An examination of the tables in the Blue Book gives an indication of the extent of economic growth over recent years.

Figure 2 based on data in the Blue Book shows the growth of national income between 1948 and 1973. During that period the value of the Gross National Product rose from £10,517 million to £33,244 million, but in terms of constant 1963 prices the change was from £18,082 million to £48,216 million, this indicating the *real* change in the Gross National Product. This is of more significance than the current figures since we are using money as the only convenient common denominator of all the goods and services produced—and it is the availability of those goods and services that affects the standard of living.

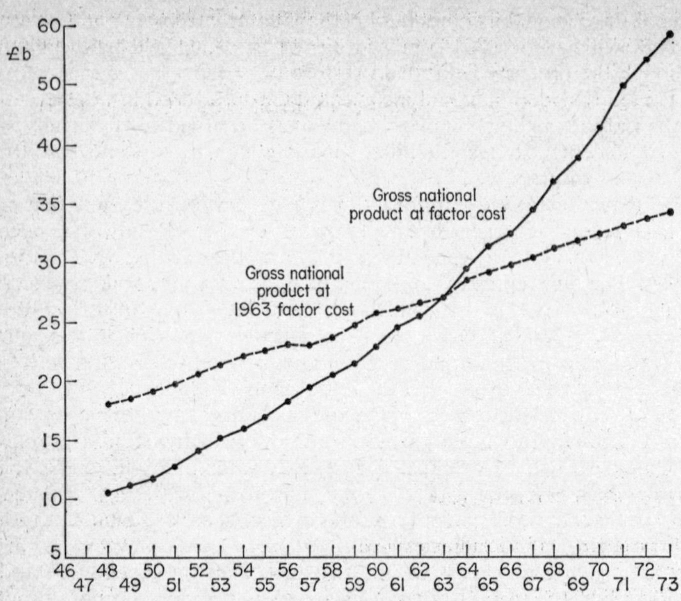

Source: National Income and Expenditure.

Fig. 2. Growth of United Kingdom National Product (1948–73)

While the current national income grew by 6·7 per cent per year over the period, the real national income grew by only 2·5 per cent. The increase in national income per head between 1948 and 1969 was from just over £200 to £700 in current values and from about £360 to £600 if 1963 prices are used. (Population grew by 10 per cent over the period.)

As the Gross National Product has been growing its composition has been changing. Table 4 shows the structure of the GNP in 1959 and 1973.

Table 4. Structure of the United Kingdom GNP (1959 and 1973)

	1959 £ millions	1973 £ millions
Consumers' expenditure	16,117	44,855
Public Authorities current expenditure	4,001	13,270
Gross capital formation	3,910	13,871
Foreign earnings (net)	225	−749
Gross National Product at market price	24,253	71,247

Source: National Income and Expenditure.

Consumption. Total expenditure of consumers has declined slightly from 66 per cent at the beginning of the period to about 63 per cent in 1973. The fall is somewhat deceptive since much Government expenditure is really on behalf of consumers. For example in both years consumers' expenditure would be much higher if it were not for Government expenditure on the National Health Service. The composition of consumers' expenditure has undergone change during the 1960s as shown by Table 5.

Table 5. Consumers' Expenditure at Current Prices (1959 and 1973)

	1959 £ millions	1973 £ millions
Food	4,158	8,460
Alcoholic drink	920	3,536
Tobacco	1,061	1,945
Housing	1,569	6,190
Fuel and Light	686	1,891
Clothing	1,525	3,774
Durable goods	1,364	4,012
Other household goods	518	1,390
Books, etc.	225	664
Chemists' goods	232	707
Recreational goods	309	1,032
Other goods	216	579
Running costs of motor vehicles	405	2,409
Travel	545	1,436
Postal, telephone, and telegraph services	132	587
Cinema	71	63
Other recreational services	193	779
Domestic service	102	203
Catering (meals and accommodation)	814	2,135
Insurance	162	714
Wages and salaries paid by non-profit-making bodies	123	667
Other services	642	1,587
Income in kind	50	59
Less tourist expenditure in the United Kingdom	−199	−793
Consumer expenditure in the United Kingdom	15,883	44,026
Consumer expenditure abroad	234	829
Total	16,117	44,855

Source: National Income and Expenditure.

Whereas in 1959 25·8 per cent of consumers' expenditure was allocated to food, in 1973 the proportion was only 19·0 per cent. Expenditure on tobacco, recreational goods, recreational services other than the cinema and other services have all doubled in money terms. But the greatest increase has been in the proportion of expenditure devoted to the running of motor-cars, the very symbol of a high standard of living.

Capital Formation. A further section of the Blue Book analyses capital formation—investment in new real assets in the various sectors of the economy. Table 6 compares the public and private sectors in 1959 and 1973.

Gross Domestic Capital Formation grew from £3,736 million in 1959 to £13,871 million in 1973, accounting for 17·4 per cent and 20·0 per cent of the GNP respectively. No significant change in the balance between private and public investment has occurred: the public sector which was responsible for 42·6 per cent of total capital formation in 1959, had maintained its share at

40·1 per cent in 1973. As it did so the proportion of public investment going into plant and machinery declined from 34 per cent to 29 per cent, while

Table 6. Gross Domestic Fixed Capital Formation (1959 and 1973)—£m.

	1959		1973	
	Private	Public	Private	Public
Vehicles, Ships, and Aircraft	423	151	1,381	180
Plant and Machinery	848	542	3,239	1,638
Dwellings	393	268	1,682	998
Other new buildings and works	480	631	2,012	2,741
Total	2,144	1,592	8,314	5,557

Source: National Income and Expenditure.

investment in dwellings and other buildings both rose significantly. Not all this investment is immediately productive—improved housing, better schools and hospitals, while commanding a high proportion of resources, may not make much of a contribution to economic growth for many years.

The Public Sector. Many people believe that a cause of the United Kingdom's relatively slow growth rate has been the increasing size of the public sector. Table 7 shows the development of public sector expenditure.

Table 7. Public Expenditure (1959 and 1973)

	1959 £ millions	1973 £ millions
Current expenditure	7,071	21,528
Capital expenditure	1,701	6,149
Debt interest	1,064	2,665
Total	8,772	30,342

Source: National Income and Expenditure.

In 1959 public expenditure (which includes Central and Local Government and the Public Corporations) amounted to 40·9 per cent of the Gross National Product at factor cost and by 1973 this had risen to 49 per cent reflecting the greater involvement of the Government in the economic and social life of the community (see Chapter Six). To the extent that public sector expenditure may be subject to less stringent criteria than private sector expenditure in terms of the prospective return on that expenditure, the increasing stake of the former may have an adverse effect on economic growth.

(6) The Sources of Economic Growth

If the economy is to grow at a satisfactory rate the balance between consumption and investment must be properly struck. While endless and aimless investment will not achieve the desired results, adequate provision must be made to increase output and to increase productivity of both labour and capital—in short to make the best use of Britain's resources. This is not easy: the Government must create the right atmosphere for investment (difficult in recent years because of the Balance of Payments constraint); trade unions and management must be prepared to respond to this in a positive manner, allowing and encouraging the development and introduction of new meth of production.

We have already observed that the Gross National Product grows by only about $2\frac{1}{2}$ per cent per annum in real terms. Apart from the years of the Industrial Revolution this is the best performance ever achieved by the United Kingdom. None the less it has given rise to a great deal of criticism in view of the fact that many other economies have been growing at demonstrably faster rates since the war and consequently improving their living standards more rapidly. Figure 3 shows the average rates achieved by selected countries.

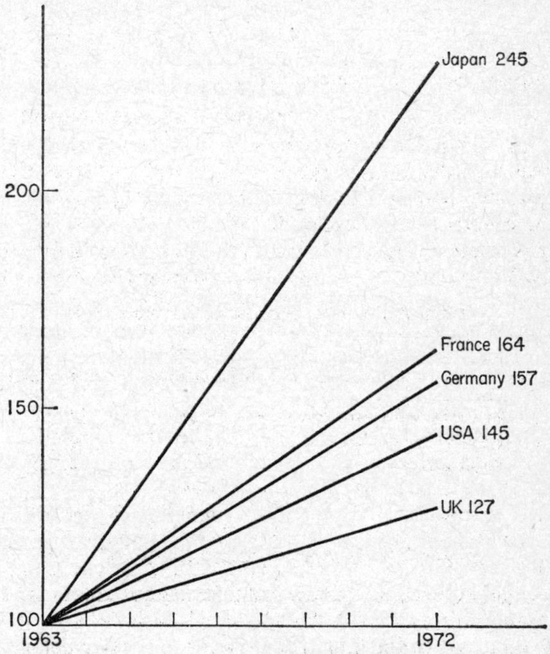

(*Source: Statistical Yearbook 1973, United Nations*)

Fig. 3. Comparative growth rates

While recognizing the difficulties of making these international comparisons there is little doubt that the general picture is the correct one.

The reasons for the relatively poor performance of the United Kingdom are more difficult to isolate. Various theories are put forward: the level of United Kingdom investment is too low, or the investment is of the wrong type; the structure of industrial relations inhibits progress which is as much the fault of management as of the Trade Unions; the supply of labour to manufacturing industry is too low or too high; the exchange rate is too high; and the European countries have enjoyed a built-in advantage in that being more damaged by the war they have been able to build up their economies from scratch using modern methods, techniques, and institutions.

In the remainder of this section we look at some of the main sources of

Table 8. A Comparison of Investment Levels and Growth Rates

	Investment (Average of 1963 and 1971 as percentage of GNP)	% Rate of Growth of GDP per year (1960–71)
Japan	33	10·6
France	24	4·8
Germany	24	4·6
Italy	22	4·6
Belgium	20	5·7
United States	17	4·2
United Kingdom	17	2·6

Source: Statistical Yearbook, 1973, © *United Nations.*

growth and try to indicate some reasons for the relatively poor United Kingdom performance.

The Level of Investment. The level of investment in the United Kingdom compares unfavourably with levels achieved elsewhere as Table 8 suggests.

Deficiencies in the level of investment (and its composition as discussed in the previous section) have been singled out by many economists as the overriding cause of the United Kingdom's relatively poor rate of growth, and it is worth examining some of the reasons for the low level of investment.

(i) High levels of investment can be supported only if profits are sufficiently good. In many sectors profits were held down by the increasing share of the Gross National Product going to labour (see page 41).

(ii) It is also likely that a steadily growing economy will induce investment whereas the stop-go nature of British economic policy made investment planning difficult in the 1960s.

The stop-go policy derived from the determination of the British authorities to maintain the exchange rate at 2·8 dollars to the pound and from contraints of running a reserve currency. Fairly certainly the restrictions imposed on the domestic economy to bolster the external position contributed to poor investment performance.

(iii) It is important to be clear that it is not particular detailed aspects of policy which have an adverse affect on investment (for instance, relatively high rates of interest are not very significant) but the general air of uncertainty that is generated when domestic economic policy is dictated largely by external events. Investment in modern plant and equipment is a lengthy and expensive process. Before committing hundreds of thousands, perhaps millions of pounds to a project an entrepreneur needs to have a fairly clear and optimistic view of the future. Without it many desirable projects will be postponed, perhaps abandoned; without such projects growth is difficult to secure. We are back to the importance of the economic atmosphere. One possibility is the use of particular incentives for export-oriented industries even when it is necessary to damp down on the domestic economy. The difficulty is, of course, that for many industries exporting is not worthwhile without a sound home market as a springboard.

Supply of Labour. Many commentators have drawn attention to the importance of the supply of labour as a source of growth. In support one might quote the case of the growth of the Japanese economy. At the end of the Second World War, over half the working force was in agriculture. Japan was able to achieve a growth of around 10 per cent per annum not only by investing something approaching 30 per cent of her Gross National Product but also by redistributing labour between the primary and secondary sectors, so that by 1969 of a labour force of 78 million, only 9 million were in agriculture. Again the members of the EEC had 21 per cent of their combined labour force in the agricultural sector in 1957, and by 1972 had reduced this to 9 per cent by transferring labour to manufacturing where marginal productivity is much higher, and workers can therefore make a greater contribution to economic growth.

The structure of employment in the United Kingdom at the end of the war was such that the country could not benefit from the kind of movement that was occurring elsewhere. Of a working force of 24 million only 5·2 per cent were on the land. And by 1965 this proportion had fallen to 3·2 per cent. In that year the ill-fated National Plan recognized the difficulty, forecasting a shortage of labour of 400,000 by 1970. The idea that labour must be moved into manufacturing gained in popularity and seems to have been partly responsible for the introduction of the Selective Employment Tax by the Labour Government on the advice of Professor N. Kaldor in 1966. The difficulty of having no agricultural sector from which to call labour was to be overcome by forcing labour out of the tertiary (service industries) sector, which is always expanding in advanced economies, into manufacturing. In some quarters it was felt that the policy was based on a misconception—manpower was absorbed into manufacturing in other countries because the economy was growing—it did not cause the growth. The great weakness of the British economy may well have been that there was already too much labour in manufacturing—that there was too much disguised unemployment (see Chapter Three).

However, given that the structure of the economy would not provide abundant labour for expanding industries the problem was allowed to become worse than it need have been: it was estimated in the National Plan that if unemployment in the Development Areas were reduced to the average level

Table 9. Activity Rates (United Kingdom 1971)

New Standard Region	Male	Female
South-East	81·9	44·8
East Anglia	80·1	38·7
South-West	78·1	37·6
East Midlands	82·3	43·3
West Midlands	84·1	45·4
Yorks and Humberside	81·2	41·7
North-West	81·6	41·4
North	80·2	40·0
Wales	78·5	35·7
Scotland	81·2	42·4
Northern Ireland	79·9	36·0
United Kingdom	81·3	42·6

Source: Regional Abstract of Statistics 1974.

for the United Kingdom 100,000 extra workers would have been employed. This is the result of lower *activity rates* in the regions. The activity rate measures the number of employed persons in an area as a percentage of the total population over school-leaving age in that area.

We shall see in Chapter Thirteen that the steps taken to overcome these differences have not met with great success, and we note here that such differences in activity rates represent lost production and a lowering of the rate of growth. Steps to persuade or encourage persons of retirement age to stay at work have been derisory for fiscal reasons, and the tax system is not always a positive inducement to married women to work. Furthermore for what may be admirable political or social reasons the decline of various industries and firms notably in coal-mining and shipbuilding has been slowed by the Government, thus further restricting the supply of labour to growth industries. However, even if the decline of such industries had been accelerated the labour that was released could not have been absorbed immediately by other industries—partly because it would have required lengthy retraining. Indeed the quality of the available labour supply has caused as much concern as the quantity and is at the root of the Government training schemes. The growth of the labour supply has also been restricted by the increasing numbers staying in full-time education after the minimum school-leaving age. Even then a lot of the education and training that they receive is not really geared to the needs of the economy. And even though economic growth may not be the end of education, it is a curious society which produces so many Doctors of Science that some of them join the dole queue for lack of work. This is not to mention deficiencies further down the scale.

In the sixties the difficulties of labour supply were aggravated by an increasing number of unofficial strikes (see Chapter Fourteen). A source of great frustration to Government, such strikes whether primarily the responsibility of management or labour can hardly be held responsible for the overall slow rate of growth, but did not help the efficient planning and smooth running of industry, and were instrumental in the slow development of some industries.

Thus for a variety of reasons, avoidable and unavoidable, the supply of labour available to contribute to economic growth has been inadequate. This is not to say that this has been the cause of inadequate growth, but it has been one of the factors contributing to the poor performance.

Incentive and Environment. In many ways the principal obligation of the Government in the matter of economic growth is to create the right environment or economic atmosphere. Principally this will be achieved if the level of demand in the economy can be maintained at a steady or gently expanding level. The plethora of bodies that were developed under Governments of left and right in the fifties and sixties with the task of fostering efficiency and encouraging growth were all based on the assumption that progress would be faster with Government involvement than without it. It seems doubtful in view of the economic performance in those years whether the cost in terms of money or effort was very effective. Certainly we need bodies to foster regional development but whether the impact of the National Economic Development Council, Industrial Reorganization Corporation, Commission for Industrial Relations, Departmental Committees, and such-like bodies produces much measurable growth is doubtful. Certainly there is a large section of academic and industrial opinion that believes what is required is less involvement by the

Government. By itself industry can make the decisions to promote its growth. The argument is that the role of the Government should be to create the atmosphere in which industralists are prepared to invest. More specifically a cut in company taxation is seen as the one great stimulant that could be administered, provided that such a cut is not accompanied by compensating increases in personal taxation or purchase tax which, leading to a fall in effective demand, could lead to a cut back in investment!

The disincentive of high taxation is not confined only to Corporation Tax. Personal incomes are taxed very severely once taxable pay rises to about £5,000 and the excessive marginal rates can hardly be an incentive to the most able to accept ever greater responsibility. This in addition to the fact that in general British managers seem to be relatively underpaid in comparison to their European and American counterparts suggests that we do not make the most of important talents.

However, this really brings us on to a further perhaps overriding reason for slow growth—the exchange rate of the pound against the dollar, and the Balance of Payments.

External Reasons. There seems little doubt the undervaluation of the Deutschmark and the Yen and the overvaluation of the pound added to the United Kingdom problems in the 1960's.

Once again it is not possible to say that this is *the* reason for the poor performance but, especially in the sixties it was increasingly difficult to make the external payments balance. This together with the important reserve currency role necessitated the frequent application of the economic brakes. Despite mounting evidence that the pound was overvalued successive Governments sought to solve their Balance of Payments difficulties through deflation. A moderate devaluation perhaps at the end of the 1950's would not have been inappropriate and would certainly have allowed a policy more geared to growth to have been implemented at home. As it was domestic goals were sacrificed to the exchange rate and Britain's reserve currency responsibilities.

Thus despite the optimism of the NEDO and National Plan the GNP of the United Kingdom has grown at an average of 2½ per cent in the 1960's. The NEDO had hoped for 4 per cent and the DEA in its national plan 3·8 per cent though nothing like this had been achieved in the immediately preceding years.

Finally, lest it be felt that this section has dwelt too heavily on the darker sides of an economic performance let us remind ourselves that in the post-war years there has been an unprecedented increase in national standards of living: the ownership of motor-cars, television-sets, durable consumer goods of all kinds; the trimmings of affluence have all increased.

Despite this, pockets of great poverty still exist: a faster rate of economic growth, achieving greater production would help to eliminate this, though it would not of itself guarantee that the extra income was channelled in the right direction. To ensure this, redistribution through the tax system is necessary (see Chapter Six).

(7) Summary of Chapter Two

(1) The aim of economic growth is to produce more goods and services each year, though there is danger in ignoring the disutilities associated with a higher material standard of living.

(2) Economic growth is measured by the change in the Gross National Product—the value of all goods and services produced. The GNP may be measured by adding all incomes, all expenditure, or all output.

(3) The British economy has not grown very rapidly since the war, though there have been changes in the pattern of demand away from necessities towards 'luxuries'.

(4) The Government is responsible for an increasing proportion of both total expenditure and total investment. This may explain the relatively low growth rate of the United Kingdom.

(5) Other factors include the supply of labour, the level of investment, and the generally fluctuating economic atmosphere.

(6) For much of the period the pound was overvalued and this added to the difficulties of the Government.

(8) Suggested Further Reading

LEWIS, W. A., *The Theory of Economic Growth*, Unwin, London, 1955.
MISHAN, E. J., *The Costs of Economic Growth*, Penguin, London, 1967.
ROSTOW, W. W., *The Stages of Economic Growth*, Cambridge University Press, 1960.

Exercises Set 2

1. Describe the difficulties involved in the measurement of the national income.

2. To what extent does a rise in the national income indicate a rise in the standard of living?

3. What are the main causes of economic growth? How can the Government stimulate growth?

4. United Kingdom Gross National Product (£ millions)

	1948		1969	
	Current Prices	1963 Prices	Current Prices	1963 Prices
Consumers' expenditure	8,552	13,808	28,618	22,629
Gross fixed capital formation	1,422	2,285	7,927	6,602
Gross National Product	10,517	18,082	38,601	31,695

Use the table to comment on the growth of the United Kingdom economy between 1948 and 1969.

5. Assess the main disadvantages that result from the pursuit of a high rate of economic growth.

6. 'The explanation of the slow rate of economic growth in the United Kingdom is that the achievement of a higher rate conflicts with the short-term aims of the Government.' Comment.

7. 'The distribution of the national income is if greater importance than its size.' Do you agree?

8. 'Economic progress cannot be measured in terms of national income per head.' Write an essay in support of this contention.

9. Using the figures in Table 5 comment on the changes that have occurred in the standard of living in recent years.

10. 'The desire for economic growth raises the conflict between consumption and investment.' Explain.

CHAPTER THREE

FULL EMPLOYMENT

(1) Introduction

Only since 1944 have British Governments been committed to a policy of full employment. In view of the experience of the inter-war years the authorities felt that if unemployment could be restricted to 3 per cent the objective of full employment would have been fulfilled. Only on rare occasions has the monthly figure been as high as this and Figure 4 shows that in contrast to

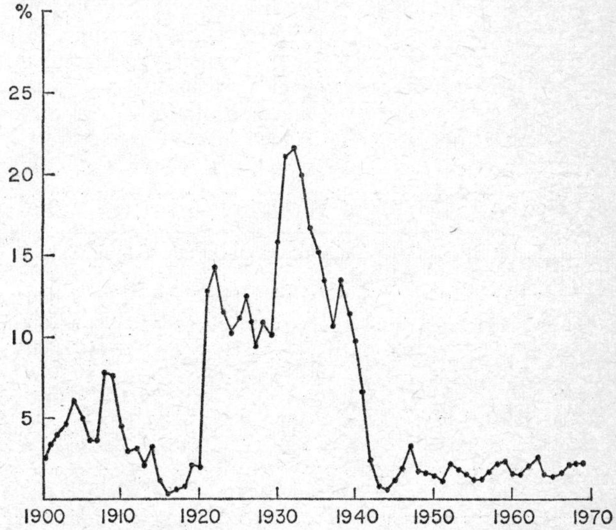

(*Source: Department of Employment*)

Fig. 4. Unemployment in the United Kingdom in the twentieth century

earlier years the post-war rate has been quite firmly under control, though as we shall see in Chapter Thirteen much greater levels have been reached in some of the regions.

The important turning-point was the publication of J. M. Keynes's *The General Theory of Employment, Interest and Money* advocating the management of Aggregate Monetary Demand via the budget. Before this the purpose of the budget was to raise sufficient revenue for the Government to meet its commitments, and the general level of economic activity was to be controlled via monetary policy and the banking system.

Keynes, stressing the importance of investment as a determinant of the level of employment showed that in conditions of heavy unemployment the onus was on the Government to inject money into the economy. While it is preferable that such injections should be in exchange for productive work, in the last resort any injection of purchasing power would do, for the recipients of the extra income would spend it on consumer goods, causing employment in consumer goods industries to rise; employees in these industries would now have more to spend which would create employment elsewhere in the economy. So the **multiplier process** would continue to raise the level of national income and employment.

(2) The Multiplier

The multiplier is fundamental to the achievement of full employment. If employment is to rise money must be injected into the economy, and spent by its recipients. The significance of any single injection will depend on the extent to which recipients are prepared to spend their new income. If they spend the greater part of any increment (that is if they have a high marginal propensity to consume) they will generate a further substantial rise in income and employment: but if they save most of the increase very little income will be passed on to create further employment. Table 10 shows what happens when £1 million is invested in the purchase of, perhaps, a power-station, when the marginal propensity to consume is four-fifths.

Table 10. The Multiplier in Action

	Rise in Income (£)	Rise in Consumption (£)	Rise in Savings (£)
	1,000,000	800,000	200,000
	800,000	640,000	160,000
	640,000	512,000	128,000
	.	.	.
	.	.	.
	.	.	.
	.	.	.
Total	5,000,000	4,000,000	1,000,000

Notes:

(*a*) The rise in investment of £1,000,000 creates incomes of £1,000,000 for the builders of power-stations.

(*b*) They save £200,000 of the increase (marginal propensity to save is one-fifth) and spend £800,000.

(*c*) This creates incomes and employment for workers in the consumer goods industries who spend £640,000 of their extra income.

(*d*) The process will eventually increase incomes by £5,000,000 and employment will rise accordingly.

(*e*) The rise in income will always be equal to the rise in investment multiplied by the reciprocal of the marginal propensity to save:

$$I \cdot \frac{1}{\text{MPS}}$$

(*f*) Thus the smaller the proportion saved, the greater the rise in income and employment.

(*g*) In conditions of full employment the multiplier would have considerable inflationary effects.

In practice there will be considerable time-lags in the operation of the multiplier which make it a difficult instrument to use for economic control. Furthermore the impact of the investment multiplier will be complicated by the action of **budget multipliers** and **export multipliers** each affecting the level of activity and employment. Just as an injection of money into the economic system in the form of extra investment will stimulate demand by much more than the original investment so a budget deficit or an increase in the balance of trade surplus generate further demand. Since all these multipliers may be in action at any time it is very difficult to assess the effects of any one of them.

(3) What is Full Employment?

(*a*) The meaning of the term 'full employment' is a matter of some debate between economists. We have seen that at the end of the war the Government felt that conditions of full employment would exist if only 3 per cent of the **insured labour force** were out of work. Such was the success of Keynesian policies that for 25 years unemployment was kept below that level. In the 1950's and 1960's the Government felt that 2 per cent was the maximum rate of unemployment they could allow. In the 1970's a higher rate has prevailed. This can be explained partly by the shake-out of labour from unproductive jobs and partly because it was thought to be a way of reducing wage demands and inflation. The Government, faced with an unprecedented combination of

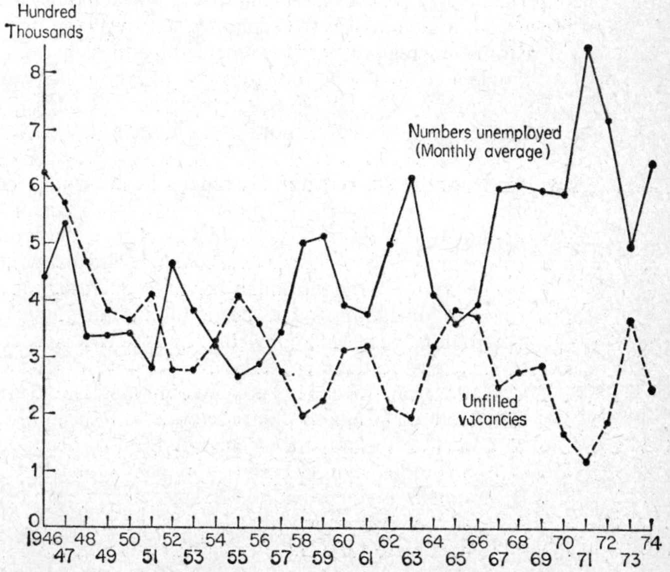

(*Source: Annual Abstracts of Statistics*)

Fig. 5. Number unemployed and number of vacancies

inflation and unemployment, determined that the reduction of inflation was more important than the immediate reduction of unemployment.

(*b*) Many feel that the crude percentage figure gives an insufficient indication of the problem and prefer to relate the numbers unemployed to the number of vacancies. If the number of vacancies is greater than the number of unemployed then conditions of full employment exist; but if there are more people out of work than there are vacancies to fill the level of unemployment is too high. Figure 5 shows that on this definition the level of unemployment has been too high almost continuously for the last decade.

(*c*) A further problem lies in the accuracy of the published statistics. The unemployed include many people not actively seeking work and people unable to work. People who stay in full-time education because they cannot find work are not included. On balance it is estimated that unemployment figures could overstate real unemployment by 20 per cent.

However, there are good social and political reasons for seeking full employment: one of the great problems that will be created as the length of the working week is reduced is the allocation of extra leisure; when that leisure is enforced through involuntary unemployment the problem is much greater. Most people actually prefer to work.

Finally, there is an equity argument in that those who are unemployed are dependent on those who are in work and excessive unemployment imposes an unacceptable burden on those paying taxes.

(4) Types of Unemployment

Cyclical Unemployment. The most serious form of unemployment and the one that most concerned Keynes is cyclical unemployment which is associated with a general down turn in demand in the economy. This was the problem that occurred with astonishing regularity in the nineteenth and early twentieth centuries. Just as a single factory will be forced to lay off labour if it cannot sell its product so the economy as a whole will experience unemployment if people at home or overseas will not or cannot purchase the goods which are being produced.

Most readers will know of the 'distress and discontent' in England after the Napoleonic Wars when the labour market, flooded by demobilized soldiers, and no longer stimulated by the war effort, could not absorb the workers available. More recently similar distress occurred in the period between the two world wars. When demand fell the multiplier began to operate in reverse —incomes falling, consumption falling, stocks accumulating, unemployment rising until over three million were unemployed. The bitterness generated during this period has its effects to the present day.

Thanks to the general adoption of Keynes's policies of monetary and especially fiscal management the fluctuations of the trade cycle have been brought largely under control, and since the war have generally been associated with deliberate acts of policy prompted by Balance of Payments considerations. The relationship between unemployment and the Balance of Payments is discussed in Chapter Seven where it is shown that in most cases the relatively high levels of unemployment have followed an increase of Bank Rate or an intensification of the fiscal squeeze.

Structural Unemployment. While cyclical unemployment is much less of a problem structural unemployment is a continuing hazard to labour. Structural unemployment results not from a general deficiency of demand but from a permanent change in the pattern of demand. Such unemployment is the inevitable result of economic development. The development of electrical power and other fuels has led to a great reduction in the numbers employed in the coal-mines. The development by African and Asian states of their own textile industries has reduced the size of the British cotton industry. The development of synthetic rubber causes unemployment in Malaysia. The development of German and Japanese shipbuilding has had grave effects on the United Kingdom industry. Many instances of structural unemployment reach the newspaper headlines, but it is in reality a long-term process, and the effect of the process may be judged from the change in the patterns of employment shown in Table 11.

There is a clear move away from the primary sector towards the secondary and tertiary sectors.

Frictional Unemployment. Structural unemployment is really a type of frictional unemployment. Since, especially when occurring in a localized industry it may cause serious problems, I have treated it separately. Frictional unemployment is, however, more clearly related to technological unemployment —which also arises through economic progress. As machines take over more and more tasks from men the pool of unemployment is swollen temporarily, while such labour undertakes retraining and is absorbed elsewhere in the economy. (Unemployment of this kind is also associated with the merger of industrial undertakings.) As labour-saving methods are introduced so the incidence of technological unemployment will increase, and so the necessity for Government financed retraining schemes increases. A major problem with such unemployment is that it is likely to be the older members of the work force who suffer most in not being able to find new jobs. Frictional unemployment may also arise where people are thrown out of work in one area and are unwilling or unable to move to similar work in another area.

Seasonal Unemployment. This may be regarded as a kind of frictional unemployment, particularly important in agriculture and the tourist trade. In these industries the problem is reduced by the coincidence of the peak season with college and university holidays which provide a large supply of temporary labour which is happy to be unemployed at the end of the season.

Disguised Unemployment. We noted in Chapter Two that the percentage unemployed will depend partly on activity rates. This figure will also depend partly on the amount of disguised unemployment. The extent of this may be difficult to assess but it is a situation which may arise for two reasons:

(i) In times of falling demand employers may deliberately refrain from dismissing labour, especially where it has invested heavily in training the workers, knowing that it will be difficult to recruit replacements when demand rises. Thus, at first overtime will be cancelled; later a four-day week substituted for a full week. An immediate effect of the Rolls-Royce collapse in 1971 was the introduction of a three-day working week by suppliers of components.

(ii) In the face of technological progress trade unions may insist on old manning ratios being maintained. A number of productivity deals in the 1960's resulting in considerable saving of labour indicate the extent of this practice. A further indication is also given by Table 5 showing international comparisons of output per head (see page 144).

Table 11. Structure of Employment in the United Kingdom
(thousands)

	1901	Percentage of total	1938	Percentage of total	1958	Percentage of total	1973	Percentage of total
Manufacturing industry	5,960	32·6	6,950	30·4	8,580	34·7	7,828	35·3
Construction	1,336	7·3	1,266	5·5	1,543·	6·2	1,380	6·1
Agriculture, Fishing, and Forestry	2,243	12·2	1,180	5·2	1,091	4.4	434	1·6
Mining and Quarrying	944	5·2	796	3·5	861	3·5	363	1·4
Transport and Communications	1,497	8·2	1,605	7·0	1,728	7·0	1,524	6·0
Distributive trades }	5,750	30·5	3,090	13·5	3,212	13·0	2,744	12·2
Other services }			4,969	21·7	6,141	25·0	8,044	36·3
Total in Employment	18,276		22,857		24,682		22,662	

Note: Items do not total since some categories are omitted.

Source: Key Statistics.

(5) Length of Unemployment

The importance of the crude unemployment figure may be exaggerated. For example, the significance of consecutive monthly figures of, say, 500,000 unemployed depends very much on whether it is exactly the same 500,000 people unemployed, or whether it is a completely new 500,000 unemployed now or whether, as is more likely, it is a combination of the two. Table 12 analyses the period spent in unemployment by those unemployed during 1974.

Table 12. Unemployed by Duration (Males)

	Thousands	per cent
Two weeks or less	67·5	10·8
Over two weeks and up to eight weeks	98·4	26·2
Over eight weeks and up to twenty-six weeks	310·4	63·0
Total	476·3	100·0

Source: Department of Employment and Productivity.

Those unemployed for two weeks or less may be regarded as being in the process of changing jobs. For the rest, the majority, unemployment is a serious problem, only slightly mitigated by the extra financial assistance available from the State (see page 32). Moreover the problems are likely to be more severe in the development regions and for older workers.

(6) The Government and Unemployment

Short-term and Long-term Difficulties. Cyclical unemployment is governed by the level of aggregate monetary demand, and it is through policies designed to affect this that the Government must seek to control the level of employment. If the achievement of full employment was all that the Government had to worry about there would be little difficulty. Demand could be stimulated until everyone who wanted a job had one. But we saw in Chapter One that the Government has many other aims and they must be balanced against each other.

Assuming that the achievement of a higher level of employment is to be given priority by the Government, consideration will have to be given to the four broad categories of monetary demand, consumption, investment, exports, and the demand for goods and services by the Government itself. If any of these is expected to increase of its own accord in the near future, the stimulation required through deliberate policy measures will be reduced. Once an estimate has been made of the degree of stimulation needed the Chancellor can consider the policies at his disposal, remembering that he will be expected to secure a fall in unemployment in the relatively short term.

It is the need to achieve short-term changes that causes problems. Most of the measures available are likely to be long-term in their effect. On the fiscal side a reduction in income tax will achieve an increase in consumption, but once the decision to reduce the tax has been taken it may be six months before the money is in the hands of the taxpayer; a more immediate change in consumption may be achieved by adjusting indirect taxes, particularly if the **regulator** is used. This enables the Chancellor to increase or decrease indirect taxes by up to 10 per cent. Monetary measures, also, may achieve some short-run change in the level of consumption: a reduction of interest rates or the removal of ceilings on loans, or the relaxation of hire-purchase restrictions may all be expected to stimulate the demand for durable consumer goods.

But the need to balance full employment against economic growth frequently dictates that any stimulation of demand should take the form of encouraging investment. Whatever monetary or fiscal measures are devised they cannot overcome the fact that investment is a very long-term process: plans are laid this year for projects to be started in perhaps two or three years' time. A reduction in interest rates, or an increase in investment incentives cannot easily accelerate the investment process. The same is true of much Government expenditure: it is often part of a long-term programme which cannot be turned on and off simply to increase or decrease the level of employment. The Government may resort to various fiscal measures to encourage exports or discourage imports so as to increase the demand for home-produced goods, but such policies are generally incompatible with our undertakings to such bodies as the General Agreement on Tariffs and Trade. In the 1930's devaluation was used as a means of increasing the level of employment (see Chapter Seven) but this is no longer allowed, and would not be of much help in the short run.

In the short run, therefore, the management of demand amounts to the management of consumption. Other factors are likely to have an impact only over a longer period.

The Mobility of Labour. Where structural unemployment is concerned the Government's main concern is to increase the mobility of industry (see Chapter Twelve) and the mobility of labour. A distinction may be drawn between **occupational mobility** and **geographical mobility** of labour. Where an individual develops skills appropriate to one particular industry, his occupational mobility is low and if made redundant he will find it difficult to find a new job: the skills of a coal-miner, for example, are highly specific and not much use elsewhere. On the other hand an electrician, thrown out of work in one industry can more easily find a new job in another. To increase occupational mobility Government Training Centres have been established where new skills can be acquired. Geographical mobility is more difficult to encourage especially where families are concerned. Such mobility is frequently encouraged by high levels of unemployment in a region when the opportunities elsewhere are obvious. But in general a worker will be reluctant to move away from an area where he has lived for a number of years, and where his wife and children have established routines. The difficulty of increasing geographical mobility has led to the Government concentrating on moving work to the worker rather than wasting effort in encouraging the greater mobility of labour.

The Cost of Unemployment. In recent years Government assistance to the unemployed has increased, and indeed one explanation of the higher level of unemployment is that people can afford to be unemployed longer in view of the increased benefits they now receive. In 1972 unemployment benefits amounted to £246 million, sickness benefit to £494 million, and redundancy payments from the Government (under the Redundancy Payments Act of 1965) to almost £70 million. While a person is certainly worse off when unemployed it is now possible for him almost to maintain his income for a short while after being unemployed especially when his tax rebates are taken into consideration. This illustrates another of the dilemmas of the Government: on the one hand, wearing its economic hat it says to the worker, 'Regrettably you have to be thrown into unemployment in the interests of our deflationary policy which for the time being requires a fall in real incomes'; on the other hand wearing its social welfare hat it says, 'We are sorry you are temporarily unemployed, and we are therefore making arrangements to insure that your real income does not fall too dramatically.' Inevitably this reduces the effectiveness of the deflationary policy.

But we are now anticipating a further conflict, that between full employment and inflation which is part of the subject-matter of Chapter Four.

(7) Summary of Chapter Three

(1) Modern Governments accept that it is their responsibility to maintain full employment.

(2) By this they mean that the general level of unemployment should not be allowed to rise much above 2 per cent of the registered labour force.

(3) Lord Keynes, in his book *The General Theory of Employment, Interest and Money* laid stress on the importance of the budget as an instrument for securing full employment.

(4) Of particular importance are the budget and investment multipliers.

(5) Unemployment may be of various kinds: cyclical unemployment is the most serious as it affects the whole economy; structural unemployment is the result of economic development; frictional unemployment is often the result of people spontaneously changing jobs.

(6) In the short term the reduction of unemployment is difficult except by increasing consumption: the other components of demand are difficult to alter in the short run.

(7) Structural unemployment may be reduced by encouraging greater occupational and geographical mobility of labour.

(8) Welfare payments may be increased to alleviate the affects of unemployment but they often run counter to the Government's deflationary policy.

(8) Suggested Further Reading

LORD BEVERIDGE, *Full Employment in a Free Society*, Allen & Unwin, London, 1960.

Department of Employment and Productivity, *Employment and Productivity* (Monthly), HMSO.

Exercises Set 3

1. How do you account for the great differences in the general level of employment in the periods before and after the war?
2. What policies are available to a Government wishing to increase the level of employment?
3. In what respects does regional unemployment represent a more intractable problem than general unemployment?
4. 'Structural unemployment should be welcomed as an indication of economic development.' Comment.

5. 'Automation leads to unemployment.' 'Automation leads to economic growth.' In the light of these statements comment on the assertion that full employment and economic growth are incompatible.

6. Why aim for full employment?

7. To what extent may unemployment problems be solved by greater mobility of labour?

8. What would be the likely effects of the Government aiming for full employment to the exclusion of other economic targets?

9. In what respects is unemployment a social rather than an economic problem?

10. Even at times of high unemployment the Government advocates higher savings. Why?

CHAPTER FOUR

INFLATION AND ITS EFFECTS

(1) Introduction

It seems to be an almost permanent feature of the economy that prices should be rising. This has not always been the case: there have been fairly long periods of price stability interspersed with sharp inflationary bursts. Since the war the United Kingdom has been experiencing a rather prolonged inflationary burst. It is the tendency for prices *in general* to rise ahead of incomes that is referred to as inflation. We are not concerned that any particular price is rising (this is bound to happen under the operation of market forces) but that the bulk of prices are rising. There are many definitions of inflation such as the popular 'too much money chasing too few goods' or the less widely quoted 'excess of aggregate money demand in conditions of full employment'. Recent experience shows that inflation can also occur when there is rather less than full employment. But however we define inflation people living in an inflationary society soon become aware of it and most modern Governments regard it as their duty to control inflation because of the harmful effects it produces.

(2) The Measurement of Inflation

Inflation implies an increase in the cost of living. As far as personal consumption is concerned changes in a range of retail prices give a broad indication of the amount of inflation; we may be interested in other aspects of inflation and in that case we could, for example, look at changes in the price of raw materials. The Government constructs an Index of Retail Prices, and since the use of index numbers is widespread in economics it is worth examining the way in which this index is compiled.

The present index runs from January 1962 and compares subsequent changes in prices with those prevailing at that date. On the basis of an extensive survey of consumers' expenditure patterns, retail goods were broken down into ten categories to each of which was attached a weight according to its importance in total consumer expenditure. There is a total weighting of 1,000 and thus any category shown to have attracted 10 per cent of consumers' expenditure would attract a weighting of 100. The categories established and the weights attached to them in 1962 and 1974 are shown in Table 13.

Thus in 1962 the extensive surveys carried out suggested that 31·9 per cent of expenditure was on food, while 10·2 per cent was on housing. A rise in the price of food would have three times the impact on the index as a rise in housing costs and the index must take account of this.

Since the pattern of consumption does not remain the same over the year the weights are adjusted annually on the basis of ascertained patterns of expenditure in the previous three years. The table therefore shows the changes that had occurred in weighting by 1974. Notice that it has been felt necessary to include an entirely new category, 'meals bought and consumed outside the

Table 13. United Kingdom Index of Retail Prices: Weighting 1962 and 1974

	1962	1974
Food	319	253
Alcoholic drink	64	70
Tobacco	79	43
Housing	102	124
Fuel and light	62	52
Durable household goods	64	64
Clothing and Footwear	98	91
Transport and Vehicles	92	135
Miscellaneous goods	64	63
Services	56	54
Meals bought and consumed outside the home	—	51
Total	1,000	1,000

Source: Department of Employment.

home' since 1968, reflecting partly the increasing importance of the leisure industry. Previously such meals were included under 'food'.

Once the base date has been chosen, and the basket of goods established, their price allowing for weighting becomes 100 at the base date. Thereafter prices of the commodities are noted weekly in a large number of towns and villages all over the country. A general increase in prices of 1 per cent would of course be reflected in the index moving to 101. In fact prices change at different rates and because of the weighting system changes in some items are more important than changes in others: thus a 5 per cent rise in food prices has a greater impact on the index than a 5 per cent rise in the cost of fuel and light.

Table 14 shows the way in which the index has moved since 1966, the rise in the price of food being a little less than all other items lumped together. The largest rise was in the cost of housing which in June 1973 stood at 213·1, reflecting the changing structure of the population (the post-war bulge in the population marrying and requiring accommodation) as well as the relative scarcity of land.

Table 14. Retail Prices Index Since 1966 (monthly averages)

	Food	All other items	All items
1966	115·6	116·9	116·5
1967	118·5	119·8	119·4
1968	123·2	125·7	125·0
1969	131·0	132·2	131·8
1970	140·1	140·3	140·2
1971	155·6	152·8	153·4
1972	169·4	162·7	164·3
1973	194·9	174·5	179·4
1974	230·0	201·2	208·2

Source: Department of Employment.

(3) Index Number Problems

The Original Sample. Clearly it is impossible for every family to be questioned in detail about its expenditure, and in fact the original sample was confined to households with an income of less than £20 per week. Thus the index can relate only to the relatively low paid and cannot be used as a guide to the changing cost of living of people earning, say, £40 per week when the sample was taken.

The Base Year. The choice of the base year may affect the rate at which prices appear to change subsequently. Thus if the base year is one in which prices have risen rapidly there may be some slowing down in subsequent years.

Quality of Goods. The index can take no account of changes in the quality of goods from one year to another. Seventy-five pounds spent on a television today may buy a better commodity than £65 spent on ostensibly the same television five years ago. This does not necessarily represent a rise in the cost of living. Some goods available now were not even invented in 1962.

Price Changes. These are notified from some five or six hundred different centres and are therefore averages. They do not represent changes in any particular area.

For these and other reasons the 'index' is at best only an indicator of the way in which prices have changed. While it is true that it gives a good general indication of such changes, it cannot really be used as an indicator of changes in the cost of living, much less the standard of living.

(4) Retail Prices and the Cost of Living

In Chapter Two we discussed the meaning of the term 'standard of living'. Equally open to misinterpretation is the term 'cost of living'. While it is true that the Index of Retail Prices is not a cost of living index, it is also true that when the index is rising it takes more money to buy a given bundle of goods. The cost of living has risen in money terms. But for many people the standard of living may not have changed—their money incomes may have kept pace with money prices. In Figure 6 the index of prices using a different base year is drawn alongside an index of average earnings and of wages and salaries per unit of output. (The rate of inflation in other countries is discussed later on pages 42.)

The first thing to notice is that earnings (both of manual workers and salary earners) have risen much more rapidly than retail prices. Anyone maintaining his earnings around the average level and buying goods and services in proportion to their weighting in the retail price index would be able to enjoy a higher standard of living than before: at the end of the period he could buy all the goods he was buying at the beginning and have money left over to buy more. Note that his cost of living will have risen: a given bundle of goods cost more at the end of the period than at the beginning. If his pattern of consumption is very different from that of the prices index then great care is necessary in relating a change in the index to his standard of living or cost of living.

(5) The Causes of Inflation

The definition of inflation offered above, 'too much money chasing too few goods', draws attention to two aspects of the problem.

The Supply of Money. If the supply of money increases so that it becomes easier for individuals to raise funds for the purchase of goods and if the supply of those goods cannot be increased prices will tend to rise; similarly if employers have easy access to overdraft facilities they will be more ready to

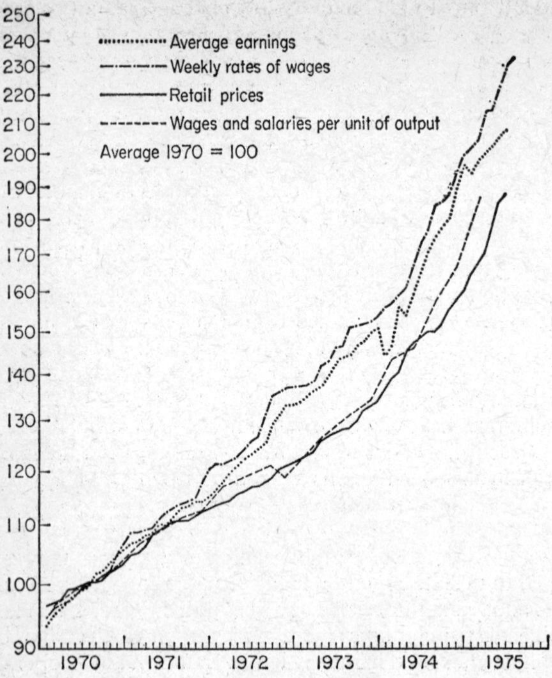

(*Source: Department of Employment*)

Fig. 6. Earnings, retail prices, wages and salaries per unit of output

concede inflationary wage claims. This view of inflation as a monetary phenomenon dates at least from the sixteenth century: the price inflation that swept Europe in that period was attributed to the influx of gold from South America. Under the more recent gold standard a Balance of Payments surplus would attract gold, increase the supply of money, and set up inflationary forces leading eventually to a Balance of Payments deficit. It was a feature of the Second World War that enemy countries tried to undermine each other's economies by forging and circulating currency notes.

Thus for many economists inflation has always been mainly a monetary problem and recent experience has reinforced their views.

Too Few Goods. The second aspect of inflation emphasized by our definition is that of 'too few goods'—that is to say too few goods in relation to purchasing power. If an economy has enjoyed stable prices for some length of time, and the output of industry suddenly falls, prices will rise unless purchasing power is reduced by an amount corresponding to the fall in output. This aspect of inflation is best looked at from the side of productivity. (*Productivity* usually means the value of output per unit of labour employed.) If a group of workers are able to secure an increase in earnings of 10 per cent and produce exactly the same number of goods as before then either prices must rise or profits must fall. Since shareholders are not likely to approve of falling dividends, the usual course is to increase prices. In recent times this 'real' aspect of inflation has attracted more attention and some feel that the cure for inflation lies in increasing productivity rather than in controlling the money supply.

Demand Pull and Cost Push Inflation. These two views of inflation—the one stressing money and the other stressing output—correspond approximately with another distinction often drawn in the discussion of inflation: the distinction between demand pull inflation and cost push inflation, the former initiated by higher purchasing power and the latter by higher production costs. In many ways such a distinction is largely academic since the effect of a demand pull inflation is to force up prices which leads some groups of workers to demand and acquire an increase in wages. Such an increase will often lead to higher prices and as such will be responsible for an element of cost inflation. The workers whose extra wages have generated some cost inflation will now have extra money to spend and therefore demand inflation continues. The interaction of cost inflation and demand inflation is the same when the cost inflation comes first. Once an inflation is underway it is almost impossible to distinguish between demand elements and cost elements, though there will normally be sufficient evidence to suggest a major cause.

Other Causes. In the rapid inflation of the 1970's the Government's own contribution was significant. It allowed Government expenditure to rise very rapidly: so rapidly that the money supply had to be increased to meet the bill. There was no corresponding rise in output. Prices rose as a result. Moreover, the increase in the price of oil and other commodities and the effects of the depreciating pound added fuel to the inflationary flames.

During the recent inflation in the United Kingdom a further cause has been very important: the role of expectations in generating price rises. Wage claims are geared not only to the rise in the cost of living that has occurred since the last wage increase and to increases granted to comparable workers, but also to the rise in the cost of living that is expected before the next increase. If workers do not adopt this attitude, and their expectations are correct their real standard of living will fall before the next increase occurs. Similarly employers will be under great pressure from shareholders to see that the real value of dividends is maintained: price increases will contain an element to allow for this. The role of expectations is quite clear in relation to interest rates. During a period of rising prices interest rates will move up as lenders of money seek to maintain the real value of their interest payments.

Whatever the cause of inflation all Governments take steps to control it. Why is it considered such a dangerous affliction?

(6) Why Avoid Inflation?

It is quite clear from the massive attempts of Governments to control inflation that they regard its effects as dangerous. If inflation is allowed to persist at above, perhaps, 5 or 6 per cent a year a number of distortions occur in the economy affecting internal and external policies. The most important of these are:

(*a*) *Fixed Income Recipients.* In a period of rising prices those who suffer most are those on fixed incomes. The outstanding group are Old Age

Pensioners whose bargaining position is very weak. To protect these (and other similar groups) the Government tries to contain price rises. It is of course a measure of its failure to control prices that Old Age Pensions and other benefits have to be increased periodically. In point of fact Old Age Pensions have more than held their own in relation to the Index of Retail Prices in the last twenty years, though this is not to imply that there is not room for further improvement.

Another group often alleged to have suffered from the effects of inflation are those holding undated gilt-edged stocks. It was once the practice to issue securities with no fixed redemption date, and a fixed interest of $2\frac{1}{2}$ per cent. Anyone holding them will receive £2·50 per year, but the purchasing power of the £2·50 has been in almost continuous decline. Moreover, owing to rising interest rates the capital value of such stocks has been eroded so that in February 1975 $2\frac{1}{2}$ per cent Consols were worth only £21·00 against their issue price of £100. This at least gives new purchasers of them a yield of almost 12 per cent $\left(\frac{2{\cdot}50}{21{\cdot}00} \times 100 \text{ per cent}\right)$.

Of course many feel that a corresponding advantage is that the real size of the National Debt is reduced by inflation and so is the value of much inherited wealth.

(*b*) *The Tax Net*. As money wages rise more people are brought into the tax net. In this way some people whose real income is too low for them to pay any income tax one year find themselves subject to tax the next year even though their real income may be unaltered. Similarly as money incomes rise to keep pace with inflation more people find themselves subject to higher rates of income tax than before. From the Chancellor's point of view this may be convenient in that it keeps the revenue buoyant, but every now and then exemption limits for income tax are raised to exclude those brought in only by inflation.

(*c*) *Hyperinflation*. There is sometimes a fear that a gentle inflation of, say, 3 or 4 per cent a year may turn into a galloping inflation of 10 or 20 or 100 per cent a year, and that this in its turn may lead to the situation of hyperinflation such as that experienced in Germany after the war when prices often doubled between breakfast and tea-time and money was abandoned in favour of cigarettes. While there is no sign of this happening it should be remembered that a constant inflation of 4 per cent per year means larger and larger absolute price increases each year. At the time of writing prices are rising at an annual rate of something approaching 25 per cent. If this undesirable target is achieved it will mean prices doubling about every three and a half years: at that rate a suit costing £40 today would cost over £300 in ten years' time. This would seem an important reason for trying to control inflation.

(*d*) *Balance of Payments*. Frequently a most compelling reason for controlling inflation is its impact on the Balance of Payments. If all countries were to inflate at the same rate even this reason would not be specially important. But when they inflate at different rates it becomes increasingly difficult for those who inflate fastest to pay their way internationally. For example, suppose at the exchange rate of 2·40 dollars to the pound goods produced in the United Kingdom for £100 can effectively compete on price with similar goods produced in the United States. If British prices double while costs in the United States increase by only 25 per cent over a period of years the British goods would now cost 480 dollars against 300 dollars for the American version. Clearly competition and a Balance of Payments surplus become impossible without devaluation—which gives a further twist to inflation (see Chapter Seven). It is this aspect of inflation that has been given greatest emphasis in recent years, and has been uppermost in the minds of the policy-makers.

(*e*) *Unemployment*. Persistent high rates of inflation lead to unemployment as employers, squeezed between price restraint and higher wage bills, are forced to lay off labour.

(*f*) *Other Distortions*. The most important are:

(i) Borrowers gain by being able to repay loans in money of lower purchasing power. Thrift is therefore actively discouraged.

(ii) To compensate for this and to persuade people to save the rate of interest rises—and in doing so adds to costs and eventually leads to further price rises.

(iii) Despite higher interest rates savers tend to look for hedges against inflation and savings are diverted from productive uses into vintage cars, works of art and the like: even office blocks which, while standing idle, appreciate in value to keep pace with inflation.

(iv) There is a danger that the shares of labour and capital in the Gross National Product may alter as either wages or profits race ahead. The relative shares of profit and income from employment in the Gross National Product are given in Table 15.

The share of profits in the national income has fallen since the war as the table shows:

Table 15. Profits and Income from Employment in Relation to Gross National Product

	1948	1959	1973
GNP at factor cost	£10,517m	£21,422m	£62,176m
Gross trading profits of Companies	£1,793m	£3,317m	£8,476m
Income from employment	£6,785m	£14,107m	£42,890m
Profits as a percentage of GNP	17·0%	15·5%	13·6%
Income from employment as a percentage of GNP	64·5%	65·8%	68·8%

Source: National Incomes and Expenditure.

There is nothing to say that the 1948 distribution is more desirable than that of 1973, nor that inflation is entirely responsible for the shift in balance. The likelihood is that inflationary wage settlements have been responsible. We have already noted (see Chapter Two) that the level of economic growth depends partly upon the level of investment and a major source of that investment is Company profits. If inflation tends to erode such profits at the expense of wages, investment, and therefore growth, becomes more difficult.

(v) The costing of major investment projects becomes difficult during a period of inflation. Prices of labour and raw materials are all likely to be rising and allowance must be made for them.

(vi) The Accountancy profession is currently devoting much consideration to the effect of inflation on published accounts. The difference between real values and money changes too rapidly during severe inflation for money values to give a true picture of a company's progress.

There are, then, good reasons for wanting to control inflation. Before investigating the means of control let us briefly look at the experience of other countries.

(7) An International Problem

Inflation is not unique to the United Kingdom. Indeed by the standards of some South American countries we are novices at the game. Table 16 shows that Britain's prices do not rise more rapidly than many other countries. The ominous point is that they do rise more rapidly than those of our major competitors.

Table 16. Comparative Inflations (1963 = 100)

	Retail Prices 1972
United Kingdom	159
United States	137
Canada	136
Germany	134
Italy	142
France	147
Denmark	164
Sweden	154
Japan	160
Argentina	811
Brazil	1,400
Kenya	118
Uganda	171
Nigeria	164
Ghana	202

Source: United Nations Statistical Yearbook 1973, p. 542.

The implication of the rapid rates of inflation endured by countries such as Argentina and Brazil is that frequent devaluation of their currency is necessary to maintain their competitive position—each devaluation setting up forces which lead to the next devaluation.

The implication for Britain is that her competitive position in export markets is being eroded by inflation: the aim must be to keep inflation at least below the rate prevailing among her major competitors. With this in view successive Governments have tried various ways of subduing inflationary forces.

(8) Policies to Cure Inflation

Monetary and Fiscal Policies. Keynsian economic policies have successfully eliminated the problem of unemployment since the war although the problems since 1971 suggest that some modification of these policies may be required. We have seen that this problem has been replaced by that of inflation. The response of Governments during the 1960's was to implement the Keynsian policies for unemployment in reverse. The idea has been that since inflation is the result of excess pressure on resources the level of demand must be reduced. Thus on the monetary side inflation has been countered by higher interest rates, attempts to restrict the growth of the money supply, and instructions to the banks about the level and direction of their lending. Each of these is designed to reduce the amount of credit available to individuals and companies, and thus to reduce the pressure of demand (see Chapter Five). Fiscal policy too attempted to take money out of the system through higher taxes thereby increasing unemployment. The higher unemployment, resulting from these orthodox deflationary policies, led to a reduction in the rate of inflation. And for most of the post-war period the policy was broadly successful as Figure 7 suggests.

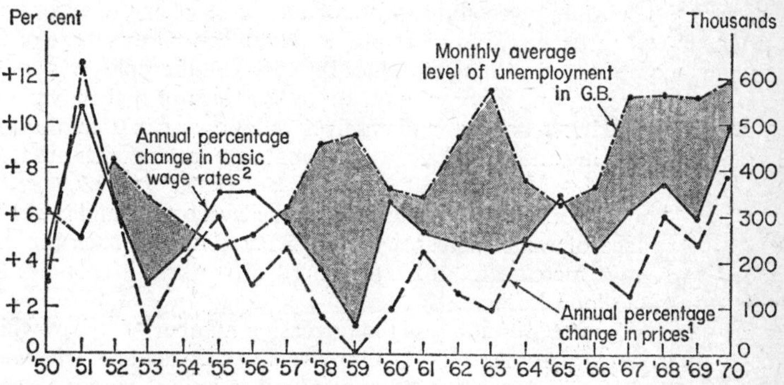

Notes
1. Retail prices (mid-Dec. to mid-Dec)
2. Hourly rates from 1956, weekly rates before 1956. 1956 figure for 11 months expressed at annual rate.
3. Figures for period to July, expressed as annual rates, in case of wages and prices.

(*Source: Barclay's Bank Review*)

Fig. 7. Level of unemployment and annual change in prices and wages (1950–70)

When deflationary policies succeeded in increasing the level of unemployment the rate of increase in prices was reduced, as for example in 1959 and 1963. And at the same time the rate of increase of wage rates was reduced, though not by so much as prices. The Government faced with the choice of higher unemployment or more rapidly rising prices could opt for extra unemployment whenever it wished (and though this was usually at times of Balance of Payments crises it still had the desired affect on inflation).

More recently, since 1967, the relationship between unemployment and prices has not been maintained. Orthodox deflationary policies have been enforced, unemployment has risen to an unprecedented post-war level but prices and wages have increased at an accelerating rate. Some people believe that the cure for inflation in such circumstances is to intensify deflationary pressure and increase unemployment until inflation does slow down. The difficulty is that no one knows how far such a policy would have to be carried;

how much unemployment would have to be created; how much production would have to be foregone; or how much social unrest would result before an acceptably low rate of inflation were achieved. This has led to a search for new approaches to the problem especially in the form of a prices and incomes policy.

Before considering this approach to the problem of inflation let us examine more closely the apparent failure of monetary and fiscal policy in recent years.

The Weakness of Monetary and Fiscal Policy

(*a*) To be effective in influencing the level of demand monetary policy needs to be vigorously enforced: marginal changes in interest rates have little effect on demand; restriction of the supply of money is difficult if gilt-edge prices are to be kept steady (see Chapter Five).

(*b*) Fiscal policy while successful in withdrawing money from the economic system is largely retrospective: although income tax can remove part of the increase in income it does nothing to reduce the costs of the employer who has conceded the increase, and who passes it on in the form of higher prices.

(*c*) Moreover, indirect taxes are themselves inflationary in that they increase the cost of living and encourage wage demands if real incomes are to be maintained.

(*d*) Orthodox deflationary policy operating on the level of demand is almost helpless in the face of wage increases of 20–25 per cent and once this has become the average increase for militant groups of workers it becomes the only desirable one for all others.

(*e*) In Chapter Fourteen we discuss the increasing number of strikes which result partly from extra vulnerability of employers to such action.

If orthodox policy is incapable of controlling inflation it may be that discipline can be imposed via an incomes policy.

(9) Incomes Policies

All Governments must have some policy towards incomes, or more precisely prices and incomes. There are really three alternatives open to them:

(*a*) To leave incomes and prices to be determined by market forces, offering interference from afar via monetary and fiscal policy. We have seen that this is not acceptable and is not likely to control inflation of the type we are considering.

(*b*) To exhort moderation. Governments may try to create an atmosphere of public opinion in which excessive increases may be resisted. They may support such a policy by setting an example in the public sector in respect of their own employees. Since 1973 the opposite has happened: public sector wages have risen most rapidly.

(*c*) To establish a formal policy, with an elaborate framework to assess and make recommendations on prices and pay. It was such a policy that the Labour Government introduced in 1965 and that has had several imitators.

The Prices and Incomes Policy

The policy began as a Declaration of Intent in November 1964. The Government together with representatives of the Trade Unions and Employers undertook urgent action to raise productivity, to stabilize prices, and to keep total money incomes in line with the growth of the real Gross National Product.

Early in 1965 the National Board for Prices and Incomes was set up to investigate changes in prices and incomes in accordance with certain criteria laid down by the Government, and from then until the middle of 1966 the policy was conducted on a voluntary basis with the object of restraining increases in incomes to a norm of 3½ per cent, while if possible stabilizing prices. During the period April 1965 to July 1966 wages rose by about 9 per cent and prices by 4 per cent.

The Balance of Payments difficulties of July 1966 confirmed to the Government the necessity for a more vigorous approach and a pay and prices freeze was imposed for six months—to be followed by a period of severe restraint during which increases were to be confined to the poorly paid and those showing increases in productivity. The Government had power to forbid individual increases but had to intervene on relatively few occasions. During the twelve months from July 1966 to June 1967 the success of the policy was marked by the fact that retail prices and wages each rose by only about 2 per cent.

The policy assumed a more moderate appearance with the passing of the Prices and Incomes Act 1967. The Government retained the power to refer any proposed price or income increase to the NBPI and to delay the implementation of any such increase during the period of investigation and for a further three months in the event of the Board finding the proposed increase against the public interest. The impact of the policy since then may be judged from figures reflecting the increasingly passive role of the Government and the increasingly voluntary nature of the policy which was effectively abandoned by the Government early in 1970, though it was not until the following year that the Prices and Incomes Board was finally abolished by the Conservative Government.

This was not the first attempt of a British Government to implement a formal Prices and Incomes policy, but the other two, by Conservative Governments met with even less co-operation from the Trade Unions, and were more or less still-born. The Labour Government's attempt is therefore the only one on which any effective debate can take place.

The National Board for Prices and Incomes

The central feature of the policy was the Prices and Incomes Board (NBPI). The task of the Board was to examine cases referred to it by the Government and in the light of criteria laid down by the Government to make recommendations about the proposed pay or price increase. It was for the Government to decide what action to take, and it usually relied upon persuasion rather than force.

The Board itself consistently emphasized the importance of productivity as a basis for wage increases and as a means of promoting price stability. Even so the Chairman of the Board estimated that between 1965 and 1968 wages rose by one percentage point less each year than would have been the case if the Board had not existed. This is hardly a great achievement but there are many who believe that a formal policy of this kind is the only alternative to the discredited traditional policies. Consider the arguments for and against.

The Benefits of a Formal Incomes Policy

(*a*) Claims can be objectively examined in the light of the criteria established by the Government for judging their macro- and micro-economic implications. When it was wound up the Prices and Incomes Board was establishing just such a reputation for objectivity.

(*b*) Inflationary claims can be exposed for what they are.

(*c*) Wage settlements are now so complex that only a highly trained team of experts can assess them. It is not just a question of hours and rates of pay: length of holidays, bonus schemes, productivity (achieved and promised), all have to be taken into account. Estimates of the rise in average earnings that would accrue to electricity workers as a result of the findings of the Wilberforce Court of Inquiry in February 1971 varied between 10·9 per cent and 18 or 19 per cent.

(*d*) Some such machinery is needed if only as a long-stop. There are bound to be disputes which drag on for weeks until the Government is forced to establish an *ad hoc* Court of Inquiry to investigate the case in the way that the NBPI would. Such a Court, though, is not backed by the highly skilled secretariat and research workers that the Board built up and its findings do not carry the same authority in the country at large.

(*e*) The interests of the low paid are likely to be better protected by a Prices and Incomes Board—acting according to appropriate criteria—than by leaving all settlements to market forces and exhortations. This may be specially important in maintaining the balance between the public and private sectors.

(*f*) The policy of de-escalation followed by the Conservatives in 1970–1 is manifestly unfair in that the acceptable level of pay rise depends too heavily on the timing of the claim. Certainly one reason for the prolonged postal strike in 1971 was the feeling that had the claim been made six months earlier the Post Office would have shown a more generous attitude. If such de-escalation is unacceptable other criteria should be used by a Prices and Incomes Board.

(*g*) Finally only by bringing wage and price increases under close public scrutiny can we establish an atmosphere in which inflation does not become a self-perpetuating and accelerating process.

The difficulties of a Formal Policy

On the other hand, trade unionists and others who have no faith in a formal framework may adduce equally powerful arguments in support of their position.

(*a*) No previous prices and incomes policy has succeeded in reducing inflation by a significant amount. Indeed research by Professor Lipsey and Professor Parkin suggests that income policies actually have an inflationary effect on wages once unemployment reaches about 1·8 per cent.

(*b*) Once a 'norm' is established it becomes the minimum. If the norm is 5 per cent no trade-union leader can accept an offer of less than that on behalf of his men.

(*c*) The very complexity of modern wage-bargaining suggests that no outside body can make an objective assessment.

(*d*) Such policies, especially when taken to the extreme length of a freeze, are followed by an increase in wage claims to make up lost ground.

(*e*) In any case the policing of such policies especially where prices are involved is virtually impossible.

(*f*) The very establishment of a 'norm' is meaningless when wage levels vary by as much as they do in a modern economy. If 4 per cent is to be the normal rise in pay and is enforced the gap between the high and low paid is widened. The alternative may be to allow everyone the same cash rise, thereby deliberately reducing differentials between high and low paid. Again such rigidity may be acceptable as an emergency measure, but would be difficult to enforce over a long period. It pays no attention to productivity, and avoids the genuine claims of workers whose skills may be in short supply.

(*g*) Further the establishment of a 'norm' assumes that the pattern of wages existing when the norm is set is the 'right' one in some way. There is also the minor difficulty that whenever the policy begins some group of workers will resent being the first to be subjected to it.

(*h*) If rises are to be decided on the basis of increased productivity at least two problems occur: how shall the wages of workers in service industries be determined? The effectiveness of a teacher is not measured by the number of examination successes his pupils achieve; nor can a policeman be judged solely by the number of convictions he secures. The second problem is the allocation of the rewards of extra productivity. If productivity rises because labour-saving machinery is employed not all the rewards should go to labour. In addition the greatest increases in productivity are likely to be achieved by work groups who have been most assiduous in enforcing restrictive practices. If such groups are to get the highest pay rises then other groups may conclude that virtue is indeed its own reward.

(*i*) Further there is the problem of deciding what is to be subject to control —individual wage rates, average earnings, or the total wage-bill of the firm?

(*j*) Perhaps the most powerful argument against a formal incomes policy is that it focuses attention on the wrong aspects of inflation. There is considerable evidence that the rapid inflation of 1974–5 stemmed largely from Government expenditure and excessive increases in the money supply. The 'social contract', in seeking to control incomes and prices, may have been attacking symptoms rather than causes.

(10) Control Through Expansion

The usual argument against expanding the economy is that the Balance of Payments will not stand the strain of higher imports and speculation (see Chapters Seven and Eight). By 1971 devaluation and deflation secured an annual Balance of Payments surplus of £600 million to £700 million, and there was clearly room for more imports. The Trades Union Congress and others could point to certain arguments in favour of expansion:

(*a*) The reduction in taxes necessary to stimulate expansion would reduce the pressure of wage claims.

(*b*) Higher demand would lead to a better use of equipment, perhaps a spreading of overhead costs, the greater price stability, as well as reducing unemployment.

(*c*) In these circumstances economic growth could increase, investment rise, and standards improve all round.

Against these arguments is the fear that expansion would lead only to further inflation. The prerequisite of expansion is control of inflation, for only then is the necessary level of investment likely to occur. There is some truth in the contention that United Kingdom policy has concentrated too much on the monetary side of inflation, and too little on the real side—on securing increases in productivity through investment.

(11) Summary of Chapter Four

(1) Inflation, like the poor, is always with us, but it has grown more severe in the last two or three years.

(2) The rate of inflation may be measured by index numbers of prices and wages, but there are difficulties associated with this, especially if the index covers a long period.

(3) The difference between real income and money income is attributable to inflation. During a period of inflation the cost of living always rises and the standard of living normally falls.

(4) Inflations may be demand inflations or cost inflations. The signs are that recent British inflation has been predominantly cost inflation attributable to high wage increases.

(5) Governments like to control inflation because of the distortions it produces: especially the hardship to fixed-income earners, and the problems caused for the Balance of Payments.

(6) Many countries suffer from a greater rate of inflation than the United Kingdom but they do not normally include our major competitors.

(7) Monetary and fiscal policies were effective in controlling inflation in the 1950's and early 1960's but more recently the use of such policies, while increasing unemployment as usual, has been accompanied by accelerating inflation.

(8) In view of this some attempts have been made to control inflation by means of an incomes policy, with little success. The debate on the merits of incomes policies continues.

(9) In view of the inability of monetary and fiscal policies and of incomes policy some believe that control could be achieved through expansionary policy, though this carries the risk of generating even greater inflation.

(12) Suggested Further Reading

HUTTON, G., *Inflation and Society*, Allen & Unwin, London, 1960.

PAISH, F. W. and HENNESSY, J., *Policy for Incomes*, Institute of Economic Affairs, London, 1967.

The National Board for Prices and Incomes, *Reports 1965–1971*, HMSO.

Exercises Set 4

1. Why do most Governments strive to control inflation?
2. Discuss the merits of the assertion that inflation is best controlled by a wages freeze.
3. What are the main difficulties associated with the implementation of a successful incomes policy?
4. Assess the contributions that (*a*) monetary policy, (*b*) fiscal policy can make in the fight against inflation.

5. 'The injustice of inflation is that those who cause it are rarely those who suffer from it.' Comment.

6. Using the information depicted in Figure 7 comment on the economic difficulties facing the Government in the 1960's.

7. Explain and analyse the role of the National Board for Prices and Incomes.

8. 'The control of inflation is necessary for international rather than domestic reasons.' Comment.

9. What are the causes of inflation? To what extent do the causes dictate the remedy?

10. Why has the traditional relationship between unemployment and inflation broken down in recent years?

CHAPTER FIVE

FINANCIAL INSTITUTIONS AND MONETARY POLICY

(1) Introduction

In the previous chapters we have discussed some of the aims of economic policy and the extent to which the Government could be considered successful in pursuing such aims. One set of policies that are available to the Government in its attempt to secure its aims is monetary policy. It is the function of the Bank of England to implement this policy by influencing the supply of money and credit and its price.

The structure of the money and capital markets is such that the Bank is forced to conduct its policies via a wide range of financial institutions, and in the following sections of this chapter we examine the functions and policies of those institutions before studying the role of the Bank of England.

(2) The Deposit Banks

These Banks are also referred to as Clearing Banks, Commercial Banks, and Joint-Stock Banks, but official statistics now refer to them as Deposit Banks.

The main Deposit Banks are the London Clearing Banks, the Scottish Banks, and the Northern Ireland Banks. In fact 90 per cent of their business is conducted by the London Clearing Banks and what is said below relates to them unless specifically stated otherwise. The distinguishing feature of the Deposit Banks is their role (via the cheque system and the Clearing House) in transferring money from one account to another. But from the point of view of monetary policy their importance lies in their power to create credit or purchasing power. A comprehensive discussion of this ability will be found in *Economics Made Simple*, but it is worth reiterating the main points here.

The Creation of Credit. The Banks know from experience that the majority of their clients will transfer the bulk of their deposits (if at all) by cheque payments. Thus if there were only one Clearing Bank the bulk of transactions would require no cash movement and could be settled by adjusting the entries in the personal accounts involved. The claim to money that is represented by each Bank deposit would be transferred from one account to another. As there are several Banks involved and it is unlikely that daily transactions between customers of any two Banks will exactly cancel each other out a relatively small cash adjustment is in fact required at the end of each day's business in the Clearing House.

The Banks have established that no more than 5 per cent of their total deposits is likely to be withdrawn on any one day and the bulk of that will quickly be redeposited by its new recipients. Therefore every time they receive a £100 of cash they can regard this as the 5 per cent cash base for deposits of £2,000, the original £100 together with an additional £1,900 which they create merely by book entries in the accounts of clients who want to borrow. It is important to realize that the £1,900 does not exist in any tangible form: it is merely a ledger entry confirming the client's claim to money. The whole system depends upon the confidence of customers that they can have cash if they want it.

Thus, the system of fractional reserve banking puts the Clearing Banks in a very powerful position, and although their own prudence will prevent them lending the whole of the £1,900 above to private sector borrowers, it is in the public interest as well as in the interest of economic policy that the direction of their lending should be subject to controls by the Bank of England. This may be explained by reference to the abbreviated Balance Sheet for the London Clearing Banks in Table 17.

Table 17. London Clearing Banks: Main Liabilities and Assets (July 1975)

Liabilities £ millions		Assets £ millions	
Current Accounts Deposit Accounts	22,654	Cash in hand	775
		Cash at Bank of England	243
		Money at call and short notice	953
		Treasury Bills discounted	938
		Other bills discounted	444
		Special deposits	552
		Investments	2,171
		Advances to customers	14,263

Source: Financial Statistics.

Until 1971 the banks were obliged to maintain a ratio of cash to deposits of 8 per cent. It is now their own business sense that prompts them to keep a ratio of approximately 5 per cent to meet any demand for cash from their customers. If the ratio falls lower than this the banks will take steps to restore it by selling some other assets. However, the ratio is kept as low as possible since cash earns the banks no money if it is left in their tills. Some of their cash is kept at the Bank of England and is used to replenish the cash in the banks' tills or to settle debts that arise between the banks. While there is no longer a formal liquidity ratio to be kept the banks make a point of holding a fair proportion of their assets in a liquid form—that is, a form that can be turned into cash within three months. The other liquid assets that appear in Table 17 include money at call and short notice which represents advances mainly to financial houses in the City for at the most fifteen days and frequently on only an overnight basis.

Treasury Bills are Bills of Exchange drawn by the Treasury on itself to finance the residual expenditure of the Government. Government income is received intermittently (with great inflows in January and July when many tax payments are due), but their expenditure is spread more evenly over the year. Treasury Bills, sold by tender to the highest bidder, are intended to fill the gap. Budget surpluses of recent years have reduced the overall significance of such Bills, as Government borrowing requirements have fallen.

Other Bills, likewise issued for three months, represent short-term finance to commerce and industry and although they have grown recently as other forms of finance have tightened they no longer hold the important position they developed in the nineteenth century.

These assets together with Company Tax Reserve Certificates, British

Government Stocks with less than one year to maturity, constitute the *Eligible reserve assets* of the banks as laid down by the Bank of England. These assets must equal at least 12½ per cent of the Eligible Liabilities of the Banks; *Eligible Liabilities* are the total sterling deposits of the banks, except for those originally made for a period of two years or more, which are not characteristic of bank operations.

The interest earned on these assets no longer bears any fixed relationship to Bank Rate, which has itself been changed to the Minimum Lending Rate, and is fixed weekly half a per cent above the rate earned on Treasury Bills rounded up to the nearest ¼ per cent. Each of the Banks has its own base rate which it sets in the light of market conditions, and the rate of interest it charges for various forms of loans is related to the base rate. The main point to note here is that the rate on short term loans is lower than on long term, but short term loans are more profitable than holding cash.

Other Assets. Of the item investments in Table 17, approximately 60 per cent are gilt-edged and themselves cover at any one time a range of liquidity: some of these investments will be due for redemption in the near future; others will have several years to run. Although the return on these investments will be higher than the return on the liquid assets the exact yield depends on the price that the Banks paid for the securities and any change in the rate of interest since the date of issue. The most profitable of the Banks' assets are their advances the interest on which is now geared to the banks' base rate. Table 18 shows the current structure of such advances and incidentally gives some idea of the importance of Overseas Banks in London.

The Special Deposits which are discussed more fully on page 63 are compulsory deposits at the Bank of England designed to reduce the overall liquidity and lending power of the Banks.

Table 18. Bank Advances in Great Britain (February 1975)

	£ millions
Manufacturing	9,843
Agriculture, Forestry, and Fishing	975
Mining and Quarrying	452
Construction	2,212
Financial	6,974
Services	7,469
Personal	4,047
Total to United Kingdom residents	31,982
To Overseas residents	14,818
Total	46,790

Source: Financial Statistics.

So we can see that the Banks have great power to create credit, and it must be remembered that the majority of purchasing power consists of such deposits. The amount of credit they can create is limited by their need to hold reserve assets to the extent of 12½ per cent of their eligible liabilities.

To some extent this requirement dictates the direction in which some credit must be created. But the banks now have considerably more freedom over the distribution of their assets than they had when both the cash ratio and the liquidity ratio were laid down for them.

(3) Recent Developments in Banking

Mergers. In common with most other industries the Banking industry has been subject to structural change in recent years. The most widely publicized mergers were the *horizontal amalgamations* (see Chapter Eleven) of the National Provincial with the Westminster Banks to form the National Westminster, which also incorporates Coutts and Company, and the absorption of Martins Bank by Barclays. The principal justification for the mergers were the expensive duplication of High Street sites, the expensive computerization of banking services, and the difficulties of recruiting staff (though this problem has been somewhat eased by the ending of Saturday banking). Ostensibly such mergers which have reduced the number of Clearing Banks result in a fall in competition in the industry, but since the Banks did not compete on price the impact was not likely to be serious as far as the banking public was concerned.

As to competition between the Banks, the report of the Prices and Incomes Board in 1966 hoped that the practice of jointly fixing interest rates and charges would be ended. This practice did cease in 1971 as a result of the new policy introduced by the Bank of England, but it is still unusual for different banks to charge significantly different rates of interest.

The Prices and Incomes Board report was also critical of the Banks' reluctance to lend on a long-term basis (most of the advances in Table 18 are for a two-year duration, although admittedly many are almost automatically renewable). The Banks' reply to this has been (and in some cases had already been) to move into the Hire-Purchase market and other areas by *vertical mergers.* Thus, the Lombard Banking Group was acquired by the National Westminster Bank. Such rationalization seems justifiable because of the clear connection and indeed overlap between the functions of the Joint-Stock Banks and the Finance Houses.

More recently the Clearing Banks have become associated with longer-term investment by forming associations with Unit Trusts and Investment Trusts, and are seemingly developing closer links with the Insurance Companies. Clearly, then, the structure of the Clearing Banks is rapidly changing and through such diversification they are coming to embrace the whole field of financial activity.

Other Developments. Perhaps the most striking development has been the move towards the cashless society symbolized by Barclaycards and Access credit cards. Starting in 1966, the former now has some 3·2 million card-holders who may use their cards at about 87,000 retail outlets. The scheme is financed partly by a commission paid by the retail outlets and partly by the interest paid by account-holders who wish to borrow against their cards, and who pay interest at 2 per cent per month. Despite the widespread use of credit cards neither Barclaycard nor Access have yet been able to make sufficient profit from their operation.

The increasing use of cash dispensers, easier withdrawal facilities at branches other than an account-holder's own branch, and the development of the Bank Giro are further examples of the ways in which the Clearing Banks are adapting themselves to change, increasingly assisted by the introduction of computers.

(4) The Discount Houses

The Discount Houses, in many ways unique to the British monetary system, were developed mainly during the period of the Industrial Revolution. Their role has changed as economic circumstances and requirements have changed and their present functions are best discussed by reference to their combined Balance Sheet in Table 19.

The principal source of their funds is, and has long been, the London Clearing Banks and the bulk of this is borrowed at a rate of interest of $1\frac{5}{8}$ per cent below the M.L.R. for a very short period (it is, of course, part of the Clearing Banks' money at call and short notice). The assets side shows, however, a less stable picture. The structure of the assets has changed noticeably in recent years. At the end of 1962 Bills of Exchange accounted for over 55 per cent of the assets and of these 73 per cent were Treasury Bills and 27 per cent Commercial Bills. By March 1973 Bills of Exchange had fallen to about 35 per cent of assets and of these Bills only 30 per cent were Treasury Bills and the remainder were Commercial Bills. Like the Deposit Banks the Discount Houses have found that as the Government has found other ways of borrowing, its need to finance itself by issuing Treasury Bills has declined. The budget surplus and the credit squeeze of 1964 was accompanied by a growth of credit in the form of Commercial Bills of Exchange and the Discount Houses were happy to advance money to business on the strength of these. But restrictions were imposed on the growth of such credit in 1965, since when it has remained subject to the same ceilings as Bank advances.

Just as the Clearing Banks have been developing new outlets for their skills, so the Discount Houses have lately been entering new fields. Though their main work is still concerned with short-term funds, there have been some moves towards longer-term activities, through liaisons with firms of stock-jobbers. In particular they have played an important part in the development of a market for dollar and sterling certificates of deposit—a new form of negotiable instrument.

Local Authority Loans. A fairly recent development for the Discount Houses has been the growth of advances normally for twelve months to Local Authorities. Not considered important enough for separate identification in the early sixties such loans accounted for over 10 per cent of assets by 1973.

The Issue of Treasury Bills. The position of the Discount Houses in the issue of Treasury Bills is of importance to the Treasury and the Clearing Banks. The London Discount Houses each enter a separate tender for the whole of any week's issue of Bills, thus guaranteeing to the Government that their residual borrowing requirement will be met. To the Clearing Banks, who never bid direct for Bills except on behalf of their customers, the Discount Houses act as wholesalers providing Bills in the quantity and of the maturity required by Banks when they want them. (There is, of course, no guarantee that the Discount Houses will be allotted any Bills, since they are allocated to the highest bidder. On three occasions in 1970 all Bills went to outside bidders; twice with the Discount Houses bidding one old penny less than the lowest price accepted.)

Lender of the Last Resort. A further traditional and important role for the Discount Houses arises in connection with the Bank of England's function as Lender of the Last Resort. If the Clearing Banks are short of cash they

Table 19. Discount Houses Balance Sheet 1962–74 (£m)

ASSETS	Total	United Kingdom Government Stocks	United Kingdom Treasury Bills	Other Bills	Local Authority	Others
End 1962	1,251	488	502	189	—	72
End 1966	1,565	542	424	404	101	95
End 1974	3,026	10	729	1,370	344	593

LIABILITIES	Total	Bank of England	London Clearing Banks	Scottish Banks	Other Domestic Banks	Accepting Houses Overseas Banks	Others
End 1962	1,186	8	706	97	—	234	140
End 1966	1,484	82	978	94	—	201	119
End 1974	2,567	—	1,120	164	97	1,135	300

Source: Bank of England Quarterly Bulletin.

call in some of their loans to the Discount Market to restore the cash ratio to 5 per cent. Since the Discount Houses have this money tied up in Treasury Bills and other assets for the next three months they try to borrow elsewhere to repay their debts. As a last resort, money being tight and unobtainable elsewhere, the Discount Houses turn to the Bank of England where they are allowed to borrow against appropriate security and at a rate set by the Bank. The Bank reserves the right to lend to them at M.L.R. or above but provided that it is satisfied with the existing money situation it will lend at up to $1\frac{5}{8}$ per cent below that Rate to enable them to make their legitimate profits. Since no other institutions normally have this access to the Bank of England the Discount Houses are the channel through which the market is kept supplied with money.

(5) Some Other Financial Institutions

Merchant Banks. The term 'merchant bank' is applied to a very large number of financial institutions, emphasizing the lack of clear boundaries between them, but is a term that was once reserved for the members of the Accepting Houses Committee, who apart from their original trading functions specialized in accepting Bills of Exchange. The endorsement of a Bill by such a house is a guarantee that the Bill will be honoured on the due date. The boundaries of merchant banking are far from clear. The accepting of Bills is still important but of growing significance are the roles of financial consultants to industry, in, for example, the question of share issues and take-over bids, the establishment of Unit Trusts and Investment Trusts, interests in property developments and insurance, in the gold market and in foreign-exchange dealings.

Overseas Banks. As an international banking centre London has always attracted a large number of foreign banks, whose activities have grown rapidly in recent years. Apart from ordinary banking functions performed mainly on behalf of clients overseas, these banks are mainly concerned with the various short-term sterling and dollar markets operating in the City.

The National Giro is a more recent addition to the scene, and is still in a somewhat minor league with gross deposits of £107 million in October 1974 against those of the London Clearing Banks of over £20,000 million. While the future of Giro is in some doubt it has provided a degree of much-needed competition to the Clearing Banks.

The common characteristic of the institutions we have discussed so far is their interest in relatively short-term finance (though many are also involved in longer-term lending and borrowing). There are many other organizations whose primary functions are in the provision of funds on a long-term basis. They are dealt with later in the chapter.

(6) The Bank of England

At the head of this assortment of banks and near banks is the Bank of England, established in 1694, nationalized in 1946, and responsible to the Government for the implementation of monetary policy. Since the Bank Charter Act of 1844 the Bank of England has for administrative and accounting purposes been divided into the Issue Department and the Banking Department.

The Issue Department. The position of the Issue Department is shown in

Table 20. Its liabilities consist entirely of Bank Notes, the majority of which are held by the public either as individuals or as institutions. The corresponding assets are for all practical purposes Government Securities. Thus every time the Issue Department wants to put new (extra not replacement) notes into circulation it does so by acquiring extra Government Stock. It is, by the way, via the Issue Department that the Bank gradually releases new issues of Government Stocks to the public and gradually buys up stock nearing redemption. By this method the authorities avoid great fluctuations in the supply of money which might be destabilizing to the securities market in particular and the economy in general.

Table 20. The Issue Department of the Bank of England (19 February 1975)

(£ millions)

Notes in circulation	5,306	Government Securities	4,834
Notes in Banking Department	19	Other Assets	491
Total	5,325		5,325

The Banking Department. The position of the Banking Department is shown in Table 21.

Table 21. The Banking Department of the Bank of England (19 February 1975)

Public Deposits	22	Government Securities	1,215
Bankers' Deposits	275	Discounts and Advances	302
Special Deposits	935	Others	84
Other Deposits	378	Notes and Coins	19
Total	1,620	Total	1,620

(i) Public Deposits. In its role as Banker to the Government the Bank of England runs all the Government accounts and the balances of those accounts appear as public deposits. It is one of the economies of the Government that they keep these deposits as low as is practicable. All Government receipts eventually find their way into these accounts and all payments by the Government come from these accounts.

(ii) Bankers' deposits refer not only to the 'Cash at the Bank of England' of the London Clearing Banks but also to the deposits of a wide range of other 'banks' including the Discount Houses and Overseas Banks. Such deposits may be used for the settlement of inter-bank debts, and settlements between the public and private sectors will be reflected by changes in public deposits and banks' deposits.

(iii) Special deposits are compulsory deposits from the Joint-Stock Banks to the Bank of England designed to reduce the liquidity and thus the lending powers of the Banks. They have become an essential part of monetary control and are discussed in that context later (see page 63).

(iv) Other accounts include those of other banking institutions and any private customers (including Bank of England employees) that the Bank still has.

(v) As with the Issue Department the principal assets of the Banking Department are Government Securities of varying liquidity, acquired and dispensed in connection with open-market operations. Discounts and advances are of importance to the implementation of monetary policy in that they are primarily acquired by the Bank in its role as Lender of the Last Resort. When the Discount Houses are short of cash the Bank advances it against the security of first-class Bills of Exchange.

(7) Monetary Policy

The most important single task of the Bank of England is the administration of monetary policy. In its efforts to control the level of economic activity and to achieve the macro-economic aims discussed in Chapter One the Government has three broad areas of policy available to it: monetary policy, fiscal policy (see Chapter Six), and direct controls mainly in the form of an incomes policy (see Chapter Four) or Hire-Purchase regulations. Each seems to enjoy its fashion and currently much emphasis is placed by some economists on the central role of monetary policy, which has in fact played a secondary part to fiscal policy for much of the post-war period. In this section we examine the traditional weapons of monetary policy together with the way in which they and newer techniques have been applied in recent years.

Traditional Techniques

Bank Rate was technically the rate at which the Bank of England would advance money to the Discount Houses against the security of first-class Bills of Exchange (either Treasury Bills or suitable endorsed Commercial Bills). Its importance lay in its influence over other rates of interest. Thus if Bank Rate stood at 6 per cent the rate on Clearing Bank deposit accounts was at 4 per cent and on loans from the Clearing Banks to most categories of borrowers at 8 per cent. This relationship between deposit rates, advance rates, and Bank Rate was a fixed one adhered to by all the Banks. The other rates in the money market are not rigidly fixed and are to a certain extent subject to market forces. Money at call and short notice would command around $4\frac{7}{8}$ per cent and the rate of interest on Treasury Bills might be 5–$5\frac{1}{2}$ per cent per annum. (Treasury Bills are issued at a discount and rates quoted on them are normally discount rates. Thus a discount rate of $5\frac{1}{2}$ per cent implies that a Treasury Bill for £10,000 has been taken up at £9,862·50, £137·50 being a quarter of £550. The purchaser of such a Bill would get a rate of interest of $\frac{137\frac{1}{2}}{9862\frac{1}{2}} \times 100$ per cent $\times$ 4 or approximately 5·6 per cent per annum.)

Other rates of interest such as those offered and charged by Finance Houses, Local Authorities, and Building Societies would respond to a change in Bank Rate, though frequently after a substantial time-lag. Such an adjustment eventually occurred since all the institutions are competing for funds from the general public. The pattern of rates that is established will reflect the risk involved and the liquidity of the funds. If one of the competing groups raises the rate it offers on deposits the pattern of rates is changed and unless the other groups adjust their rates they will normally lose funds as investors seek a higher return on their money.

Bank Rate was not always the leader of other rates. Operators in the market adjusted rates according to the supply of funds whether Bank Rate changed or not. The role of Bank Rate was to establish a framework within which such market adjustments occurred, and those adjustments often anticipated a change in Bank Rate.

The Effect of a Change in Bank Rate

Now with Bank Rate at 6 per cent suppose that a Discount House borrows £100,000 from the Clearing Banks at $4\frac{3}{8}$ per cent and invests in Treasury Bills yielding $4\frac{5}{8}$ per cent interest per annum. Over the three months' life of the Bills a profit of £62·50 can be expected. (Remember $4\frac{3}{8}$ per cent and $4\frac{5}{8}$ per cent are the annual rates.) But if the Clearing Banks immediately demand repayment of the call money the Discount Houses are obliged to find the cash which is, of course, tied up for three months. In such circumstances the market may be forced to borrow from the Bank of England at Bank Rate against the security of Treasury Bills. At worst they must borrow £100,000 at 6 per cent for three months. In other words while they have gross receipts of £1,156·25 on the Treasury Bills they spend £1,500 on their loan from the Bank of England, though the penalty will be smaller, the older the Treasury Bills.

This is clearly not a profitable proposition and in future the Discount House will charge more for lending to the Government via Treasury Bills, and rates in the discount market will creep up. Moreover, should the Bank of England want to increase rates in general it need only increase Bank Rate (and thus increase the penalty on Discount Houses forced into the Bank).

The Bank's aims are:

(i) To raise the rates on Trade Bills to deter some entrepreneurs from marginal projects.

(ii) To raise the rates on Commercial Bills thus indirectly increasing Hire-Purchase rates.

(ii) To force up other rates: the Clearing Banks put up their rates to keep their competitive position relative to other institutions. The important point is that it is through the Discount Houses that the Bank gets rates to rise.

It should be noted that the Bank of England did not have to alter Bank Rate to alter interest rates: marginal adjustment to money rates may be achieved by open-market operations (see below); by altering the supply of money available the Bank can (and does) achieve alterations in the rate of interest.

The Effectiveness of Bank Rate

It is difficult to assess the effectiveness of a change in Bank Rate since any change was usually part of a package deal involving monetary and fiscal policy.

While a change in Bank Rate can involve profits or losses of thousands of pounds in the Discount Market its effectiveness as a weapon of general economic policy has long been doubted.

Indeed for nearly twenty years until 1951 the rate was fixed at 2 per cent and not used at all. In 1958 the Radcliffe Committee heard evidence that the rate of interest was among the last items considered by large firms investing in new plant. There is evidence, too, that in the market for durable consumer goods it is the physical controls over Hire-Purchase credit (raising deposits, reducing repayment periods) rather than changes in the rate of interest that deter borrowers. Despite historically high rates for house mortgages there is no shortage of applicants.

For the Bank Rate to be effective on its own (e.g. to bring about changes in the level of fixed-capital formation) changes in the Rate might have to be of the order of 6 or 7 percentage points at a time. This would be quite unacceptable for several reasons.

(i) The price of gilt-edged securities varies inversely with the rate of interest.

If the Government issues £100 of stock at 5 per cent the holder knows that he will receive £5 of interest per year. Now if by the time the Government wants to issue more stock the long-term rate of interest has risen to $7\frac{1}{2}$ per cent a person with £100 to invest can obtain £7·50 per annum by buying the new security. He will not be interested in buying the old one unless its price falls to £66·66$\frac{1}{2}$ $\left(£100 \times \frac{5}{7{\cdot}5}\right)$ so as to yield £$7\frac{1}{2}$ per cent. Obvious violent changes in Bank Rate would effect great changes in the price of fixed-interest securities, and bring chaos to the markets. In practice the Bank lays great emphasis on maintaining a stable gilt-edge market.

(ii) A heavy rise in Bank Rate in the United Kingdom would lead to a great inflow of currency from abroad seeking the highest return. Initially this would benefit the Balance of Payments but eventually this would be counteracted by the higher interest paid to overseas depositors. Such destabilizing influences would be unacceptable to the international monetary authorities.

(iii) The Government, being normally the largest borrower in the country, has an interest in keeping Bank Rate as low as possible. Despite this Figure 15 shows the unmistakable upward trend of Bank Rate since 1950, partly reflecting inflation and anticipation of inflation, as well as the conditions of demand and supply of money.

We may conclude that the role of Bank Rate was an indicative one. Most of what has been said about Bank Rate applies to the new Minimum Lending Rate.

Open-market Operations. While Bank Rate is designed to influence the price of money directly, open-market operations are concerned mainly with the supply of money, influencing the price only indirectly. The significance of open-market operations rests upon the fractional reserve principle. We have already observed (see page 50) that the Clearing Banks are able to create credit far in excess of any cash that they receive. If the authorities can increase the amount of cash in the hands of the banks they can secure a much larger increase in Bank advances, and in purchasing power in the economy.

An Example of Open-Market Operations

Let us suppose that the Clearing Banks are in a position where their cash ratio and liquidity ratio are at the required minimum of 8 per cent and 28 per cent.

	£ millions		£ millions
Deposits	10,000	Cash	800
		Other Liquid Assets	2,000
		Other Assets	7,200

Suppose, also, that the level of unemployment being too high the Government is intent on expanding economic activity by encouraging Bank lending. The Government Broker is instructed to buy gilt-edged securities in the Stock Exchange. (He will frequently buy the most short-dated bonds to facilitate the management of the National Debt.) The sequence of events is as follows:

(i) The Bank of England pays for the securities it buys with a cheque drawn on itself. (The Bank can always find a buyer or seller by adjusting the price it asks or offers.)

(ii) The recipients of such cheques pay them into their accounts at the Clearing Banks.

(iii) The Clearing Banks present the cheques to the Bank of England and their accounts at the Bank are then credited with the cash.

Assuming the Bank of England bought securities for £300 million the position of the Clearing Banks would now be:

	£ millions		£ millions
Deposits	10,300	Cash	1,100
		Other Liquid Assets	2,000
		Other Assets	7,200

(iv) They now have a cash ratio of 10·68 per cent and a liquidity ratio of 30·1 per cent, and are therefore in a position to increase their profits by increasing their 'other assets', investments and advances thereby increasing deposits until the cash and liquidity ratios are restored to the required level.

(v) A cash base of £1,100 million is able to sustain deposits of £13,750 million (i.e. £1,100 million is 8 per cent of £13,750 million). But if the Clearing Banks were to move immediately to this position

	£ millions		£ millions
Deposits	13,750	Cash	1,100
		Other Liquid Assets	2,000
		Other Assets	10,650

creating all the extra credit of £3,450 million in the form of advances and investments the liquidity ratio would be too low at about 22½ per cent.

The extra assets must be created in such proportions as to preserve the appropriate liquidity ratio.

(vi) The final outcome is therefore

	£ millions		£ millions
Deposits	13,750	Cash	1,100
		Other Liquid Assets	2,750
		Other Assets	9,900

By purchasing £300 million of securities in the market the Bank of England has been able to increase the other assets of the Clearing Banks by over £3,000 million. Purchasing power in the economy is therefore increased and the level of economic activity should also rise, though because the credit is created partly in a liquid form and partly to finance investments, by no means all of it is available to the public.

If the Bank of England wished to reduce the level of activity it would of course have to sell securities in the market.

Difficulties in achieving the desired results in this direction led to the introduction of Special Deposits.

The effect of open-market operations will not be restricted to their impact on the cash position of the Clearing Banks. Indeed this may not be the main aim of sales and purchases. If the Bank of England wishes to influence rates of interest it can do so by buying and selling securities. Thus, if the Bank is selling securities their price tends to fall and yield on them rises; Bank purchases on the other hand increase prices and reduce yields. Such operations which occur on a daily basis are frequently referred to as *smoothing operations* —designed to level out fluctuations in the rate of interest, a matter of some importance to the Government as a major borrower.

Effectiveness of Open-market Operations

(i) Open-market operations are likely to have a far greater impact in expanding the economy (where the Banks will be eager to co-operate, thereby pleasing their customers and their shareholders) than in restricting activity. The authorities have in the past experienced difficulty in containing Bank lending when the liquidity ratios have been kept substantially above the minimum.

(ii) The two aims of fixing interest rates and controlling the level of the Banks' cash reserves are not entirely compatible. If, for example, the authorities wish to reduce the cash holdings of the Banks they must sell securities. This causes yields to rise and interest rates in general increase. But if the Bank of England is reducing the powers of the Clearing Banks to create credit it presumably wishes to accompany this with higher interest rates. Clearly interest rates and liquidity cannot both be fixed.

The clash between interest rates and liquidity in controlling the banks set a limit to the scale of open market operations. Accordingly, open market operations have been relegated to a minor role in monetary policy since 1971.

The emphasis now is on the rate of interest rising to find its market level and Special Deposits being used to control the supply of money. At the same time other difficulties persuaded the monetary authorities that a new and more comprehensive policy was required. Most monetary measures now cover the whole range of banking institutions, not only the main deposit banks.

Modern Techniques

It was apparent in the 1960's that changes in Bank Rate and the use of open-market operations could not bring about the restraint on credit that was required. The authorities have therefore relied heavily on *Special Deposits* and *Directives or Requests.*

(*a*) *Special Deposits.* The lending power of the Banks is related to the size of the liquid assets: the greater they are the more credit the Banks can create. Furthermore, if the liquidity ratio is too high the use of restrictive open-market operations is impeded. For example, suppose the Banks have to maintain a liquidity ratio of at least 30 per cent but in fact have a ratio of 35 per cent:

	£ millions		£ millions
Deposits	10,000	Cash	1,000
		Other Liquid Assets	2,500
		Other Assets	6,500

If the Bank of England wishes to restrict lending it sells securities in the open market. If it sells £100 million worth, then £100 million is transferred from the Clearing Banks to the Bank of England leaving the Clearing Banks with a fractionally depleted cash ratio of 9·9 per cent:

	£ millions		£ millions
Deposits	9,900	Cash	900
		Other Liquid Assets	2,500
		Other Assets	6,500

But this is easily restored to 10 per cent by calling in loans to the Discount Houses of £90 million, and since the liquidity ratio is still comfortably above the required minimum there is no impact on advances.

	£ millions		£ millions
Deposits	9,900	Cash	990
		Other Liquid Assets	2,410
		Other Assets	6,500

The Special Deposits scheme is designed to counter both these problems. First used in 1961 the scheme empowers the Bank of England to call for Special Deposits from the Clearing Banks equal to a given percentage of their total deposits. The volume of special deposits required will depend upon the Government's view of the economy. The need to restrain bank lending will prompt the Bank to call for more special deposits. Money thus frozen is not available for lending elsewhere. On the other hand, if the Bank of England releases special deposits it will not normally be difficult for the banker to find an outlet for the extra money now available. Even so, it will be difficult for the government to decide on the best level of special deposits to demand.

The Clearing Banks felt a certain sense of injustice in that the Special Deposits scheme applied only to them and not to all the other institutions with the power to create credit. But since the introduction of the new monetary policy in 1971 a wide variety of financial institutions have been subject to Special Deposits when they have been called. These deposits are now the main method of control.

(*b*) *Requests*. An increasing use has been made of directives as well. Such directives are used mainly to fix ceilings on Bank lending, though in recent years they have also tried to influence the direction of such lending. When directives were used in the 1950s they applied exclusively to the Clearing Banks, but from 1971 all other Banks have been subject to general directives. The most active use of this device has occurred since 1965. One such request was made in 1970 when the banks were requested to see that lending did not expand by more than 5 per cent in the ensuing twelve months. But it was not simply the scale of lending that concerned the authorities. The following ex tract from the notice issued by the Bank of England and Finance Houses indicates the qualitative as well as the quantitative nature of requests:

> Any increase in lending should be directed to the finance of export transactions . . . and to finance for production and investment which can be expected to contribute to the Balance of Payments over the coming years by making possible increased exports, high invisible earnings or savings in imports. It is not intended that there should be any increase in finance for personal consumption . . .

While it is difficult to argue with the aims of such requests there has been considerable criticism of the use of ceilings and their arbitrary effects. The choice of base dates is important and any given percentage rise that is allowed is a greater penalty to Banks that are underlent than to those that have exceeded previous ceilings. Further, although the requests apply to all Banks and Finance Houses there is a wide range of financial institutions to whom they only became applicable in 1971. The Bank hopes to keep such requests to a minimum.

Such requests also tend to remove the implementation of monetary policy from the Government and the Bank of England to the Clearing Banks and their branches. It is there that decisions have to be made as to which applicants for loans shall be satisfied.

Conclusions on Monetary Policy

These, then, are principal aspects of monetary policy. To them may be added the practice of *funding* whereby the Bank buys up short-dated Government Stock from the market and sells instead long-dated stock; and physical controls over Hire-Purchase credit.

The overall effectiveness of monetary policy in controlling the economy is difficult to assess, because, as we noted earlier it is always associated with various fiscal measures. It is, however, essentially a macro-economic policy in that it affects all sectors of the economy at the same time: if interest rates rise in one sector, they rise in all sectors. It is not therefore a policy for the fine-tuning of the economy—fiscal policy is probably better for this in that taxes can be levied on particular sectors of the economy.

As we saw in Chapter Four the supply of money is of importance in the regulation of the level of demand and in the generation of inflation, and in the next section we examine briefly what is to be understood by the term the 'supply of money'.

(8) **The Supply of Money**

The renewed interest in the money supply as an important factor in the generation of inflation led the authorities in 1970 to reconsider their definition of the supply of money.

Quite clearly something much broader than notes and coins is required and Bank deposits have always been included as the major part of money. The important question to be answered is how far one goes in including such deposits: the 'supply of money' will obviously vary according to the number of institutions that qualify as banks.

The authorities have overcome this problem by providing not one but three definitions, the narrowest of which M_1 covers notes and coins and all Bank deposits belonging to the private sector and denominated in sterling and transferable by cheque on demand. It thus corresponds closely with the idea of money as a medium of exchange. Somewhat broader was M_2, no longer much used. It adds to M_1 the private sector deposit accounts with the Deposit Banks and the Discount Houses, both of which, though subject to seven days' notice, may be regarded as completely liquid for practical purposes. Finally M_3 includes notes and coins, and all resident deposits with the United Kingdom banking sector in sterling or foreign currency. The differences between the definitions amount broadly to differences in liquidity, since the items included in M_3 can be turned into cash in a fairly short period if necessary.

As a concluding point of interest the value of M_1 and M_3 have changed as follows in recent years.

Table 22. Money Supply (Average Amounts Outstanding)
(£ millions)

	M_1	M_3
1968	8,044	14,978
1969	8,075	15,618
1970	8,489	16,570
1971	10,023	18,831
1972	11,682	22,941
1973	12,842	29,148
1974	13,370	34,983

Source: Financial Statistics.

A more detailed examination of the changes in the supply of money would reveal that the Government's borrowing has contributed significantly to the increase.

(9) The Capital Market

The institutions we have studied so far in this chapter are primarily concerned with the provision of short-term funds. But business and Government departments often require funds on a long-term basis, and for these they have resort to the Capital Market, where through a variety of institutions the surplus savings accumulated by various sectors of the economy are made available to other sectors whose savings are insufficient to meet their capital requirements. In this section we briefly examine the supply of those savings and some of the channels through which they travel.

Savings and Capital Requirements. Table 23 shows the main sources of savings and the application of those funds in 1972.

Before any investment in real assets can occur the funds have to be made available either by the savings of the individual or organization who is to undertake the investment or by someone else foregoing consumption. In 1972 over 25 per cent of total savings was undertaken by the personal sector and this represented approximately 6 per cent of total personal income, and almost 8 per cent of total disposable income. Such savings may be used within the personal sector or, via the financial institutions, in other sectors.

While the Government's savings far exceed its own capital requirements most of the balance is absorbed either by the Public Corporations or the

Table 23. Capital Receipts and Expenditure (United Kingdom 1972)

Receipts	£ millions
Savings	
Personal Sector	3,486
Companies	4,981
Public Corporations	844
Central Government	1,379
Local Authorities	834
Additions to dividend and interest reserves	
Companies	4
Public Corporations	40
Additions to tax reserves	
Personal Sector	231
Companies	27
Public Corporations	5
Total saving before providing for depreciation and stock appreciation	11,831
Less Stock Appreciation	
Personal Sector	−213
Companies	−1057
Public Corporations	−49
Central Government	—
Total	−1,319
Residual error	345
Total	10,857
Expenditure	
Gross domestic fixed capital formation	
Personal Sector	2,300
Companies	4,275
Public Corporations	1,782
Central Government	642
Local Authorities	2,215
Total	11,214
Value of physical increase in stocks and work in progress	
Personal Sector	47
Companies	−533
Public Corporations	19
Central Government	27
Total	−440
Net investment abroad	83
Total investment	10,857

Source: National Income and Expenditure 1972.

Local Authorities, or in repaying parts of the National Debt. The new funds coming to the Capital Markets come therefore mainly from the personal sector. Table 24 reveals how the personal sector acquired and allocated its funds in 1972.

Table 24. Personal Sector: Acquisition and Use of Funds (1972)

	£ millions
Acquisition of funds	
Saving	3,714
Capital transfers	308
Borrowing	
Bank advances	1,963
Money at call	−36
Hire-purchase	241
Loans for house purchase	2,679
Other loans and mortgages	123
Other items (mainly unidentified)	681
Use of funds	
Taxes on Capital	680
Investment in Fixed Assets and Stocks	2,560
Kept as notes and coin	246
National Savings	829
Tax Reserve Certificates	−8
Short-term Local Authority Debt	35
Deposits with Banking Sector	1,767
Deposits with Building Societies	2,139
Deposits with Finance Houses	−29
British Government Securities	9
Other Local Authority Debt	−117
Company Securities	−812
Life Assurance and Superannuation	2,374

Source: Financial Statistics.

Let us look at some of the means of saving mentioned in the table paying particular attention to the direction in which institutions invest the money they collect.

National Savings. The small saver may initially decide that the most straightforward way for him to save is through the Post Office, which offers him a variety of vehicles, such as National Savings Certificates, Savings Bonds, Defence Bonds, National Development Bonds, Premium Bonds, Save-As-You-Earn schemes, ordinary savings accounts, and Trustee Savings Bonds. The great attraction of saving in one of these ways is that the money is absolutely safe. Because of this, interest rates are generally lower than in the private sector where risks may be slightly higher, but in recent years competition from the private sector and the erosion of values caused by inflation has forced up rates offered by the Post Office schemes so that many of their schemes provide a very attractive investment. The introduction of more attractive schemes was necessary to stop the flight into the private sector.

The fact that such funds are channelled into the public sector where they are at the disposal of the Exchequer means that they are not of importance to the Capital Market except in so far as they deprive the private sector of funds. The main categories of National Savings are given in Table 25.

Table 25. The Structure of National Savings (December 1973)

	£ millions
National Savings Certificates including accrued interest	2,617
British Savings Bonds	897
Defence and National Development Bonds	1
Save-As-You-Earn Balances	84
Premium Bonds	1,015
National Savings Bank Accounts	2,060
Trustee Savings Banks	3,366
Other National Savings	335
Total	10,375

Source: Financial Statistics March 1974.

However, our small saver may want to try something slightly more ambitious and so he moves out of the public sector and begins to invest his funds via the many institutions available in the private sector.

Building Societies. If the small saver looks beyond the Post Office he could save in the Clearing Banks but it is more likely that he will decide to place his savings in a Building Society, where a high degree of safety is combined with good interest rates. In general their funds are not available to commercial organizations seeking capital but they are important to them in that they provide a convenient vehicle for personal savings that might otherwise have reached the commercial market. By the end of 1973 their assets were just over £15,000 million and of this almost £13,000 million was in the form of house mortgages, the balance being mainly public sector investment.

The Insurance Companies provide a wide variety of opportunities for the saver, especially in the form of endowment policies and policies linked to Unit Trusts. In 1972 the personal sector subscribed £2,374 million to life assurance and superannuation funds. As far as the supply of capital funds is concerned, it is only the life assurance business of the companies that is important. In the case of general insurance, such as motor insurance, the bulk of premiums are needed to meet current claims and cannot therefore be tied up in long-term assets.

The life premiums collected by the companies, on the other hand, are available for longer-term investment, since the liabilities of the insurance companies are in general long term. By careful investment in Government and Company Securities the insurance companies achieve sufficient income to meet their administrative costs, to add to their portfolio each year and to share the proceeds with some classes of policy-holders. Table 26 shows the structure of their portfolio at the end of 1972.

The person contributing to a life assurance policy is thus indirectly contributing funds to a very wide range of activities. Recently the balance of investments has changed in favour of Company Securities, Government Stock

Table 26. Insurance Companies Life Funds at Book Values (31 December 1972)

	£ millions
Short-term Assets	551
British Government Securities	4,104
Local Authority Securities	389
Overseas Government Securities	132
Company Securities	8,126
Loans and Mortgages	2,553
Land, Property, and Ground Rents	2,354
Other Assets	891
Total	19,101

Source: Financial Statistics March 1974.

representing less of a hedge against inflation, but at all times it is the object of the companies to balance income carefully against safety. While it is true that most of the liabilities are long term the companies ensure that an adequate proportion of investments is in a liquid form.

Superannuation Funds. The superannuation funds are really an extension of the life assurance business, where contributions are deducted weekly or monthly from one's pay packet or made by one's employer. Table 27 shows the distribution of the investments (the structure of which varies greatly from fund to fund) at the end of 1972.

Table 27. Superannuation Funds: Investments 1972 (market value)

	Public Sector (excluding Local Authorities)	Local Authorities	Private Sector
Short-term Assets	76	65	226
British Government Securities	212	327	696
Local Authorities Debt	39	249	107
Overseas Government Securities	5	4	22
Company Securities	1,358	987	5,273
Loans and Mortgages	223	—	44
Land, Real property and ground rents	328	16	549
Others	19	197	193
Total	2,260	1,845	7,109

Source: Financial Statistics March 1974.

Obviously with money being contributed each week by employees all over the country the superannuation funds are an important source of savings for the capital market. Once again we notice that a balance is struck between safety in the form of public sector investments and income in the form of company investments, but that balance varies considerably between the various types of funds.

Unit Trusts and Investment Trusts. Unit Trusts provide an important channel for the savings of individuals, who while not wanting to risk direct investment in commercial enterprises via the Stock Exchange, are looking for something more than they can earn on Bank or Building Society Deposits. The investor buys 'units' from the managers of the Trust, who, deducting a small percentage for management expenses, invest the money in shares appropriate to the Trust deed. (Unit Trusts frequently specialize in particular sectors of industry but they spread their risks by investing in a large number of companies.) One of the disadvantages of the Unit Trust is the rigidity imposed on managers by the requirement to invest in predetermined directions. The price of units is quoted daily in the Press and reflects the underlying movements in the prices of the securities owned by the Trust; and the managers stand ready to buy or sell units at the quoted price. If unit-holders in general want to sell, the managers will have to sell investments in order to buy back units. Any income accruing to the Trust in the form of interest or dividends must be distributed to unit-holders, though they can opt to have it turned into further units. Table 28 reflects the aims of the Trusts.

Table 28. Investments of Unit Trusts (December 1973)

	£millions
Short-term Assets	333
British Government Securities	8
United Kingdom Company Securities	1,241
Overseas Company Securities	304
Total	1,886

Source: Financial Statistics March 1974.

They invest almost entirely in Company Securities and a further analysis reveals that all but £62 million of those securities are Ordinary Shares. While spreading their risks the Trusts have two aims—to secure a high income for unit-holders and to achieve capital appreciation. The two aims are not easily reconciled and frequently a Unit Trust will quite deliberately aim for one at the expense of the other. A measure of the growing popularity of this form of investment is provided by the fact that in 1960 total funds totalled only £200 million.

Another convenient way of obtaining a stake in a wide range of industry is to buy shares in an Investment Trust, which is really a Joint-Stock Company which specializes in buying the shares of other companies. Like the Unit Trusts, the Investment Trusts are mainly interested in the acquisition of Company Securities as Table 29 reveals.

Again the overwhelming majority of Company Securities are Ordinary or Deferred Shares. Since they are not restricted by Board of Trade regulations the Investment Trusts can follow a more flexible and frequently more profitable investment policy. And since they acquire their own funds through the issue of Ordinary or Preference Shares or Debentures they do not have to sell their investments if holders of those shares wish to encash them. A further difference is that the Board of the Investment Trust need not recommend that all

Table 29. Investments of Investment Trusts 1973

	£ millions
Short-term Assets	440
British Government Securities	65
United Kingdom Local Authority Securities	25
United Kingdom Company Securities	2,915
Overseas Company Securities	2,063
Other Investments	92
Total	5,600

Source: Financial Statistics March 1974.

income be paid to shareholders—reserves can be accumulated for subsequent investment, although this is of course subject to the approval of the Annual General Meeting—a safeguard not available to and (because of Government control) not required by the unit-holder.

Direct Investment. If our investor had sufficient funds and, more important, sufficient experience he could by-pass all the institutions and get a stockbroker to buy shares for him on the Stock Exchange. Such an exercise is in fact fraught with danger for the inexperienced investor: movements in prices can be sudden and ruinous to the investor who has not spread his risks. Unfortunately the principles of Stock Exchange investment lie beyond the scope of this book. Our imaginary investor must be content like most of us to allow the institutions to manage his funds for him.

There are, of course, other directions in which personal savings may be placed, but those we have looked at are the most important, and whichever of them is chosen the saver can be sure that his money will normally be safe and that he will get a rate of interest that reflects the risk he is taking and the liquidity of his funds.

(10) The Finance Corporations

In 1931 the Macmillan Committee investigating the financial system of the United Kingdom recommended the establishment of a specialist institution to fill the gap between those bodies providing short-term funds and those providing long-term capital. But it was not until 1945 that any action was taken.

The Industrial and Commercial Finance Corporation owned by the Bank of England, the London Clearing Banks, and the Scottish Banks is prepared to advance between £5,000 and £300,000 to new clients. Although owned by the Banks the ICFC is financed mainly by Debentures issued to the public (yet another channel for savings) and the funds are applied mainly in the form of secured loans, and subject to the careful appraisal of applications. In addition to the provision of capital on this basis the corporation (like the FCI it is really a public joint-stock company) has developed a wide range of other services for industry, overlapping with the management consultancy field.

The Finance Corporation for Industry operated along the same lines but was mainly concerned with the provision of sums of over £200,000. Like ICFC it now comes within a new umbrella organisation, Finance for Industry.

Other Corporations. The oldest of the finance corporations in the United Kingdom is the *Agricultural Mortgage Corporation* established in 1928 lending for up to sixty years against the security of agricultural freeholds.

The Estate Duties Investment Trust, a subsidiary of the ICFC, specializes in assisting small businesses who have difficulty in raising cash to meet death duties because of the non-marketability of their shares.

Perhaps the most interesting of the finance corporations was the short-lived *Industrial Reorganization Corporation* established in 1966 to foster rationalization and amalgamations between small firms but wound up in 1971 as an unjustifiable interference with the market mechanism before it really had time to show its value.

(11) **Summary of Chapter Five**

(1) The Deposit Banks are in a powerful position since they can create credit, the extent of which depends on their cash ratio and the direction of which depends partly on the need to keep some of their assets in a liquid form.

(2) Like other industries the Banking industry has undergone considerable structural changes in recent years.

(3) The Discount Houses have an important role to play in the smooth running of the short-term money market, especially in connection with the issue of Treasury Bills, but are subject to control by the function of the Bank of England as lender of the last resort.

(4) There are many other institutions—such as Overseas Banks, the Post Office Giro—that are involved in the management of short-term funds.

(5) At the head of all these institutions is the Bank of England responsible to the Government for the development of monetary policy, which includes Bank Rate, Open-market operations, Directives, and Special Deposits.

(6) 'The supply of money' is open to a number of interpretations and the Government currently gives three definitions.

(7) The Capital Market is concerned with the channelling of longer-term funds and there are a variety of institutions collecting small amounts from many people and investing large sums in industry, commerce, and the public sector.

(8) Specialist Finance Corporations have been established to fill gaps left by privately developed institutions.

(12) **Suggested Further Reading**

Bank of England Quarterly Bulletin.

DAY, A., *An Outline of Monetary Economics*, Oxford, 1958.

MIDGLEY, K. and BURNS, G., *Business Finance and the Capital Market*, Macmillan, London, 1969.

Report of the Radcliffe Committee on the Working of the Monetary System, HMSO, 1959.

The National Board for Prices and Incomes, *Report 34. Bank Charges*, HMSO, 1967.

Exercises Set 5

1. Why did the Radcliffe Committee conclude that the liquidity ratio is more important than the cash ratio?

2. The British Clearing Bank is required to keep a cash ratio of 10 per cent and a liquidity ratio of 30 per cent. It is in equilibrium:

Liabilities (£ millions)		Assets (£ millions)	
Deposits	5,000	Cash	500
		Other Liquid Assets	1,000
		Advances	3,500

Describe and explain how equilibrium is restored if the Central Bank buys £100 million of securities in the open market. How will the Central Bank's accounts be affected?

3. Explain the importance of the work of the London Discount Market to the smooth running of the monetary system.

4. Why has the Bank of England found it necessary to develop new methods of monetary control?

5. In what ways do you think that more competition between the Deposit Banks would lead to a better service for clients?

6. 'Recent structural changes suggest that the Clearing Banks are becoming all-embracing financial institutions.' Comment.

7. 'Bank Rate is of little importance to the domestic economy.' Why?

8. What do you understand by the term 'money supply'? Why is it important to the authorities to know the level of the money supply?

9. A friend has £1,000 which he wishes to invest. Advise him of the possibilities available to him and the advantages and disadvantages of each.

10. Distinguish between the roles of the Finance Corporation for Industry and the Industrial and Commercial Finance Corporation. Why were these bodies established?

CHAPTER SIX

PUBLIC FINANCE

(1) Introduction

The public sector is responsible for approximately half of total expenditure in the United Kingdom and the way in which this proportion has risen in recent years has been held responsible by many economists for the extent of our economic difficulties. In this chapter we shall examine the main principles underlying the income and expenditure of both the Central Government and Local Authorities—but not of the rest of the public sector, dominated by the nationalized industries.

(2) Principles of Taxation

The principles of taxation were first enumerated by Adam Smith in *The Wealth of Nations* as follows:

(*a*) Certainty: it should be clear to taxpayers how much tax they have to pay and when they have to pay it.

(*b*) Costs: the cost of assessing and raising taxation should be kept to a minimum.

(*c*) Convenience: within reason taxes should be payable at times most convenient to the taxpayer.

(*d*) Equality: members of the community should pay taxes in proportion to their incomes.

(*a*) *Certainty.* As far as individuals are concerned the British system of taxation does in general meet this requirement at least in respect of taxes on income. Despite the complexities of the system most of us do know in advance at least our approximate liability for tax; and if we do not know it, it is possible to ascertain. This is only possible because the rates of tax are declared in advance and the circumstances in which taxes are payable are very closely defined. An undesirable exception occurred in a recent budget when a retrospective levy was imposed on the investment income of certain surtax payers. The taxation of companies is also retrospective in that the rate of Corporation Tax declared in the April budget applies to companies' financial years which in many cases have already finished. But this sort of uncertainty is preferable to the legalized robbery of tax-farming whereby the revenue of an area was the responsibility of a tax-gatherer who was entitled to any surplus he was able to accumulate.

Apart from the obvious inequity of retrospective taxation the difficulties of business planning and industrial investment would be multiplied if tax rates fluctuated retrospectively or frequently, and in fact it is unusual for rates to change by very much, thus enabling acceptable forecasts of liability to be made.

(*b*) *Costs.* The cost of collecting tax amounted to 1·32p in the pound for the year 1968/69 as far as the Inland Revenue was concerned and 0·91p for the Customs and Excise department. It is one of the advantages of the British system of 'Pay-As-You-Earn' that a large proportion of the collection costs fall upon the thousands of employers up and down the country who are required to deduct tax and forward it to the Revenue. Thus the figure quoted above somewhat underestimates the cost of collection. Adam Smith had nothing to say about the costs of compliance. It is one of the weaknesses of the British system that its increasing complexity necessitates the employment of thousands of accountants on taxation matters when they might be more usefully employed on other financial problems: experts are paid to devise taxes, other experts are paid to show how to avoid them, and yet others to adjudicate between them, quite apart from the regiments of clerks needed to arrange the routine imposition and collection of the tax.

As the tax system continues to grow, somewhat haphazardly with the Government closing various loopholes only to open others, the costs of compliance and of minimizing liability can only increase. This is only one of the reasons why the British system of taxation requires a drastic overhaul.

(*c*) *Convenience*. The United Kingdom system certainly meets this requirement as the bulk of tax is payable (and deducted) as income is earned or when goods are bought. Certainly the PAYE system is far more convenient for the majority of taxpayers (and the authorities) than the previous system where tax was payable in two lump sums in January and June of the fiscal year in which the income was earned, by which time many taxpayers had to default on their payments. This system does, of course, still apply to other taxes such as Surtax and Corporation Tax payable in lump sums in the following year, but even this is convenient to the taxpayer in that he is in effect receiving an interest-free loan from the Government from the end of his financial year to the day he pays his tax.

(*d*) *Equality*. There are three methods by which a tax system may achieve some kind of equality among taxpayers:

(i) Poll taxes, where everyone pays the same amount in taxation irrespective of his income; the National Insurance contribution is such a tax.
(ii) Proportional taxes, where everyone pays the same percentage of his income in tax so that the rich pay more than the poor.
(iii) Progressive taxes, where the rich pay a greater proportion of their income in taxation than the poor.

It is, of course, the latter system that prevails today, for while the other systems have the evident merit of simplicity they make no attempt to relate the individual's *tax burden* to his *taxable capacity* or ability to pay.

The interpretation of these latter concepts has given rise to considerable academic discussion in recent years. We may note here that one's tax burden is the actual amount of tax paid expressed as a percentage of income. A refinement of this is to express the tax paid as a percentage of total income minus that part of income which is necessary for subsistence purposes; that is as a percentage of taxable capacity.

We may say that progressive taxes such as British income tax and surtax aim at *vertical equity* so that the rich pay a greater proportion of their income in tax than the poor. It is important that there is continuity within such a system so that there are no large jumps in tax liability following small changes in income. The assessment of Estate Duties in the United Kingdom allowed for marginal adjustments to avoid this kind of discontinuity, where an estate only just qualified for a higher rate of duty.

A tax system should also aim for *horizontal equity* in that two individuals with the same income and the same family commitments should pay the same amount of tax. This concept would also require all similar activities to be taxable at the same rate if any one of them were taxable. Many of the objections to the Selective Employment Tax were based on what critics felt were artificial distinctions between activities, resulting in glaring unequities.

Before examining in detail some individual taxes we must consider the general structure of taxation in the United Kingdom and the broad aims of taxation.

(3) Government Income and Expenditure

Table 30 shows the main sources of Government income and expenditure for 1973.

Table 30. Government Income and Expenditure 1973
(£ millions)

CURRENT ACCOUNT

Receipts			*Expenditure*		
Taxes on income		9,143	Current expenditure on		7,653
Income tax	6,929		goods and services		
Surtax	342		Military defence	3,316	
Profits tax	1		National Health Service	2,497	
Corporation tax	1,871		Miscellaneous	1,840	
			Subsidies		1,351
Taxes on expenditure		6,457	Housing	313	
Beer, wines, and spirits	978		Agriculture	287	
Tobacco	1,100		Nationalized transport	162	
Hydrocarbon oils	1,620		Employment premiums	114	
Protective duties	434		Miscellaneous	348	
Purchase tax	380		Current grants to personal		
Betting and gaming	184		sector		6,000
Motor Vehicle Duties	518		National Insurance	3,927	
SET	132		War Pensions	158	
VAT	2,043		Supplementary benefits	705	
National Insurance			Family allowances	360	
Contributions		3,636	Universities, Colleges	387	
National Health			Miscellaneous	463	
Contributions		237	Interest on National Debt		1,801
Redundancy Fund			Current grants to local		
Contributions		53	authorities		4,099
Gross Trading Surplus		6	Other grants		347
Rent		107	Total Current Expenditure		21,251
Interest and Dividends		1,633	Surplus		953
		22,204			22,204

Source: National Income and Expenditure.

It was once the aim of the Chancellor of the Exchequer merely to balance his budget, to set an example to the rest of the community by living within his means. Lord Keynes demonstrated the futility of such a passive role and showed that the budget might be used as the principal method of economic management if the Government were to spend more than it took in taxation when unemployment were high or spend less than its income in times of high activity. The use of the budget for control has led to the Chancellor having to weigh up a great number of economic goals when framing his budget for the year ahead.

The Purpose of the Budget. The aims of the Chancellor may be divided into macro-economic aims which are really the broad aims of economic policy and micro-economic aims affecting various sectors of the economy.

(*a*) *Macro-economic aims:* the Chancellor will consider the likely effect of his proposals on:

(i) the level of employment; including regional employment;
(ii) the rate of economic growth (can he encourage productivity?);
(iii) the standard of living;
(iv) the Balance of Payments;
(v) the general level of prices.

(*b*) *Micro-economic aims:* any taxes the Government raises or any expenditures affect individual sectors of the economy. Thus the Chancellor will have to consider whether motor exports will react to an increase in purchase tax on cars; he must carefully consider the distribution of indirect taxes; he must weigh the advantages and disadvantages of an increase in income tax against an equally productive rise in purchase tax; will money be better used to increase family allowances or to give greater subsidies to farmers, reducing the price of food and the need for family allowances? Is a reduction in taxation preferable to an increase in old-age pensions? The Chancellor is faced by these and hundreds of similar choices and he must answer them in the sure knowledge that whatever he does he will be wrong, in the eyes of at least half of the population.

He must also consider the effect of taxation on the nation's resources. A rise in income tax may reduce the supply of labour and the allocation of indirect taxes and subsidies will transfer resources from the taxed industry to the subsidized as Figure 8 illustrates.

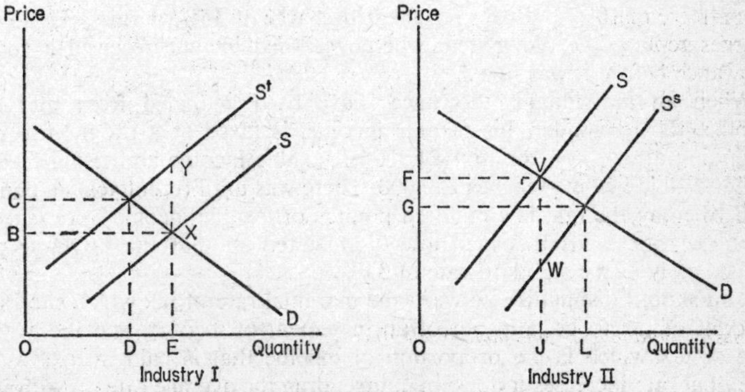

Fig. 8. Effects of indirect taxes and subsidies

Notes:

(*a*) In the absence of Government action industry I would be in equilibrium at price OB and output OE and industry II at OF and OJ.

(*b*) By imposing a tax of XY per unit on industry I the Government forces the supply curve upwards, showing that any given quantity will now be put on the market at a higher price than before.

(*c*) The subsidy of VW to industry II enables it to place goods on the market at a lower price than before.

(*d*) As a result industry I reaches a new equilibrium at price OC and output OD.

(*e*) Industry II expands its output to OL at the lower price of OG.

(*f*) If the Government persists in such a policy resources must be released from industry I and absorbed by industry II.

(*g*) The greater the elasticity of demand for the products the greater will be the effect on the size of the industries which is one reason why Governments like to levy taxes on products with inelastic demand. (The reader should redraw the diagrams using much less elastic curves to satisfy himself on this point.)

We now turn to an examination of the main taxes levied in the United Kingdom.

(4) Income Tax and Surtax

Although these were technically separate taxes administered by separate departments of the Inland Revenue the budget of 1971, beginning the long overdue process of reform, made provision for them to be consolidated into a single progressive personal income tax with effect from April 1973.

Income tax was introduced in the United Kingdom as a temporary measure in 1799 and with a break from 1816 to 1842 has been with us ever since. Historically the tax had been made progressive partly by a system of allowances which are deducted from gross pay before arriving at taxable pay and partly by allowing some income to be taxed at preferential rates.

Thus in 1974–75 a single person could claim a personal allowance of £625 and a married man £865. There are additional allowances in respect of children: £240 for those under 11, £275 for those of 11–16 and £305 for those over 16 and in full time education. Unearned income over £1,000 is subject to a surcharge of 10% and over £2,000 a surcharge of 15% applies. These surcharges replace the old system whereby earned income received a special allowance before it was taxed.

When an individual's allowances have been deducted from his gross income, the remainder, his taxable income, is taxed at a progressive rate, beginning at 33% on the first £4,500 of taxable income and rising to 83% when taxable income reaches £20,000. There was until recent years a concession whereby the first few hundred pounds of taxable income were taxed at very low rates, but this has now disappeared so that the taxpayer pays immediately at the standard rate of 33%.

You should distinguish between the marginal rate of tax which shows the amount of tax to be paid out of an increment of income, and the average rate of tax which is the proportion of income that is paid in tax. As the marginal rate increases it does, of course, drag the average rate up with it, as you can see in Fig. 9.

Table 31 shows the rates of tax applicable to various slices of income in 1974–75. Rates frequently change, but the basic principle remains the same.

Table 31. Income Tax Rates, 1974–75

Taxable income (£)	Percentage rate on last slice of income
0–4,500	33
4,500–5,000	38
5,000–6,000	43
6,000–7,000	48
7,000–8,000	53
8,000–10,000	58
10,000–12,000	63
12,000–15,000	68
15,000–20,000	73
over 20,000	83

Source: Inland Revenue.

Figure 9 shows the proportion of income payable in income tax and surtax for various incomes up to £20,000 per year, for a single person with no dependants, when income is either wholly earned or wholly unearned.

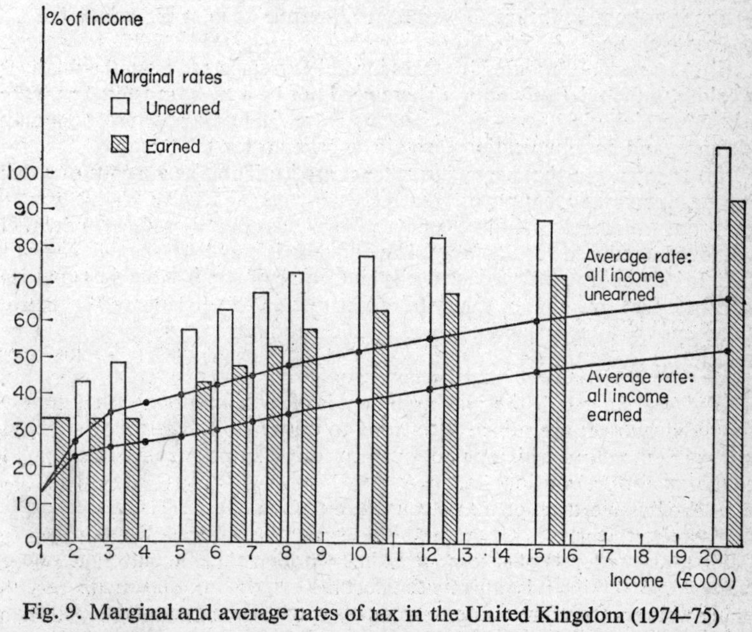

Fig. 9. Marginal and average rates of tax in the United Kingdom (1974–75)

Notes:

(*a*) The continuous lines represent the effective rate of tax: that is tax paid as a percentage of total income.

(*b*) The columns represent the marginal rate of tax: that is the percentage of the last pound of income taken in tax.

(*c*) The marginal rate remains constant between columns.

We noted earlier the distinction that is drawn between earned and unearned income. The diagram shows that the discrimination against unearned income is inconsistent in that, for example, in the middle ranges the difference is considerable (see marginal curves) while at the upper end of the scale it almost disappears.

(*a*) *Advantages of Progressive Taxes.* Despite these inconsistencies there are compelling reasons for raising a large part of Government Revenue through progressive taxation. Among the more important advantages are:

(i) In general the contributions made are related to ability to pay. And there is clearly a rough-and-ready justice about a system in which the £1,000-a-year man pays 12½ per cent of his income in tax while the £20,000-a-year man pays 53 per cent. The difficulty, of course, is not that there should be a difference but to decide what the difference should be, and what the rate of progression over the whole range should be. There is no way in which we can establish what are the 'correct' rates, but the aim of encouraging the optimum use of the national resources must be remembered and if it can be shown that a change in the tax system would lead to an increase in national income without reducing Government Revenue then it is, prima facie, a desirable change.

(ii) As a result of progressive taxes income is transferred from the relatively wealthy to the relatively poor. (There need not be a cash transfer. The wage-earner receiving £20 per week benefits from State expenditure on police, defence, and communications even if he pays no tax.)

(iii) Many argue that heavy direct taxes are justifiable as a means of reducing large economic rent payments which many people receive. In this way the pop-stars who receive hundreds or even thousands of pounds weekly have their net income reduced considerably. The difficulty is knowing where to draw the line. It may be true that no one needs an income of £20,000 per year, but it is also true that this kind of salary has to be offered to persuade top executives to accept extra responsibilities, and to allow room for a proper salary structure lower down the scale.

(*b*) *Disadvantages.* The equity argument is of such importance that none of the disadvantages are sufficiently strong to outweigh it. The following arguments are therefore criticisms not of the principle of progressive taxation but of the rate of progression.

(i) Progressive taxation has strong disincentive effects. There seem to be two aspects to this:

First, at low levels of income overtime working raises the average rate of tax payable (though it is unlikely to affect the marginal rate). It is alleged that many workers therefore refuse to work overtime. They prefer an extra hour's leisure to the extra income they could earn. It is fair to say that there is very little documentary evidence to support this claim. Indeed many would argue that many of the restrictive practices referred to in Chapter Fourteen are partly the result of progressive taxes. Thus if taxes reduce net pay below acceptable levels it may lead to delaying tactics to create overtime working. On the other hand there may be groups of workers who are actually prepared to work harder when taxes are increased in order to maintain their standard of living, though they are more likely to demand extra pay to achieve this.

Secondly, among higher-income groups high rates of taxation may reduce mobility of labour. Thus a move to a more responsible position with another company may well put an executive into a higher tax bracket. There will be many cases where the net gain in salary is insufficient to compensate for the extra responsibility and the upheaval to domestic life of moving, perhaps, from one end of the country to another

(ii) As a result, particularly of the difficulties of this group of workers, progressive taxation encourages the development of all kinds of non-taxable incomes. After all, for a person paying tax at 73 per cent a rise of £1,000 allows him £270, the remainder going to the Exchequer. If his employer can create non-taxable benefits for him which cost less than £1,000 both the employer and his employee are better off. Only the Exchequer loses. (Before the changes of April 1971 the taxpayer would have retained only £87·50 of an increment of £1,000.)

(iii) The Chancellor then has to close the loopholes, creating in the process an even more complex system, and adding to the third drawback of progressive taxation—the difficulty and expense of administering it with the mass of accountants and tax lawyers that this involves.

(iv) Steeply progressive rates of tax might be justified if they were productive of great amounts of revenue. But surtax raised only £350 million per annum for the Exchequer in its last year of operation. Its recent reduction and the proposed merger with income tax will be advantageous to the Inland Revenue in reducing assessment costs, and might have beneficial effects on important sections of management who are subject to it. Furthermore as with many other taxes a reduction in the rate is called for if only to eliminate the effects of inflation which results in the real burden of taxation growing as inflation proceeds, and which also brings into the tax net people previously exempt. (In fact there should be annual adjustments to ensure that the incidence is geared to real incomes.)

(v) The systems of allowances designed to secure vertical equity are of necessity arbitrary and as such are productive of much dissatisfaction. But it must be remembered that these are primarily social rather than economic decisions and it is not the task of the economist to justify them. However, they do have economic effects and one of the most obvious is the treatment of the single person compared with a married man with a family. Table 32 shows the tax paid by a single man and that paid by a married man with two children under eleven at various levels of income (all earned).

Notice that the discrimination in favour of the married man diminishes as income increases and his extra allowances account for a smaller proportion of total income.

This discrimination is just one of many areas of contention in the incidence of direct tax in the United Kingdom. The treatment of married women, for example, has always caused dissatisfaction. Until 1972/3 it had been the

Table 32. Tax Incidence in United Kingdom

	Tax paid by a	
	Single man	Married man, 2 children under 11
Income (£)	(£)	(£)
700	24·75	—
1,000	123·75	—
1,500	288·00	68
2,000	453·00	233
3,000	783·00	563
4,000	1113·00	893
5,000	1443·00	1,223
10,000	3912·00	3,525

Source: Inland Revenue.

practice to treat a married couple as one person for surtax purposes, with the result that a married couple, able to claim only one set of allowances, were paying more in tax than two single persons with the same incomes as the married couple. From April 1972 such couples may opt to be taxed separately.

(5) Corporation Tax

Until 1966 company profits were subject to income tax and a profits tax of 15 per cent, but since then the dual system has been replaced by Corporation Tax which has fluctuated between 40 per cent and its present level of 52 per cent. There was formerly a discrimination against distributed as opposed to retained profits. Companies were required to deduct income tax at the standard rate from dividends sent to shareholders. This extra levy did not apply to retained profits. The system was criticised on the grounds that it tends to stagnate the capital market and inhibit the flow of funds to new channels. On the other hand the retention of profits is presumably a stimulus to investment and might be justified on these grounds, except that there is no guarantee that the firms retaining the profits are those that should be doing the investment, or even that they will invest. It was for this reason that the Conservatives amended the system established by its predecessors by eliminating the discrimination against distributed profits. This is unlikely to be the last change. It is probable that further modification will be required in due course as the process of tax harmonisation within the European Economic Community gets under way.

A further effect of the Corporation Tax has been to encourage the raising of further capital through the issue of Debentures rather than Ordinary Shares since the interest on the former is deductible from profits before assessing Corporation Tax. Thus the incidence of the tax depends partly on the capital structure of the company which does not meet all the requirements of equity.

(6) Capital Gains Tax

It was not until 1962 that capital gains were taxed in this country, and then it was only short-term gains (where assets were realized within six months of purchase) that were involved. In 1965 the qualifying period became twelve months, and at the same time a more comprehensive long-term tax was introduced whereby, with certain exceptions, all gains were taxable at 30 per cent, or if the gains are less than £5,000 for a particular individual, at half the marginal rate of income tax plus surtax that would be applicable to them if they were unearned income. In the 1971 budget the distinction between long-term and short-term gains was abolished and the gains involved where annual disposals were less than £500 were exempted from the tax. The taxation of capital gains had been the subject of a long campaign on grounds of equity. It was argued that if an investment of £100 appreciated to £200 on subsequent sale the £100 gain should be treated as income for taxation purposes. However, if prices have doubled in the intervening period the investor is clearly no better off even if there is no tax. And if there is a tax he is worse off than before. Assessing the 'correct' rate of tax is clearly a difficult problem.

Nevertheless in the 1950's many people did make substantial and rapid, often speculative, gains and it was incumbent upon the Government to introduce some tax.

The taxation of capital gains like Corporation Tax inevitably affects the capital market: funds tend to be immobilized, certain types of investment may be adversely affected, and new enterprises may find it difficult to raise capital. This is not to say, however, that at a time of high taxation of income capital gains should not be taxed.

(7) Taxes on Capital

Death is regarded as the realization of assets and any gains are subject to Capital Gains Tax, though such tax payments may be set against death duties. For a long while Death Duty was regarded as an optional tax in that it could be avoided by the disposal of assets three years before death; later this only applied to gifts made over seven years before death. Estate duty then began at 25 per cent on estates of £20,000 rising to a maximum of 75 per cent on estates of £1 million and over.

The motives for death duties as with the Capital Gains Tax were based partly on equity. This is related to the windfall nature of inheritance but the tax as it stood did not really foster the principle of equity. For example, a person may be the sole beneficiary of an estate of £100,000. After death duties had been paid he would receive between £40,000 and £50,000. But were he the beneficiary of ten estates of £10,000 he would receive £100,000. Of course, viewed from the side of the estate, the equity principle is fulfilled by the progressive rates.

This is one factor that has led to demands for a more comprehensive wealth or gifts tax or both. The outcome was the present Capital Transfer Tax which is levied on virtually all transfers of capital whether they are made during a person's life time or at death. In this way the optional aspects of estate duty have been removed. Small transfers (up to £100) are exempt, but the rate on estates begins at 10 per cent on £1,500, and rises to 75 per cent where £2,000,000 are involved. The tax payable on an estate of £2,000,000 would be £1,289,000.

Now under consideration is the introduction of an annual wealth tax on personal wealth of, perhaps, more than £50,000 or £100,000. Problems of the rate of the annual levy, types of wealth to be exempted, and the means of assessment immediately arise. The rate to set depends largely on the purpose of the tax: if the aim is to break up large estates, a high rate is necessary, but the higher the rate the greater the adverse effect on saving. If exemptions are allowed, personal wealth will gradually become concentrated in the exempt category. Death duty requires the valuation of only a fraction of personal wealth each year; an annual wealth tax requires much more: probably a system of self-assessment would be necessary.

A further alternative is the introduction of an inheritance tax where each individual legacy is taxed at a progressive rate as opposed to the current system where the whole estate is taxed rather than the beneficiaries themselves. While an inheritance tax is more complicated it has much to recommend it particularly if it is related not only to the size of the legacy but also the wealth of the recipient. But such a tax would encourage many small legacies and little of the estate would be returned in the form of tax to the public.

(8) Purchase Tax, Customs and Excise Duties

The progressive element in the United Kingdom system of taxation is achieved by the different rates of income tax and estate duties. Expenditure taxes of various kinds are often criticised for their regressive nature but they too have their progressive features. Expenditure taxes account for a large proportion of Central Government revenue, and in particular the excise duties levied on tobacco, alcoholic drink, and petroleum products are very important sources of revenue to the Chancellor of the Exchequer. The principal justification for this is that demand for such products is highly inelastic and therefore the disruptive effects on resource allocation are minimized. (See Figure 8 where output is drastically reduced when the elasticity of demand is high.) In the case of tobacco and alcohol there are also strong moral arguments that the Government should discourage their consumption in the interests of the health of the community.

Although no one would argue that the indirect taxes are not regressive an attempt to make them conform to principles of fairness is made by taxing rich men's goods more heavily than others. Thus the rate of purchase tax on certain luxuries was 55 per cent while the excise duty on whisky is much higher than on beer.

Purchase Tax was levied at the wholesale stage on an *ad valorem* basis at four different rates arbitrarily applied to different commodities (Table 33).

The great merit of the tax was that it was easily collected at about 70,000 points (compare the problem associated with a value added tax; see page 87) and that in general it steers clear of necessities such as food. However, it is in some respects highly regressive—for example, the tax on television represents a much greater burden to the poor than the rich, because of the greater utility to the poor man of each of his scarce pounds.

Similar considerations apply to *excise duties* except that they are applied at the point of manufacture and are specific taxes: for example, the tax on tobacco is £6·44 per pound, and on whisky £20·43 per proof gallon. (Or 29p for twenty cigarettes and £2·40 for a bottle of whisky.)

These rates are so high that there is no incentive to producers to increase efficiency: if petrol costs 10p to produce but is retailed at 35p because of excise duty a reduction in costs of 5 per cent, while a significant achievement by the

Table 33. United Kingdom Rates of Purchase Tax (1971)

Rate of tax (%)	Examples of items
$11\frac{1}{4}$	Sewing thread
	Plastic wall coverings
	Paper handkerchiefs
	Cutlery
18	Potato crisps
	Pet foods
	Confectionery
	Ice-cream
30	Refrigerators, washing-machines
	Sports equipment
	Motor-cars
	Soap, shaving cream
45	Fur garments
	Jewellery
	Cameras
	Cosmetics

Source: H.M. Customs and Excise.

manufacturer, is of only marginal significance to the consumer. This is because prices are nowhere near costs of production.

One disadvantage of indirect taxes that has received considerable attention in the last few years is the impact that they have on the cost of living and inflation. To the extent that trade unions are free to secure wage increases and management is free to pass on rising costs, increases in indirect taxes must give some impetus to price inflation. For as taxes increase the cost of living, wage increases are secured to cover the rise and the wage increase is passed on in the form of higher prices. To the extent that wages and prices are properly controlled, of course, then rises in taxation may be expected to be deflationary (see page 44). The unpalatable truth is that what is needed is that the rise in prices must be accompanied by steady wages to secure a fall in real incomes.

The concentration of indirect taxes on smoking, drinking, and motoring has prompted many suggestions for broader-based taxes, partly on grounds of equity and partly on the grounds of resource allocation. It was the desire for a broader-based system as well as the prospect of British membership of the European Economic Community that led the Conservatives in the 1971 budget to propose the introduction of a Value Added Tax to replace Purchase Tax and Selective Employment Tax. Another important influence was their dislike of the Selective Employment Tax.

(9) Selective Employment Tax

This controversial tax was introduced in the budget of 1966, and was repealed in 1973 to make way for the Value Added Tax. It was a tax levied on all employers in respect of each employee. Three groups were distinguished:

(*a*) Manufacturing industries which paid the tax but received a refund of the tax plus $37\frac{1}{2}$p per worker after three months.

(*b*) A neutral band of non-manufacturing activities such as agriculture and transport where the tax was refunded after three months but no premium was payable.

(*c*) The construction, distribution, and service industries which received no refund at all.

The rates which the tax has been levied have fluctuated, but since July 1971 the charge has been £1·20 for men, £0·60p for women and boys under eighteen, and £0·40p for girls under eighteen. Only in the development areas do manufacturers now receive the premium, the Regional Employment Premium of £1·50 and that is to be abolished in 1974.

The required qualification for the rebate of the tax is that over half the employees of an establishment should be engaged in an appropriate activity.

The apparently arbitrary distinctions made in the administration of the tax have given rise to much criticism. The distinction between services and manufacturing is an artificial one and although one of the aims was to redress the balance of indirect taxation between manufactured goods and services many services nevertheless escaped. Thus a company maintaining a head office in one place and a factory in another found that it received no rebate in respect of head-office typists, but received a rebate plus the 37½p premium in respect of typists at the factory providing over half the employees were in a qualifying manufacturing activity.

The 50 per cent rule was a direct encouragement to companies to ensure that an establishment contained at least 51 per cent of personnel in qualifying activities. This undoubtedly caused considerable rearrangement of activities within firms to avoid the tax. In this connection there was a sharp and socially undesirable fall in the number of employees in some industries and a corresponding rise in the number of self-employed contractors as companies sought to avoid the tax, which was not levied on self-employed persons. This loophole has since been closed by the 1970 Finance Act.

In all advanced economies an increasing proportion of labour is absorbed into the services sector. Many critics therefore regarded one of the stated aims of the tax—to encourage labour out of services into manufacturing—as fundamentally misconceived, especially as they felt that the basic weakness of our manufacturing industry was (and is) not a shortage of labour but an excess of it in relation to capital investment. It was argued that what was required was proper encouragement to investment.

Furthermore, although it may have had some slight affect in reducing the export prices of manufacturers, at a time of acute Balance of Payments difficulties the Selective Employment Tax was bound to hit the one really strong sector—the invisible exports such as investment and insurance.

Prompted, no doubt, partly by criticisms along these lines and by the allegedly inflationary nature of the tax the Treasury commissioned the Department of Applied Economics at Cambridge to make an impartial assessment of the effects of the tax. At the time of writing only the first part of their report dealing with the distributive trades has been published and the principal conclusion of Professor Reddaway who conducted the project was that the introduction of SET had resulted in an increase in productivity in the distributive trades over and above what could have been expected if the tax had not been introduced, as is shown in Table 34 reproduced from the report.

The increase in productivity for 1968 represents something like 130,000

Table 34. Effect of Selective Employment Tax on Productivity. Gain in Productivity as a result of abnormal new factors (1965 = 100)

	Actual productivity	Expected productivity	Differences as percentage of expected productivity
Retailers			
1966	102·5	100·8	1·7
1967	106·0	102·6	3·3
1968	111·1	105·6	5·1
Non-Industrial Wholesalers			
1966	103·1	101·0	2·0
1967	105·5	100·5	5·4
1968	110·2	104·2	5·8

full-time workers and, the report urges, this saving allowed the costs of SET to be very largely absorbed.

At its height the Selective Employment Tax was raising over £600 million per year for the Government. Many people felt that its abolition would prove difficult, but it was subsequently achieved by absorbing the tax (as well as purchase tax) into a new Value Added Tax.

(10) Value Added Tax

Explanation. The negotiations surrounding Britain's application to join the European Economic Community has already led to a great deal of discussion of the VAT in the United Kingdom, when in 1971 the Government announced its intention to replace Purchase Tax and SET by a VAT in 1973. Such a tax will have been adopted in five of the six member countries by 1972 though not at a uniform rate. It may be regarded as a comprehensive multi-stage tax on consumer spending. The tax is imposed every time goods change hands on the value that has been added to those goods by the firm now selling them. If the seller of the goods has already paid tax on them when he bought the raw materials, the components or the goods themselves, he is entitled to a rebate of the tax paid.

Consider the case in Table 35 taken from the report of the National Economic Development Office on Value Added Taxation:

Table 35. Impact of Value Added Tax

Value added		Purchase price to seller ex VAT	Purchase price including VAT	Selling price excluding VAT	VAT liability	VAT credit	VAT due
100	Farmer sells to manufacturer	0	0	100	10	0	10
100	Manufacturer sells to wholesaler	100	110	200	20	10	10
50	Wholesaler sells to retailer	200	220	250	25	20	5
50	Retailer sells to consumer	250	275	300	30	25	5
	Cost to consumer = 330 of which VAT = 30						

Source: National Economic Development Office.

A farmer sells to a manufacturer who sells to a wholesaler and retailer. A Value Added Tax of 10 per cent is levied.

The farmer having added £100 of value to the raw material is liable for tax of £10. It is his responsibility to pay this to the Government, but he passes it on to his customer in the form of higher prices (£110). Since the manufacturer has already paid tax of £10 he can set this against his tax liability. Thus by the time he sells the goods £200 of value has been added to them and purchasers therefore must pay £220. The manufacturer is liable for £10 of tax. As the process continues the Government eventually collects (from four different sources) £30 and the whole of the tax is shifted forward to the final consumer who pays £330.

The computation of the tax would be complicated by the introduction of exemptions and by the introduction of two or three different rates of VAT, but the basic principles would be unaltered.

The arguments for and against are fairly evenly balanced:

(*a*) *Advantages*

(i) *The tax is non-discriminating*. A Value Added Tax would be an improvement on the present system of indirect taxation which discriminates between particular forms of consumption. It would, however, be fatuous to expect the introduction of a single-rate, all-embracing Value Added Tax to be accompanied by the disappearance of Purchase Tax and Excise Duties. Such a move would lead to a significant rise in the price of food together with a large fall in the price of whisky and cigarettes. Even if some economic justification for this could be found there would be overwhelming social and political considerations against it. None the less it must be acknowledged that a Value Added Tax has allowed some reduction in the high rates of indirect taxation endured by the motor vehicle and other consumer durable goods industries.

Many people feared that the introduction of a Value Added Tax would involve a multi-rate tax which is unnecessarily complicated. This was not necessary but a special tax was imposed on new cars and Excise Duties were retained to maintain the structure of indirect taxation. Value Added Tax avoids the artificial distinction previously made between 'productive' and 'service' industries, which had been partly eliminated by the Selective Employment Tax. Value Added Tax is applied to hair-cuts as well as scissors.

(ii) *A tax on costs*. Since Value Added Tax is a tax on costs it falls most heavily on those with the highest costs and it is claimed that it is an incentive to efficiency and better management. One would have thought this true of existing *ad valorem* indirect taxes.

(iii) *Efficiency*. There is a presumption that a Value Added Tax which is not levied on capital investment and which is substituted for Corporation Tax would encourage mechanization, efficiency, and economic growth. But the NEDO report points out that this depends on the changes in relative costs of labour and capital. Since no one will want to take advantage of tax-free investment if it is more economic to use labour-intensive methods because of the low level of wages compared to the high cost of capital. The likelihood is, however, that the substitution of a Value Added Tax for Corporation Tax could result in increased efficiency and an improved Balance of Payments, but since VAT replaced other expenditure taxes, not Corporation Tax, the theory has not been put to the test.

(iv) *Balance of Payments*. The Balance of Payments might be expected to benefit initially at least since the Value Added Tax would be levied on imports and rebated on exports, but the effect on exporters would depend partly on the general impact on costs and prices of the Value Added Tax and more importantly on whether VAT were used as a rebate for Corporation Tax (in which case exporters would benefit) or Purchase Tax (in which case they probably would not benefit, since they do not pay Purchase Tax on their exports).

(v) *Diminishing returns from other taxes*. NEDO points out, and their evidence is supported from other sources, that in the United Kingdom we are rapidly reaching the point of diminishing returns from some of our indirect taxes, notably those on tobacco and alcohol, and therefore new sources of revenue are important.

(vi) *European Economic Community*. One of the main arguments in favour of the adoption of a Value Added Tax was said to be that the system would become obligatory if the United Kingdom joined the EEC.

(*b*) *Disadvantages*

(i) *Administrative complexity*. If the VAT were substituted directly for Purchase Tax the number of collection points would be increased from about 70,000 to something over two million. Anything other than a flat-rate tax without exemptions would further increase the problems of the tax authorities not to mention the firms paying the tax.

(ii) *No benefits to exporters* will occur if the tax is a substitute for Purchase Tax, since exports are not subject to Purchase Tax. Thus to benefit exporters the VAT would have to replace to some extent Corporation Tax, since all exports embody an element of Corporation Tax. If that tax were replaced entirely by a VAT, rebatable on exports, this particular tax element in export prices would disappear. But as we saw earlier the British already pay a high proportion of tax indirectly and thus there are good reasons for not substituting VAT for Corporation Tax. In any case there are probably more effective ways of helping exporters.

(iii) Many of the benefits could be achieved by the extension of the previous system of Purchase Tax into a general Retail Sales Tax.

(iv) Since the VAT is a regressive tax it might require increases in social-security payments to shield the poor from its effects. Moreover, such a tax is bound to be inflationary as it increases the cost of living.

The Rate of VAT. Clearly the rate at which VAT would need to be levied would depend on the tax or taxes it was wholly or partly to replace. If VAT were to replace Purchase Tax:

In 1969 Purchase Tax yielded £1,110 million. Consumer expenditure excluding taxation was of the order of £21,000 million. So a flat rate no exemption VAT would need to be levied at about 5·3 per cent to produce sufficient revenue. To produce sufficient revenue to replace all customs and excise duties VAT would need to be levied at a flat rate of about 23 per cent and to replace Corporation Tax a rate of 6 or 7 per cent would be necessary. To replace Purchase Tax and Selective Employment Tax a rate of 9 or 10 per cent proved to be necessary and 10% was the rate chosen.

Conclusion. The introduction of VAT at a flat rate of 10% (with a number of exceptions) in April 1973 went fairly smoothly, but many traders were suspected of cashing in on the price changes that occurred. Since then VAT has become an established part of the Chancellor's policy. The nature of the tax has changed: it is becoming a multi-rate tax, returning to the principles of purchase tax in discriminating against less essential goods.

(11) Government Expenditure

In 1900 Government income from taxation, including Local Authority rates, amounted to £166 million or about 8·4 per cent of the Gross National Product. In 1972, by contrast, total public expenditure was about £29,000m or about 54% of GNP.

Table 30 shows the main divisions of Government expenditure in 1972. Central and Local Authorities are now responsible for approximately half of total expenditure. This is a reflection of:

(*a*) The increasing extent to which Governments have felt it necessary to intervene first in micro-economic problems of industry: thus in 1972 the regional employment premiums cost £106 million; and investment grants, like the REP introduced only in 1967, amounted to £331 million.

(*b*) The extension of the social services in recent years (Table 36).

Table 36. Public Expenditure on Social Services (£m)

	1959	1972
Education	848	3,508
National Health Service	788	2,644
Local Welfare Services	28	108
Child care	25	85
School meals, milk	82	163
Social Security Benefits	1,450	5,119
Total	3,221	11,627

Source: National Income and Expenditure.

The extension of the social services reflects not only attempts to broaden the scope of the services but also an increase in the size of the dependent population—those below working age and those over retirement age. The costs of Further and Higher Education have also risen because a higher proportion of those of working age stay in full-time education.

The acceleration of Government expenditure may also be seen in terms of the proportion of an increase in national income that is devoted to public expenditure. Between 1958 and 1969 the Gross National Product rose by just over 80 per cent while public expenditure rose by over 125 per cent.

Between 1958 and 1959 extra public expenditure absorbed 65 per cent of the rise in GNP of £810 million. In 1965, 67 per cent of the rise in GNP went to public expenditure and in 1968 about 90 per cent of the rise was absorbed by the Government.

Although public expenditure has been rising so rapidly the demand for the services provided is insatiable. Every service the Government provides could be improved and extended and almost every one has its own public and private lobbies pressing its claims which are difficult to resist. Of course we need more hospitals and personnel to man them; of course there are too many antiquated schools and too few teachers. Of course there is insufficient house building; regrettably some still live in poverty and of course the road system is inadequate to meet modern requirements. To meet the steadily rising demand the Government may resort to one of three broad policies:

(*a*) Extra taxation. But rates of taxation are already high, and increases in direct taxes are likely to have disincentive effects on effort; and increases in indirect taxation are likely to be inflationary.

(*b*) A reshuffling of Government expenditure. The social services could be improved if Government expenditure on, for example, defence could be cut; but defence expenditure has in any case not grown so rapidly as other expenditure and reductions are not really politically possible.

(*c*) Charging for services or being more selective in providing them. Charges are already made for some of the social services: optical and dental treatment, medical prescriptions, school meals are all subject to charges though exemptions are made for those on low incomes. Family allowances are no longer universal: recent increases have not been available to those paying income tax at the standard rate.

Selectivity and charges are all very well, but those who are most clamorous in their support of extra welfare payments are usually those who are most critical of any discrimination between groups. The great difficulty is to know where to draw the line, and to establish the appropriate level of benefit.

The Case for Selectivity

The main arguments in favour of selective social services may be summarized thus:

(*a*) Because of high taxation the expansion that is needed in the social services cannot be financed by the taxpayer. Those that can afford to pay should be made to do so.

(*b*) Universal benefits necessarily imply spreading those benefits and giving them to those without need. There are, for example, many parents to whom the family allowance has very little utility. By transferring payments from them to those more obviously in need the effectiveness of welfare payments would clearly be increased.

(*c*) Many people prefer to pay privately for services, and should be encouraged to do so by a system of tax rebates.

The Case Against Selectivity

The main argument against selection and charges is that it would involve a means test, and then any savings effected by the ending of universality would be offset by administrative charges. The likelihood is that the Conservative Government will reject this argument and take steps to see that the cost of the social services is more equally distributed between users and taxpayers.

But a return towards the market in social services is a move back to the jungle. To charge people for medical treatment is to deter them from seeking advice; to vary educational services according to ability to pay is not only socially undesirable, but also wasteful if talented children are deprived of appropriate education because of their parents' poverty. Not only that, there is no firm evidence that more selectivity would lead to improvements in the services provided and it is fairly certain that selective benefits would be a disincentive to the poor to improve their earnings since this would involve a reduction in benefits.

An alternative proposal to such selectivity involves the introduction of a *negative income tax*. At present if a person's income is lower than the allowances he can claim he pays no tax and that is the end of the matter. A negative income tax would provide him with a payment in addition to his wages to bring his income up to some predetermined level, without the need for a *means test*, detestation of which is the source of many objections to selective social services.

(12) The National Debt

Contrary to popular belief the National Debt is not simply money owed by the United Kingdom to countries overseas. It consists of money borrowed by the Government in the past from residents or institutions in this country or overseas. Table 37 shows the way in which the National Debt has grown since its inception in 1694.

Table 37. Growth of the National Debt (1694–1973)

Year	£ millions
1694	1·2
1714	49
1785	244
1815	878
1914	617
1920	7,800
1938	7,100
1945	23,000
1973	35,000

Source: H.M. Treasury.

Apart from the last twenty-five years the Debt has always grown most rapidly during time of wars and much of the existing Debt represents war borrowing for which there are no tangible assets today. The post-war borrowing has been largely to finance a series of budget deficits and in particular to finance a great deal of investment by Local Authorities and the Nationalized Industries.

Table 38 shows the structure of the National Debt as at 31 March 1973:

Of the total debt, £1,954 million consisted of Nationalized Industries' stocks guaranteed by the Government. This does not represent all the borrowing of the Nationalized Industries for they now borrow directly from the Government. Their total borrowings are discussed fully in Chapter 12.

The Redemption of the Debt?

All Governments have dreamt of eliminating the National Debt, and there have been periods when the Debt has been reduced. In fact there was a slight fall between March 1968 and March 1969 thanks to an overall Central Government surplus of £273 million that year. The point is that if no stocks

Table 38. Structure of the National Debt (31 March 1973)

(nominal value £ millions)

(*a*) By maturity	
Treasury Bills	3,093
0–5-year stocks	6,923
Over 5 years or undated	20,146
Non-Marketable Debt	6,346
Total	36,526
(*b*) By holder	
UK Official Holdings	10,183
Market holdings:	
Other Public Bodies	171
Banking Sector	2,619
Other Financial Institutions	8,072
Overseas Residents	4,857
Other Holders	10,624
Total	36,526

Source: Bank of England Quarterly Bulletin.

mature during the year and the Government cannot raise sufficient revenue through taxation then it must borrow and thereby increase the National Debt. Great pressure is put upon Governments these days to improve the services it provides and it is likely to be only in years of severe restraint that taxation covers expenditure requirements. Consequently the Debt will continue to grow.

Problems of the National Debt

(*a*) *The Debt as a Burden.* It is frequently argued that the Debt should be written off or reduced because it is a burden to the country. In fact, of course, only that part of it held overseas is in any real sense a burden to the United Kingdom since the interest payments and the repayment of the overseas debt represent a drain on the Balance of Payments. The domestically held debt (over 80 per cent) is not a burden on the nation: the annual interest payments represent a transfer from taxpayers to debt-holders. It is only to the extent that debt-holders are not taxpayers that any suggestion of undesirable cross-subsidization is raised.

(*b*) *Interest Costs.* Even if the real burden of the National Debt is sometimes exaggerated the interest charges in 1972 amounted to £6,599 million and in a period of high taxation it is desirable to keep this to a minimum. The Bank of England have developed a number of techniques to this end and for example if borrowing is necessary in a period of high interest rates they borrow on a short-term basis.

(*c*) *Administrative Costs.* Similarly the costs of management must be kept to a minimum and for this reason the issue of longer-term bonds may be preferred to shorter-term to avoid frequent costs of issue and redemption. There is often a clash between interest and administrative costs. In a period of high interest rates it does not pay to issue long-term securities since it may be possible to reduce the interest rates at a later date.

(*d*) *Monetary Policy*. Table 38 shows that the financial institutions hold about 25 per cent of the National Debt. Any reduction of the Debt, while it may be beneficial to taxpayers, creates difficulties in the conduct of monetary policy which is heavily dependent on the existence of a large body of marketable debt—open-market operations rely on such securities. Moreover, reductions in the Debt put money into the hands of the general public and thence into the banking system, compromising any attempts the Government may be making to deflate the economy. Retirement of the Debt is therefore preferable at times when the Government wants to expand the economy.

(*e*) *Private Investment*. If the Government is forced to resort to borrowing either to meet its own commitments or those of the nationalized industries it tends to force up interest rates in the capital market and add to the difficulties of the private sector in raising capital. If private sector investment is more conducive to economic growth and welfare than public sector investment this is likely to have an adverse effect on the development of the economy.

(*f*) *Inflation*. Almost the whole of the National Debt consists of fixed-interest securities. The difficulties of issuing these are increased by the consistent 5·6 per cent inflation that the United Kingdom endures these days. Many economists advocate the issue of some kind of equity stock carrying interest related either to the cost of living or the Gross National Product. However, one advantage to the Government of the continuing inflation is that the burden of interest is annually reduced unless there is rapid increase in the size of the Debt. But continuing inflation also necessitates higher interest rates being offered by the Government to persuade the public to hold new securities.

(13) Local Authority Finance

Our study of public finance would be incomplete without an examination of the finance of Local Authorities. Table 39 shows that only about a quarter of Local Authority revenue is derived from local taxation, the remainder being obtained through Central Government grants, borrowing, rent and trading.

Table 39. Local Authority Finance (Current Account) 1972 (£m)

Receipts		Expenditure		
Current grants from Central Government	2,923	Current expenditure on goods and services of which		4,816
Rates	2,377	Education	2,349	
Gross Trading Surplus	162	Police	475	
Rent	1,194	Roads	339	
Interest	128	Sewerage and Refuse	330	
		Others	1,323	
	7,162	Housing subsidies		74
		Grants to personal sector		253
		Debt interest		1,164
		Total expenditure		6,328
		Surplus		834
				7,162

Source: National Income and Expenditure.

Rates. Rates are in effect taxes levied on property within their boundaries by Local Authorities to meet the cost of the provision of local services, to the extent that this is not covered by Central Government expenditure. The liability for rates depends on the *rateable value*, a notional value placed upon the property by the rating officer and revised from time to time and representing the rating officer's idea of the annual rent chargeable for the property in a given base year. Variations in the amount to be collected are fixed annually on the recommendation of the Local Authority's Finance Committee at a figure per pound of rateable value.

Despite the fact that rates account for only 10 per cent of all taxes payable (including National Insurance contributions) they arouse a great deal of resentment and criticism on various grounds:

(*a*) Rates are regressive. They are in effect a tax on wealth or a certain kind of wealth and as such are unrelated to ability to pay, but the rate rebate scheme is designed to reduce the regressiveness and the incidence is roughly in proportion to income.

(*b*) Moreover the incidence of rates varies from area to area, and it has been found necessary to introduce special grants called *Rate Deficiency Grants* to help areas where rating revenue is low.

(*c*) Although rates are intended to pay for local services, the amounts paid by occupiers is not related to the benefits they receive. However, it should be remembered that the system would be even more regressive if contributions were on the basis of benefits received.

(*d*) Inequities arise through rates being levied only on unmovable property. The most glaring example is perhaps that of central-heating where the installation of most systems increases the rateable value of a property, but the installation of electric night-storage heaters leaves it unaffected.

(*e*) Because rates are based on rental values they are frequently regarded as a tax on thrift: if a householder improves the amenities of his house by building a garage or an extension he increases the rental value and his liability to rates.

(*f*) People working but not living in an area derive benefit from the rates paid by other people.

But all taxes have their critics and it is as well to remember the merits of the present system and to consider the alternatives. The main advantages of the present system are:

(*a*) Although rates may be regressive and not related to ability to pay, they do meet with most of the other principles of taxation—they are certain in their impact, convenient to pay, and cheap to collect, as well as being very easily understood.

(*b*) It is argued that rates bring into the tax net people who would otherwise make very little contribution to the cost of services used.

(*c*) Since many services are administered locally it is appropriate that a proportion of the cost of those services be raised locally, and since the domestic rate amounts to only about 10 per cent of total taxation its regressive effects are likely to be of only minor importance. The regressive taxes on tobacco and alcohol are of far greater significance to many people.

(*d*) If rates were abolished £2,300 million would have to be raised elsewhere. Among the possibilities are:

(i) *The Exchequer*. This would mean extra Central Government taxes, and since the main objection to rates seems to be their regressiveness the extra money would need to be raised through extra direct taxation equivalent to 20p in the pound on income tax.

(ii) *A local progressive income tax*. This would suffer from the same weakness and also be expensive to administer, though a flat-rate income tax need not create the same problems. Glaring inequities would arise where neighbouring local authorities demand the tax at different rates—a difficulty that would also arise with local sales taxes.

(iii) *Increased charges for services*. At present only about 20 per cent of Local Authority income is derived from charges, and the majority of that is from housing. The main areas in which charges could be made include roads, the health service, education, and libraries. It seems that charges could not be made for most of these services because, being more regressive than rates or requiring means tests to assess the charges payable, they would be more expensive to administer.

In conclusion it may be said that if Local Government is to thrive then it must be allowed a degree of financial responsibility. One merit of the present rating system is that it allows this, and since the taxes are local they encourage local economy.

(14) Summary of Chapter Six

(1) Taxation should be certain and equal in its incidence, convenient to pay, and economic to collect.

(2) Equality implies vertical equity and horizontal equity.

(3) The budget is perhaps the most important economic regulator—having macro- and micro-economic effects.

(4) While income tax achieves vertical equity, horizontal equity is prevented by the discrimination against unearned income.

(5) Purchase Tax and Customs and Excise Duties introduce an important regressive element into the tax system. Such regression might be increased by moving to a Value Added Tax which would have a much broader base than present indirect taxes.

(6) The Selective Employment Tax has been introduced partly to bring services within the scope of indirect taxes.

(7) In recent years Government expenditure has increased more rapidly than national income, and in the face of increasing pressure on the social services, it is likely that charges will have to be introduced.

(8) The National Debt represents Government borrowing of all kinds, and was largely accumulated during wartime. It is only a burden to the nation in so far as it is held overseas.

(9) Rates are local taxes based on accommodation and despite their critics are superior to alternatives such as local income taxes or local sales taxes.

(15) Suggested Further Reading

A Value Added Tax (National Economic Development Office), HMSO.
PREST, A., *Public Finance*, Weidenfeld & Nicolson, London, 1963.

SHOUP, C. F., *Public Finance*, Weidenfeld & Nicolson, London, 1969.
The Annual Report of the Inland Revenue, HMSO.
The Annual Report of the Customs and Excise, HMSO.

Exercises Set 6

1. What are the main principles of taxation? To what extent does the British fiscal system deviate from these principles?
2. With the aid of diagrams show the importance of the elasticity of demand and the elasticity of supply in the determination of the incidence of indirect taxes.
3. Consider the advantages and disadvantages of a system of income taxes that rises to 83% in the pound on marginal increments of earned income.
4. Write a critical analysis of the Selective Employment Tax.
5. In what respects would the United Kingdom's fiscal system be improved by the adoption of a Value Added Tax?
6. 'The purpose of progressive taxation is the redistribution of income.' Comment.
7. 'The trouble with Government expenditure is not that there is too much of it, but that too much of it goes in the wrong direction.' Discuss.
8. What is the National Debt? Comment on its importance to the monetary system and the fiscal system.
9. 'Local Authority rates are not an ideal form of taxation but no one has suggested an acceptable alternative.' What are the merits of rates and the demerits of the alternatives?
10. What are the principal considerations influencing the Chancellor of the Exchequer in the formulation of his budget?

CHAPTER SEVEN

THE BALANCE OF PAYMENTS

(1) Introduction

International trade involves not only the exchange of goods but also the exchange of currencies. The foreign exchange market exists to provide the currencies that are required in international trade. When a country is importing a greater value of goods and services than it is exporting a Balance of Payments deficit emerges. The country is earning less foreign exchange than it requires and to pay its creditors is therefore forced to draw on its reserves of gold and foreign currency or to borrow the currency from overseas countries or international institutions. In this chapter we examine Britain's experiences in foreign trade in recent years, and the steps taken to overcome the difficulties that have emerged.

(2) The Balance of Payments Accounts

The Basic Balance. Table 40 shows the normal presentation of the Balance of Payments accounts in publications prior to 1970. Most readers will be familiar with this presentation which gives the figures for 1968, the last year for which they were published in this way.

Table 40. United Kingdom Balance of Payments 1968
Basic Balance (– indicates an adverse balance)

	£ millions	£ millions
1. Current Account		
Visible Trade	–796	
Invisible Trade	+377	
Current Balance		–419
2. Long-term Capital Account		
Official (Net)	+ 23	
Private (Net)	– 62	
Long-term capital balance		– 39
Balance of current and long-term capital accounts		–458
Balancing items		– 87
3. Monetary Movements		
International Monetary Fund Loan	+525	
Other Borrowing	– 94	
Gold Reserves	+114	
Total		+545

Source: United Kingdom Balance of Payments 1970.

The current account includes both visible trade (tangible items that can be counted as they enter or leave the country) and invisible trade in the form of services of various kinds. (See page 108 for a discussion of these services.) The monthly figures to which considerable publicity is given in the Press and on television normally refer to the balance of visible trade and only a quarterly estimate is made of the invisible balance, though it may generally be safely assumed to be a surplus of some £40 million to £50 million per month for the United Kingdom, frequently more than enough to offset any deficit that may emerge on visible trade.

Capital movements are divided into the *long-term capital account* and *monetary movements* (once known as the short-term capital account). This is clearly a somewhat arbitrary distinction (and one that eventually led to the end of this system of presentation). Included in the long-term capital account were investments, loans, and repayments of loans between Governments (but not the interest on those loans which is an invisible import or export), and investments, loans, and repayments involving private citizens or companies. Investments might be of various kinds—direct investment in, for example, plant and machinery overseas, or portfolio investment in securities relating to overseas companies or governments.

The balance of the current and long-term capital accounts is referred to as the *basic balance*.

Also included in the long-term capital account is the balancing item, errors and omissions, which represents the difference between all the identified current and long-term capital transactions on the one hand and all the monetary movements on the other. Since the accuracy of the monetary movements (recorded through the Bank of England and other banks) is more trustworthy than that of the trade figures which are subject to timing difficulties, the balancing item is placed in the long-term capital account, associating it with the basic balance. Although an error of £87 million may seem large in itself, taken in relation to the total value of transactions it is almost insignificant and is usually reduced as the years go by and the errors are discovered.

The items recorded in the current and long-term capital accounts have usually been regarded as *autonomous* movements since they occur irrespective of their effect on the Balance of Payments, but it was always possible that some long-term items were in fact *accommodating*, occurring, like the monetary movements, because of the surplus or deficit elsewhere in the current or long-term capital accounts.

The monetary movements show the ways in which a deficit in the other two accounts is financed or the ways in which a surplus is disposed of. Figures are provided by foreign exchange dealers, the clearing banks and overseas banks to the Bank of England. They show acquisitions and sales of foreign currency. These accommodating payments measure the extent of the deficit or surplus, that is to say the overall increase (in the case of a surplus) or decrease (in the case of a deficit) in the net overseas assets of the United Kingdom. A surplus may be added to the reserves or invested in overseas securities—or used to reduce overseas liabilities.

The Total Currency Flow. The Balance of Payments Pink Book for 1970 introduced the new currency flow presentation of the accounts, thought to be more appropriate to present conditions. The figures for 1973 are given in Table 41.

Table 41. United Kingdom Balance of Payments 1973
Total Currency Flow (£m.)

Current account		
A. Visible trade		
(a) Exports (f.o.b.)		11,435
(b) Imports (f.o.b.)		13,810
Visible balance (a minus b)		−2,375
B. Invisibles		
Government services and transfers (net)		−790
Private services and transfers (net)		+860
Interest, profits, and dividends		
Private sector		+1,290
Public sector		−195
Invisible balance		+1,165
C. Current balance (A + B)		−1,210
1. Capital transfers		−59
Investment and other capital flows		
2. Official long-term capital	−252	
3. Overseas investment in UK public sector	+312	
4. Overseas investment in UK private sector	+1,440	
5. UK Private investment overseas	−1,382	
6. Borrowing to finance UK public sector	+831	
7. Import credit	+128	
8. Export credit	−232	
9. Other short-term flows	+226	
10. Total investment and other capital flows		+1,012
11. Balancing item		+408
12. Total currency flow		+210
13. Allocation of Special Drawing Rights		—
14. Gold subscription to IMF		—
15. Total—rows 12 to 14		+210
Official financing		
Net drawing from (+)/net repayments to (−)		
16. IMF	—	
17. Other monetary authorities	—	
18. Drawing on (+)/additions to (−) official reserves	−210	
19. Total official financing		−210

Source: United Kingdom Balance of Payments 1974.

The kind of things that are recorded are of course identical, but the picture is clearer. Some items formerly included as monetary movements have been removed from the official financing which therefore now shows the extent to which the Government has had to raise loans to meet the deficit.

The current account remains unaltered by the new presentation, and of course still retains its importance in showing whether or not we are paying our way in the world. Most other payments, however, are now thrown together under the heading '*Investment and other capital flows*'. These represent flows of capital for a variety of purposes, many of which were formerly included as monetary movements and which may be briefly explained as follows: items (2) and (3) represent public sector lending and borrowing overseas on a long-term basis; items (4) and (5) are the corresponding investment figures for the private sector; (6) shows the extent to which the Government allowed public bodies (mainly the nationalized industries) to borrow overseas to finance their activities. Such borrowing causes the invisible payments to increase later. (7) and (8) represent credit extended by both private and public sectors abroad and at home during the normal process of trade; (9) is an omnibus item indicating the extent to which overseas holders of bank accounts in London have changed their balances during the year. Also included here are a number of other transactions involving foreign currency.

Taken with the current account, these figures give initially a total currency flow from the United Kingdom of £198 million (a current account deficit of £1,210 million and inward capital flows of £1,012 million). Ostensibly there was a net flow of currency from the country of £198 million which would have to be borrowed or taken from the reserves. However, the Bank of England knows from the 'official financing' figures that there was actually a net flow of currency into the country of £210 million. Errors and omissions have occurred in the current account of the capital flows to the extent of £408 million, which amount becomes the balancing item.

The last part of the accounts shows that the £210 million was added to the official currency reserves. This could have been used to repay loans.

(3) The Post-war Performance

Table 42 summarizes the United Kingdom Balance of Payments record since the war, using the new presentation.

Of the twenty-four years presented here fourteen show an overall deficit while the current account was in surplus on thirteen occasions. The gradual post-war deterioration of the current account is indicated by the fact that in the years from 1951 to 1960 there were three deficit years involving a total deficit of £789 million against surpluses for the decade of £1,353 million, while from 1961 to 1969 five deficits amounted to £1,107 million against surpluses of £685 million. The deterioration of the visible trade balance has been even more severe even if no allowance is made for the quite exceptional deficit for 1951 attributable to a steep rise in commodity prices due to the Korean War. The increasing difficulties are further indicated by the duration of current account deficits. In the 1950's the deficits of 1951 and 1955 were quickly eliminated; the current account was then in surplus till 1960 which saw a deficit which persisted until 1961. There was, however, only two years' respite before the next deficit in 1964 which, of course, with the exception of the small surplus in 1966, persisted until 1969. (See page 115 for a discussion of the policies for removing deficits.)

We turn now to an examination of the various components contributing to the Balance of Payments.

Table 42. United Kingdom Balance of Payments (1946–69)

	1946	1947	1948	1949	1950	1951	1952	1953
A. Current account								
Visible trade	−103	−361	−151	−137	−51	−689	−279	−244
Invisibles	−127	−20	+177	+136	+358	+320	+442	+389
CURRENT BALANCE	−230	−381	+26	−1	+307	−369	+163	+145
B. Currency flow and official financing								
Current balance	−230	−381	+26	−1	+307	−369	+163	+145
Special grants	—	+30	+138	+154	+140	+43	—	—
Investment and other capital flows	+235	+342	−128	−106	+128	+92	−404	+119
Balancing item	+50	−150	−100	−50	—	−100	+66	+32
TOTAL CURRENCY FLOW	+55	−159	−64	−3	+575	−334	−175	+296
Gold subscription to IMF	−1	−51	−6	—	—	—	—	—
Total of above	+54	−210	−70	−3	+575	−334	−175	+296
Financed as follows:								
Official borrowing drawn (+)/ repaid (−)	—	+58	+15	—	—	−10	—	−56
Official reserves (drawings on, +; additions to, −)	−54	+152	+55	+3	−575	+344	+175	−240

	1954	1955	1956	1957	1958	1959	1960	1961
A. Current account								
Visible trade	−204	−313	+53	−29	+29	−117	−406	−152
Invisibles	+321	+158	+155	+262	+315	+260	+141	+148
CURRENT BALANCE	+117	−155	+208	+233	+344	+143	−265	−4
B. Currency flow and official financing								
Current balance	+117	−155	+208	+233	+344	+143	−265	−4
Investment and other capital flows	−48	−195	−409	−300	−121	−103	+291	−310
Balancing item	+57	+121	+42	+80	+67	−22	+299	−25
TOTAL CURRENCY FLOW	+126	−229	−159	+13	+290	+18	+325	−339
Gold subscription to IMF	—	—	—	—	—	−58	−32	—
Total of above	+126	−229	−159	+13	+290	−40	+293	−339
Financed as follows:								
Official borrowing drawn (+)/ repaid (−)	−39	—	+201	—	−6	−79	−116	+370
Official reserves (drawings on, +; additions to, −)	−87	+229	−42	−13	−284	−119	−177	−31

	1962	1963	1964	1965	1966	1967	1968	1969
A. Current account								
Visible trade	−102	−80	−519	−237	−73	−552	−643	−141
Invisibles	+214	+194	+124	+160	+116	+240	+324	+557
CURRENT BALANCE	+112	+114	−395	−77	+43	−312	−319	+416
B. Currency flow and official financing								
Current balance	+112	+114	−395	−77	+43	−312	−319	+416
Investment and other capital flows	+5	−103	−289	−308	−564	−560	−1010	+48
Balancing item	+75	−69	−11	+32	−26	+201	−81	+279
TOTAL CURRENCY FLOW	+192	−58	−695	−353	−547	−671	−1410	+743
Gold subscription to IMF	—	—	—	—	−44	—	—	—
Total of above	+192	−58	−695	−353	−591	−671	−1410	+743
Financed as follows:								
Official borrowing drawn (+)/ repaid (−)	−375	+5	+573	+599	+625	+556	+1296	−699
Official reserves (drawing on, +; additions to, −)	+183	+53	+122	−246	−34	+115	+114	−44

(4) Exports

The monetary value of Britain's exports has increased steadily over the post-war period; partly due to inflation and partly because of the great expansion of world trade that has occurred. Even so Britain has not been able to keep the proportion of world exports that it once enjoyed. Table 43 shows the way in which Britain's exports have fallen as a percentage of world exports over the post-war period.

Table 43. Growth of Exports (1948–72)
(thousand millions of dollars)

	1948	1958	1968	1972
World exports	53·2	95·7	205·3	285·2
World exports manufactures	24·7	50·8	127·6	186·6
UK exports (almost entirely manufactures)	6·5	9·5	15·3	24·3
EFTA and EEC (excluding UK)	7·2	24·7	67·2	128·8

Source: United Nations Statistical Yearbook 1973.

As a proportion of world trade British exports declined from 12·2 per cent to 8·5 per cent over this period and as a proportion of world exports of manufactures from 26·1 per cent to 13 per cent.

This of course is not surprising. At the end of the war the continental countries' economies were in no position to export, the Japanese were in similar difficulties, and consequently, Britain, thanks to a strong export drive, was able to win a large proportion of the export market, and her share of world trade in manufactures actually increased from 20 per cent to 25 per cent between 1938 and 1950.

In the 1950's the economy of Europe, and especially of Germany, recovered, accompanied by a typically vigorous export drive from Japan. Commonwealth countries looked increasingly to Japan and the United States for supplies, and were producing for themselves what they formerly bought from the United Kingdom. In these circumstances it would have been surprising indeed if Britain had managed to maintain its share of world markets in the 1950's.

The commonly accepted explanation for the continuing fall in Britain's share of world trade since 1950 draws attention to the structure of British exports both by destination and commodity. The argument is that since for historical reasons we began the post-war period selling much of our exports to Commonwealth countries whose economies tend to have rather slow growth, and since moreover we concentrated on the export of traditional products, we could not expect to match the growth of world trade influenced as it has been by the rapidly growing European market and by the increasingly technological products of the twentieth century.

Figure 10 illustrates the structure of British exports by destination and commodity at selected times in the post-war period.

The concentration on sterling area exports had been increased during and immediately after the war by the network of restrictions imposed on international trade by all countries in their anxiety to conserve foreign currency. (Even so in the years from 1935 to 1939, 44 per cent of British exports went to sterling area countries.)

British exports have always been predominantly manufactured goods and this bias is clear from the diagram. It might have been expected that the dependence on manufactured exports would have served Britain in good stead after the war for during the period from 1949 to 1969 world trade in manufactured goods rose by over 500 per cent. Disappointingly British exports rose by only 135 per cent in this period. The dependence on textiles and similar traditional and slow-growing markets and the link with the Commonwealth were once thought to be the main reason for this poor performance.

Board of Trade studies in 1957 and 1965 discounted the influence of area/commodity considerations as a source of the slow growth rate of British exports, the reason being that the British performance was not strikingly different even in rapidly growing markets. In most markets, and with most commodities British, exports grew more slowly than our rivals. Thus between 1956 and 1966 British exports to the EEC grew at 8·3 per cent against the growth of world exports to the EEC of 13·7 per cent. United Kingdom exports of electrical machinery grew at 5 per cent against 11·8 per cent for world exports, and for textiles the comparable rates were 4·9 per cent and 5·6 per cent.

Figure 10 shows that the 'area' composition of exports has undergone considerable change in twenty years and even if one is reluctant to accept the Board of Trade contention that the area structure was unimportant, it cannot explain the continued poor performance in the second half of the 1960's when only just over 25 per cent of exports went to the sterling area and over a half to western Europe or the United States, and when the bulk of exports were modern technological products. It is therefore necessary to find other explanations. It is difficult to find conclusive evidence, and the following is a summary of the major arguments that have surrounded this topic in recent years.

(*a*) The resurgence of Germany and Japan. It is argued, especially in the case of Germany, that post-war reconstruction permitted the immediate introduction of modern techniques which gave them (and apparently still give them) a competitive advantage over the United Kingdom. But while there were clear advantages in starting from scratch, it might have been expected that the effects would have been declining by the 1960's if this were the main cause of our difficulties.

(*b*) Inflation. While it is only in the last few years that inflation has reached dangerous proportions it has been a permanent post-war problem forcing our prices up more rapidly than those of our competitors. Once again firm and strictly comparable evidence is difficult to find but Table 44 gives some indication of the extent of the problem.

From 1953 to 1963 our rate of inflation was exceeded only by that of France, while since 1963 our prices have risen more rapidly than the rest.

These figures are for consumer goods, not exports, but like much other evidence they suggest that price inflation was somewhat more severe in Britain than elsewhere. In competitive export markets where the elasticity of demand is high our relatively high prices contributed to the weak performance.

(*c*) Many felt that non-price factors were important. Salesmanship, after

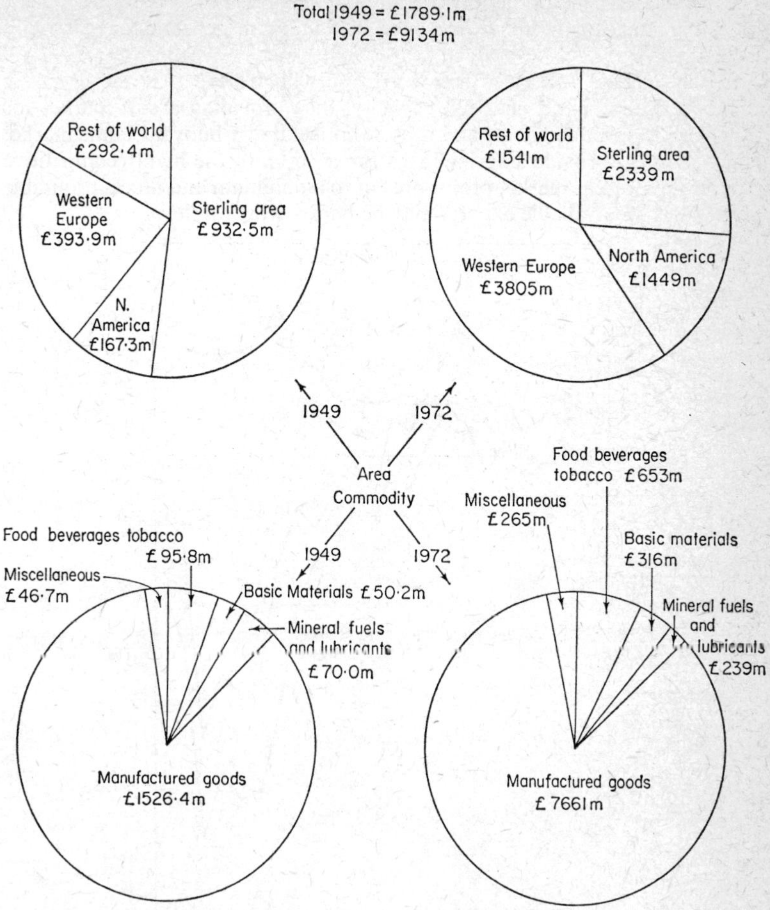

(*Source: Annual Abstracts of Statistics*)

Fig. 10. United Kingdom exports by area and commodity (1949–72)

Table 44. Index Numbers of Consumer Prices (1963 = 100)

	1953	1972
France	69	147
Germany	82	134
Italy	75	142
United Kingdom	75	159
United States	87	137

Source: United Nations Statistical Yearbook.

sales service, design, availability of spare-parts, poor delivery dates, and a lack of export finance have all at times been held partly responsible for balance of trade deficits.

(*d*) The debate continues between those who believe that the domestic economy was run too near full capacity, thus providing a soft market for otherwise exportable goods, and those who feel that a buoyant home market is necessary to provide a springboard for exports. In the highly competitive overseas motor-car market profits are cut to a minimum and unless profitable home sales are available exports may be hardly worthwhile.

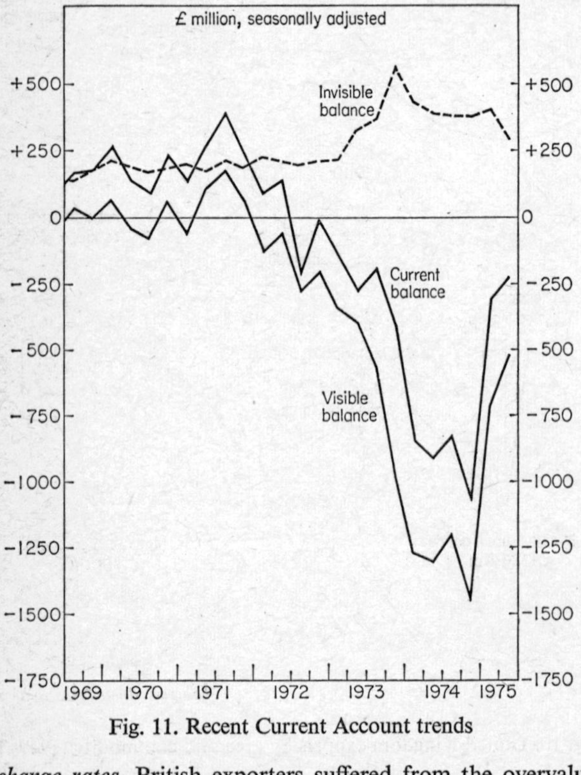

Fig. 11. Recent Current Account trends

(*e*) *Exchange rates.* British exporters suffered from the overvaluation of sterling certainly from 1960 to 1967, and also for the bulk of the post-war period the Deutschmark has been undervalued making it even more difficult for us to compete.

It is important that exchange rates should be so adjusted as to enable goods to be *traded at their real cost*. The great weakness of present international monetary arrangements is that the necessary adjustment does not occur very frequently (see page 117). The exports of countries with an undervalued currency are able to undercut the prices of other countries' exports even if their real cost of production is the same. Only after the devaluation of sterling in 1967 and the revaluation of the mark in 1969 were exchange rates at anything like appropriate levels (and British inflation was soon rendering them obsolete).

(5) Imports

We need not spend so much time on imports. Figure 12 shows the structure in 1949 and 1972. The main change since then has been the upsurge in oil prices which has slowed down the trend towards the import of manufactured goods. This trend has been in accordance with that of other industrialized countries, and in the case of the United Kingdom the reasons for it are similar to those explaining the poor export performance; inflation reducing the ability of British industry to compete effectively with imports from other advanced nations.

Imports seem to be even more clearly related to Balance of Payments deficits than exports. The cycle is as follows. During the stop-phase of the

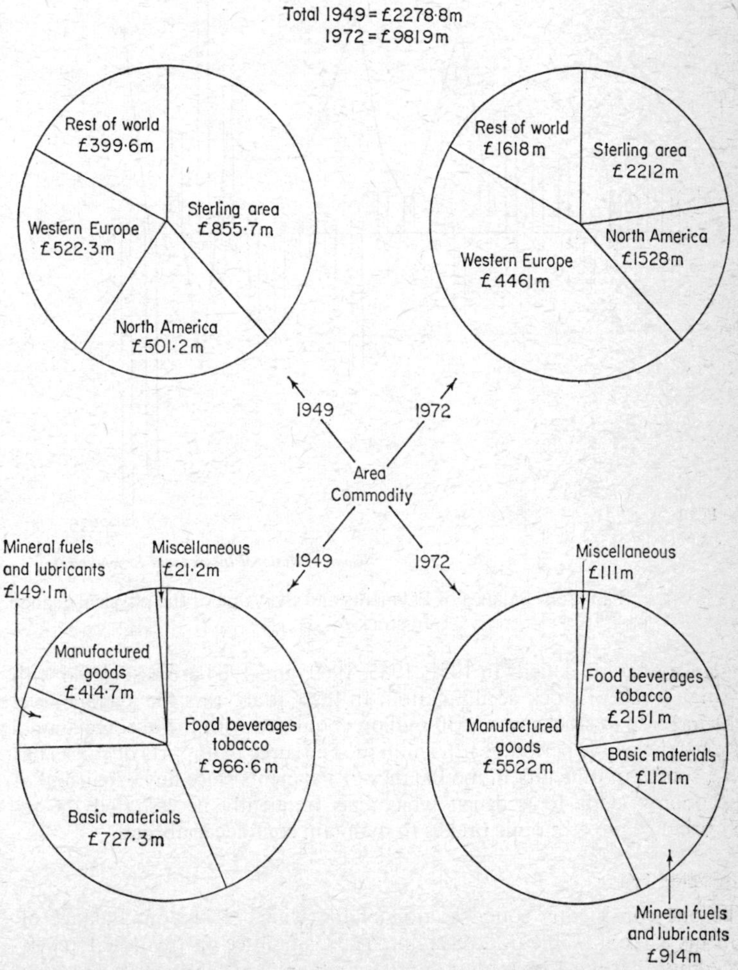

(*Source: Annual Abstracts of Statistics*)

Fig. 12. United Kingdom imports by area and commodity (1949–72)

stop-go cycle industry runs down its stocks of raw materials and finished products. The Balance of Payments for this and other reasons eventually moves into surplus. Then as the brakes are taken off the economy expands and aggregate monetary demand rises, imports of manufactures rise because stocks at home are inadequate, and the imports of raw materials rise very steeply to satisfy the increased production that is anticipated. This relationship between the level of industrial stocks and the current account of the Balance of Payments is shown in Figure 13.

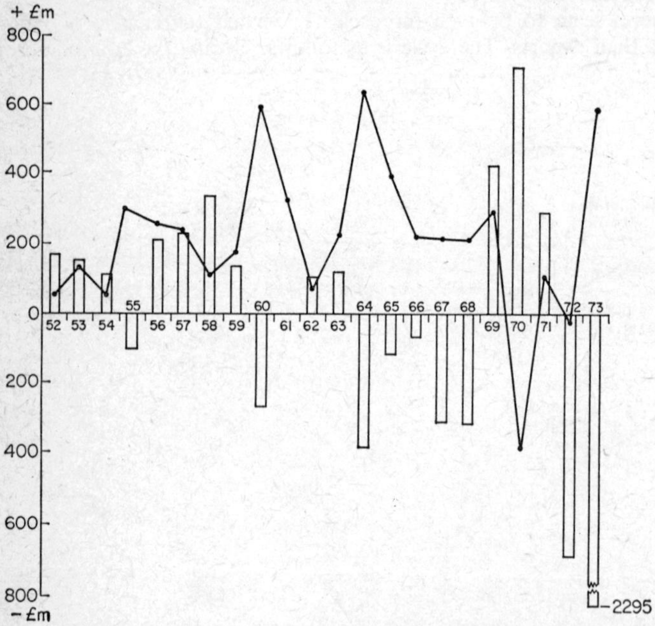

(*Source: National Income and Expenditure*)

Fig. 13. United Kingdom Balance of Payments and the value of the physical change in stocks

Balance of trade deficits in 1951, 1955, 1960, and 1964 are associated with very high levels of stock accumulation. In these four years the average level of the increase in stocks was £530 million compared with the average annual figure for the whole period of £266 million. The surge in imports of stocks has been a source of difficulty in the Balance of Payments since any expansion of the economy leads to a deficit which has frequently necessitated the re-application of the economic brakes to maintain confidence abroad.

(6) Invisible Trade.

The one consistently sound section of the United Kingdom Balance of Payments is the invisible trade account. The Committee on Invisible Exports pointed out that the account has been in continuous surplus since the beginning of the nineteenth century. During the same period the visible trade account showed a surplus on only seven occasions. Consequently current account surpluses have depended on the ability of the invisible surplus to finance visible deficits. Table 45 shows the breakdown of invisibles for a number of post-war years:

Table 45. United Kingdom invisible trade 1959–72 (£m)

	1959	1964	1972
Credits			
Government Services	43	45	75
Shipping	620	685	1,645
Civil Aviation	82	143	410
Travel	143	190	551
Other Services	440	558	1,516
Interest, Profits, Dividends	656	890	1,585
Private Transfers	100	131	211
Total	2,084	2,642	5,993
Debits			
Government Services	270	477	623
Shipping	606	724	1,699
Civil Aviation	64	116	346
Travel	164	261	529
Other Services	224	291	613
Interest, Profits, Dividends	396	495	1,129
Private Transfers	100	154	286
Total	1,824	2,518	5,225
Net			
Government Services	−227	−432	−548
Shipping	+ 14	− 39	− 54
Civil Aviation	+ 8	+ 27	+ 64
Travel	− 21	− 71	+ 22
Other Services	+216	+267	+903
Interest, Profits, Dividends	+260	+395	+456
Private Transfers	—	− 23	− 75
Total	+260	+124	+768

Source: U.K. Balance of Payments 1973.

The invisible account may be divided into public and private sections.

The Public Sector

The Government consistently shows a deficit and has done so in every post-war year. Excluding the Government's external transactions the invisible surpluses for the years 1959, 1964, 1969 were £487 million, £556 million, and £1015 million. The difficulty on the public side has been the static position of Government credits, which throughout the 1960's fluctuated only between £36 million and £46 million, while Government debits have shown a steady increase. The position is even worse than Table 45 suggests if Interest Profits and Dividends are broken down into public and private balances:

Table 46. Interest, Profits and Dividends 1959–72 (£m)

	1959	1964	1972
Government:			
Debits	150	162	314
Credits	22	43	167
Net	−128	−119	−147
Private:			
Debits	246	333	815
Credits	634	847	1418
Net	388	514	603

Source: U.K. Balance of Payments 1973.

Only recently have credits begun to rise while debits have grown consistently. This tendency in the public sector for payments to outstrip receipts not only damages the invisible account as a whole but impairs the ability of the private invisible surplus to finance the visible deficit.

During the interwar period the invisible surplus covered about one third of the visible import bill. By 1967 it covered only about 4 per cent. In 1973 it covered about 8 per cent of imports thanks to high overseas earnings of interest, profits and dividends. This trend, of course, is not only because of inadequacies on the public side, but the fact is that 'since 1964 more than 70 per cent of the net earnings on the other invisibles has been necessary to cover the (Government) deficit'.

Among the reasons for the deterioration in the Government trading account are the following:

(*a*) The position was eased in the 1950's by the continued receipt of military aid from the United States. This has ceased in the period under consideration.

(*b*) Government employees overseas, military and diplomatic, have received substantial pay rises in the 1960's, thus increasing Government expenditure.

(*c*) Economic grants from Britain (which appear here, not in the capital movements) have continued to increase.

(*d*) The general increase in interest rates together with a rise in the overseas holdings of British Government securities has accounted for the increasing public deficit on interest profits and dividends.

(*e*) Since 1967 British payments have of course been increased by devaluation, and the gradual depreciation of the pound.

The Private Sector

Table 45 shows the importance of the contribution made to the Balance of Payments by private invisible exports. That contribution is best understood by an examination of the individual categories, the trends of which are illustrated in Figure 14.

(*a*) *Interest, Profit and Dividends.* This has always been a most important part of the British Balance of Payments. Enormous earnings here have often supported deficits elsewhere in the accounts. The earnings represent payment for investments of all kinds by British residents and companies overseas. There are two main categories, portfolio investment (or investment in overseas securities) and direct investment (or investment directly in factories and subsidiaries overseas).

During the Second World War many overseas assets were sold and Britain's overseas earning power was therefore somewhat reduced for a while, though receipts have continued to rise throughout the post-war years. They have not unfortunately risen as rapidly as payments which have been inflated by the interest and dividends payable on the increased overseas investment in the United Kingdom.

(*b*) *Transport*. If people overseas travel to this country in British ships or

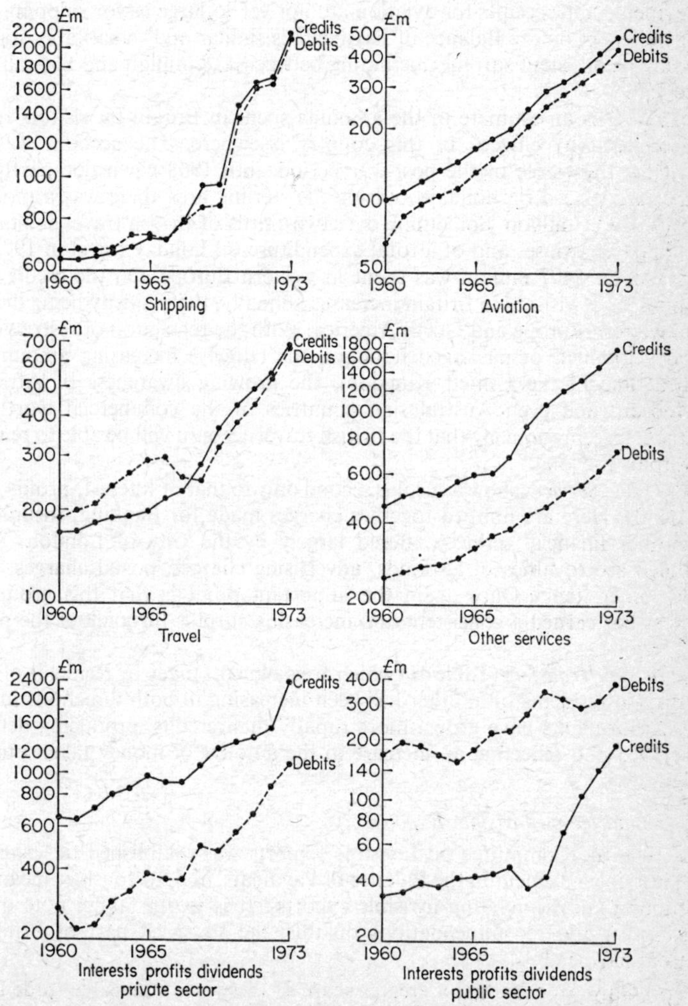

(*Source: UK Balance of Payments*

Fig. 14. Trends of selected United Kingdom invisibles (1960–73)

aircraft the Balance of Payments is credited; if United Kingdom residents travel in American aircraft the British Balance of Payments is debited. In the inter-war years earnings from shipping were an important source of foreign currency for Britain. The post-war years have seen only modest surpluses, however, as other countries have developed their own sea-going fleets, often heavily subsidized. Payments on both sides of the shipping account are still considerable but the balance over the recent years has fluctuated between a deficit of £76 million and a surplus of £60 million, and in a very competitive industry it is unlikely that there will be any upsurge in earnings to assist the overall balance.

Payments and receipts for aviation are not yet so large as for shipping but their net effect on the Balance of Payments is similar and remarkably stable, showing a consistent surplus fluctuating between £18 million and £64 million since 1959.

(*c*) *Travel* is an estimate of the amounts spent in Britain by visitors from overseas and by citizens of this country elsewhere. The account was in deficit for the whole of the post-war period until 1968 when due partly to restrictions placed on holidays outside the sterling area there was a modest surplus of £11 million. Something over two-thirds of British travel debits are for holiday purposes and of a total expenditure on holiday travel in 1973 of £467 million £407 million was spent in western Europe. On the credit side the number of visitors to Britain increases annually, the majority being drawn from western Europe and North America. With the relaxation of restrictions, the development of packaged holidays, the (slowly) increasing amount of leisure time in the United Kingdom, the growing awareness of African, Caribbean, and even Australasian countries of the commercial worth of tourism, it seems unlikely that the British travel account will be able to remain in surplus for long.

(*d*) *Other Services* show a surplus second only to that of interest, profits and dividends. Here are lumped together charges made for Banking, Insurance, and other financial services offered largely by the City of London. Also included are royalties of all kinds, advertising charges, postal charges, and many other items. Once again the important point is that this group of services has earned a consistent and increasing surplus throughout the post-war period.

(*e*) *Private Transfers* (Table 45) which are payments made by residents of one country to residents of another has been increasing in both directions in the 1960's, but debits have grown more rapidly than credits, producing deficits since 1963 and reflecting an increase in the amount of money taken out by emigrants.

The Committee on Invisible Exports

In 1966 the Committee on Invisible Exports was established to 'examine the "invisible" element in the Balance of Payments' and 'to consider means of promoting and stimulating invisible exports'. It is worth taking note of its conclusions and recommendations on this, the strongest part of Britain's external payments.

(*a*) Only America had a greater share of the world's invisible trade than Britain.

(*b*) The encouragement given to invisible exporters was scant indeed.

Particular attention was drawn to the Selective Employment Tax which was a burden to invisible exporters but not exporters of manufactures. Furthermore the export rebate scheme operating from 1964 to 1967 was not applicable to most invisible exporters.

(*c*) It warned of increasing competition likely to be experienced by some services in future. Among the principal recommendations was a call for the removal of exchange regulations which hindered the international role of the Banks. It was also felt that more Government assistance was needed by the tourist industry.

(*d*) The removal of obstacles interfering with the free flow of capital would probably improve invisible earnings.

(7) Capital Movements

Residents of a country may demand foreign currency for investment as well as trading purposes, and this is just as likely to produce a Balance of Payments deficit as excessive importing.

The controversy over international investment has been a long one and it continues. The arguments cannot be discussed in detail here but may be summarized as follows:

(*a*) *Arguments against overseas investment*

(i) Any overseas investment imposes a strain on the Balance of Payments when it occurs. This strain may be intolerable when there are deficits elsewhere in the accounts. Thus in 1964 United Kingdom investment overseas amounted to £399 million when there was already a current deficit of £395 million. Not surprisingly restrictions were imposed on overseas investment in 1965.

(ii) Greater benefit would be derived from investing the funds at home. (This assumes that the funds *would* be invested at home.)

(*b*) *Arguments in favour of overseas investment*

(i) The importance of overseas investment may be gauged from the contribution of interest, profits and dividends to the invisible surplus.

(ii) Overseas investment is more profitable than domestic investment. (In fact the Reddaway Report on foreign investment cast serious doubts on this contention.)

(iii) Overseas investment creates export orders. While this is certainly true the exact relationship is obscure and it is not clear that the long-term benefits justify the short-term costs.

(8) The Stop-Go Cycle

Figure 15 attempts to show the relationship between the Balance of Payments on current account and the level of economic activity as measured by the percentage unemployed from 1950 onwards. The changes in the Bank Rate are also included to give an indication of the direction of domestic economic policy. The diagram, in which the Balance of Payments surplus or deficit is measured on the left-hand axis in £m, the percentage unemployed on the top half of the right-hand axis, and the Bank Rate on the lower half of the right-hand axis, shows quite clearly the stop-go aspect of the economy's progress. A balance of trade deficit is generally associated with a fall in the level of unemployment and a surplus with rising unemployment. This is not

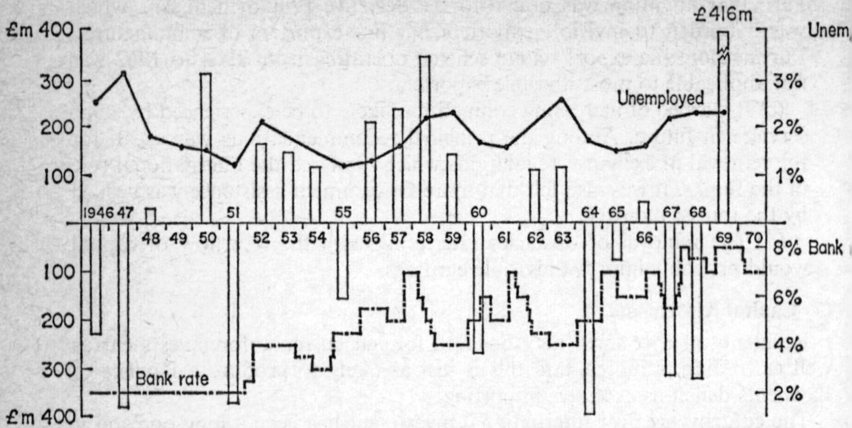

(*Source: Annual Abstracts of Statistics*)

Fig. 15. The Stop-Go cycle

the place for a year-by-year analysis of Britain's Balance of Payments but it is worth looking at the nature of the cycle before looking in more detail at the policies available for dealing with deficits.

The Cycle

The early post-war years are largely irrelevant for our purpose owing to the distortions resulting from the wide range of direct controls, the exceptionally severe winter of 1947 which led to record levels of unemployment, and the Korean War which caused a heavy adverse movement in the terms of trade, largely responsible for the 1951 deficit. The period from 1952 obviously falls into distinct cycles, 1952–5, 1956–60, 1961–4, but the last few years do not conform to the pattern. In each of the cyclical periods we begin with a balance of trade surplus associated with unemployment rising or about to rise. It is important to be clear that the determining factor in the cycle is the Balance of Payments. When the deficit emerges the Government is forced to impose restraints on domestic activity. After the surpluses of 1952 and 1953 the position began to deteriorate in the second half of 1954. The level of activity at home rises and the level of unemployment falls. As the level of demand rises so do imports, both of raw materials and manufactured goods which domestic industry cannot deliver in sufficient quantities. The incentive to export is reduced by the existence of an easy home market and the current balance then deteriorates on two counts. In the case of the United Kingdom the difficulties are compounded by the reserve currency role of sterling and the inadequacy of the gold reserve in relation to short-term liabilities. This is discussed further in Chapter Eight, but it is noted here that this deficiency results in a loss of overseas confidence in the pound which leads overseas holders of sterling to convert their sterling into gold or other currencies. This outflow of capital is in addition to the current account difficulties. Each of the deficits of 1955, 1960, and 1964 conformed to this broad pattern. In each case defensive measures were forced on the Government whose main objective was maintenance of the external value of the pound at 2·80 dollars.

One frequently used device was to increase Bank Rate. This not only acts as part of the deflationary package on the domestic economy but also attracts currency from overseas, thus initially having a favourable impact on the Balance of Payments. (If interest rates remain high the invisible side of the current account suffers as extra interest has to be paid out not only on new deposits but on those that were already here.) Bank Rate rises were normally accompanied by the whole crop of monetary measures designed to reduce demand. Open-market sales of stock, special deposits (in the 1960's), and directives as well as hire-purchase restrictions. Moreover, international monetary assistance was frequently sought to supplement the reserves during the crisis, and to avoid devaluation (see Chapter Eight).

Faith in monetary measures has not been sufficient during the post-war period to entrust to it the removal of deficits, and the deflationary package must also include fiscal measures. The credit squeeze is reinforced by an increase in taxation, and repeated attempts to reduce Government expenditure (which, at best, result in a reduction in the rate of its growth).

This normal deflationary package may be accompanied from time to time by direct controls in the form of import tariffs, export subsidies, or exchange controls, with, in particular, controls on the export of capital.

The effect is for unemployment to rise as the rate of increase of aggregate demand falls, and eventually for the Balance of Payments to improve. The relationship between unemployment and the Balance of Payments has not been so consistent in the 1970's, largely because the domestic economy has not responded in the orthodox way to monetary and fiscal controls. There is no longer the overwhelming priority of maintaining the exchange rate; inflation has forced high levels of unemployment upon us and oil prices have compelled the abandonment of growth.

Policies that have been used to turn deficits into surpluses fall under three headings: deflation, direct controls, and devaluation or depreciation.

(9) Policies for a Surplus

Deflation. We have noted elsewhere the nature of deflationary measures of monetary and fiscal policy, and Figure 15 shows the way in which Bank Rate has been increased to deal with trade deficits. It does not show the whole picture. Many Balance of Payments crises had little to do with the current account, but were nevertheless attacked with the usual package. In September 1957, for example, Bank Rate rose from 5 per cent to 7 per cent, public expenditure cuts were announced, and restrictive monetary measures introduced, not to correct the current account but to stem the speculative tide against the pound—all these despite the fact that the economy was not by any means fully employed, and the current account was in substantial surplus. Not only does the use of deflationary measures imply a rather barren attitude to the aims of economic activity, but it seems to have been increasingly difficult to improve the Balance of Payments by this method. Whereas a turn round in the Balance of Trade was fairly easily achieved in the 1950's by orthodox methods, the deficit of 1964 persisted more or less permanently until 1968. The reasons for this are not obscure:

(i) As time goes by the exchange rate gets more and more out of line, gradually reducing the United Kingdom's competitive strength as inflation proceeds at a faster rate than other people's. This being so, increasingly severe doses of deflation are required to compensate for the overvaluation of the pound.

(ii) The more severe the deflation the greater the impact on real earnings that is sought (prices do not fall but take-home pay does fall). Trade unions not unreasonably react by demanding higher wages and giving a further twist to the inflationary spiral.

(iii) Similarly deflationary measures if anything push up industrial costs, and lower sales make it more difficult to cover overhead costs. Prices tend to rise.

(iv) In the absence of an effective prices and incomes policy both these effects are likely to hamper an improvement in the trade balance.

(v) The purchasing power of the unemployed, while not absolutely maintained, is, thanks to improvements in the welfare state, much higher than it was. So the impact of a given level of unemployment on the level of demand and of imports is reduced.

Not only have deflationary methods had little success, but they also cause untold harm to the general development of the economy—growth depends on efficiency which depends on investment which will not flourish unless entrepreneurs are fairly sure of the future.

(*b*) *Direct Controls.* In the immediate post-war years the elaborate framework of direct controls established during the war was maintained. With the gradual expansion of world trade, restrictions were removed and by the end of 1953 the bulk of restrictions had gone. As with deflationary measures the use of direct controls of various kinds for purely 'Balance of Payments' reasons is dictated by the totem-pole-like sanctity of the exchange rate. Like the deflationary measures, they too face an increasingly difficult task and in the long run have little effect on the underlying weaknesses. The general post-war trend under the auspices of the General Agreement on Tariffs and Trade and the IMF has been for such controls to be reduced. The severity of the 1964 difficulties necessitated the introduction of a 15 per cent import surcharge on most manufactures and semi-manufactures, an export rebate which amounted to 2 per cent of turnover, and the £50 limit on non-sterling holiday expenditure. The trade deficit and the unemployment crisis of 1975 led to demands for selective import controls. These measures conflict with our undertakings to a number of international organisations but are generally excused on the grounds of exceptional Balance of Payments problems.

The trouble with such restrictions is of course the cushion they give to home industry. We have already noted the great increase in the level of manufactured imports in the course of the 1950's and 1960's and certainly this represents an alarming trend. But the long-term answer still lies in greater efficiency, and protective devices, while they may secure short-term Balance of Payments advantages, do nothing to improve the competitive edge of home industry. Indeed one of the arguments in favour of joining the European Common Market is the extra competition that this now involves and the impetus that might be given to efficiency.

Once again though our attention is thrown back to the exchange rate. Before looking at it more closely, it is worth considering the extent to which the Balance of Payments (and especially the Balance of Trade) may be regarded as a domestic problem.

Balance of Payments as a Domestic Problem

Under a managed flexibility system the value of a currency is fixed within very narrow limits except in the case of 'fundamental disequilibrium'. Prices in international trade consist of two elements, the domestic cost and the exchange rate, and if the exchange rate is fixed any adjustment of export prices must be achieved through changes in the domestic unit costs. This, of course, is the rationale of using deflationary policies, but since deflation at best achieves only a reduction in the rate of increase of prices, the emphasis needs to be put on reducing costs by increasing productivity—or at least encouraging increases in productivity to ensure that United Kingdom prices do not rise as rapidly as those of our competitors. If this fails the deficit country finds it increasingly difficult to balance its books and must have recourse to devaluation, but even though this may be regarded as turning the Balance of Payments into an external problem, its success depends largely on the condition of the domestic economy.

(*c*) *Devaluation.* Devaluation was used as the last resort in dealing with Balance of Payments deficits. This derives from the system of managed flexibility operated by the International Monetary Fund. The British and American authorities seeking a compromise between the rigidities of the gold standard (which implied a high level of unemployment) and the excesses of free exchange rates as they operated in the 1930's, eventually agreed on the system known as the gold exchange standard whereby the US dollar stood fixed in terms of gold at 35 dollars per ounce and all other currencies expressed their par value in terms of the dollar. The monetary authorities of each country undertook to maintain the value of its currency within a very narrow band approximately 1 per cent either side of par. Thus the Bank of England would ensure that the pound did not move outside the range of 2·38 to 2·42 dollars, and until November 1967 they were obliged to maintain the rate between 2·78 and 2·82 dollars.

Without anticipating too much of the section on the IMF it is fair to say that the founders of the Fund did not envisage their system as one in which exchange rates should become fossilized for eighteen years at a time. But the British authorities certainly did all they could to avoid devaluation during the 1960's.

Despite their efforts the pound was devalued in 1967. Why? We take the story up in 1964, though this is not to imply that there was no currency weakness before then. The Labour Government, coming to power in October 1964, reacted to the enormous Balance of Payments deficit it inherited by using the weapons which had had such limited success under their predecessors: the import surcharge, and export rebates came first, followed shortly by an increase in income tax and National Insurance contributions, increased petrol tax and restrictive monetary measures. At the same time enormous sums were raised overseas to ward off speculation against the pound encouraged only partly by the election result itself. As month succeeded month deflationary measures were heaped on deflationary measures until in the summer of 1966 the Prime Minister himself introduced the July measures, a deflationary package of exceptional severity, including an incomes freeze, which did succeed in moving the Balance of Payments into surplus for the last part of 1966 producing a small current surplus for the year.

The year 1967 saw a slowing down of world trade, Britain's exports grew by only 2 per cent up to October compared to 1966, while imports rose by 5 per cent. The trading picture was distorted by the closure of the Suez Canal and a dock strike, but there was no disguising the deterioration in the position: the quarterly figures for 1966–7 are given in Table 47.

Table 47. United Kingdom Quarterly Balance of Trade 1966–7 (£m)

	1966				1967			
	1	2	3	4	1	2	3	4
Imports	1,367	1,309	1,313	1,232	1,382	1,395	1,348	1,450
Exports	1,289	1,217	1,209	1,395	1,359	1,280	1,268	1,116
Balance	−78	−92	−104	+163	−23	−115	−80	−334

Source: Bank of England Quarterly Bulletin (March 1968 *and September* 1968).

Confidence in sterling declined, the crisis fed not only by the trade figures, but also by the Suez crisis, and the United Kingdom's renewed application to join the European Economic Community. The Bank of England had resort to credit lines of all kinds, from the IMF, the Group of Ten, the Bank for International Settlements, and a variety of Central Banks in its efforts to stem the speculative tide during the autumn. But the October trade deficit announced on 14 November was the worst ever (partly because of dock strikes) and on 18 November devaluation of the pound from 2·80 dollars to 2·40 dollars was announced. This devaluation of one-seventh meant that the value of currencies not devalued rose by one-sixth. Thus goods produced in this country for £100 and (ignoring transport and other freight charges) selling in America for 280 dollars would now sell for 240 dollars, and goods selling in the United Kingdom for £100 before devaluation would now cost £116·66.

In fact an exporter may decide to raise the sterling price of his exports thereby increasing the profitability of exporting, but causing dollar prices to fall by less than 40 dollars.

One of the immediate drawbacks of devaluation is that it turns the *terms of trade* against the devaluing country. The terms of trade may be measured by

$$\frac{\text{Index of import prices}}{\text{Index of export prices}} \times 100 \text{ per cent}$$

If the terms of trade fall the terms are said to have improved in that a given volume of exports will allow the purchase of a greater volume of imports. The immediate effect of devaluation is to reduce export prices and increase import prices, causing an adverse movement in the terms of trade indicating that a given volume of imports now requires a greater volume of exports to pay for it. For this reason the respective elasticities of demand are important.

The success of the operation depends on the elasticity of demand for traded goods being greater than one. Then as the price of British exports falls overseas foreign currency earnings will increase and the rising price of imports will result in lower expenditure of foreign currency. The effect of the change in price is to cause the demand for exports and in the demand for import substitutes to increase. If the economy cannot meet this demand because it is already running at or near full capacity, prices will rise and the competitive advantages gained through devaluation will be surrendered. Therefore a successful devaluation requires that the elasticity of supply of exports should be high.

Devaluation is therefore often accompanied by measures designed to reduce demand at home so as 'to make room for more exports'. The measures in 1967 were familiar: Bank Rate up to 8 per cent, restrictions on lending with priority to be given to the finance of exports or productive investment and various tax increases were forecast for the forthcoming spring budget. In some respects the task was made more difficult by the postponing of restrictive domestic measures until the spring and allowing a considerable consumer boom to persist for three or four months.

Before considering the effects of devaluation on the United Kingdom Balance of Payments why did the Government delay the operation for so long? The following seem the most likely reasons:

(i) The Government was bound by its electoral undertaking that the pound would not be devalued. To this may be added the feeling that devaluation in some way amounts to a national disgrace.

(ii) They believed that devaluation was immoral in that it automatically reduced the foreign exchange value of the sterling balances of other countries who held foreign exchange for a variety of reasons, and indeed many of the loudest protests were to come from such countries.

(iii) Further there was the idea that since inflation was the main cause of our troubles we should deal with it by domestic policies.

(iv) Apart from the six-month wage freeze at the end of 1966 the period was one of continuous inflation. There was no desire to add the inflationary pressure of devaluation to those already existing.

(v) The Americans and the IMF were anxious that devaluation should be avoided because of the disruption it might cause to the world payments system.

Effects of Devaluation

It is, of course, impossible to say precisely what were the effects of devaluation and what was attributable to other aspects of policy but Figure 16 shows the changes in imports and exports for the years 1967–70.

Although devaluation was followed by a sharp increase in exports, imports refused to react to higher prices and rose just as rapidly as exports, giving an even greater visible trade deficit for 1968 than 1967, but an improvement was achieved in 1969 giving al arge current surplus (though visible trade showed its usual deficit) and in 1970 there was actually a small visible surplus. Thus the target was eventually achieved, though it looks as though the relevant elasticities take much longer to work themselves out than had been anticipated—and in any case many other factors were at work by then.

(10) **Continuing Difficulties.** Although the Balance of Payments has moved into surplus the economy has had to endure continuing inflation, claimed by many to have been sparked off by the devaluation.

The more recent introduction of a floating exchange rate has, if anything, made matters worse. The gradual depreciation of sterling has forced up import prices and made inflation difficult to contain. We must now look more carefully at this and other means of settling international debts.

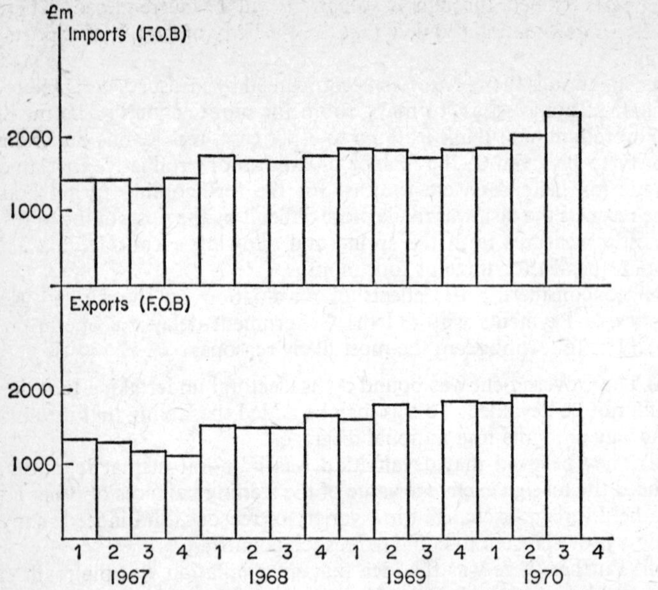

(*Source: UK Balance of Payments*)

Fig. 16. Changes in United Kingdom exports and imports (1967–70)

(11) Summary of Chapter Seven

(1) Balance of Payments problems develop when a country has insufficient foreign currency to finance its imports.

(2) All economic transactions between countries should find their way into the Balance of Payments. The method of presentation of the accounts has recently been changed from the 'Basic Balance' to the 'Total Currency Flow' method.

(3) The British Balance of Payments performance gradually deteriorated in the 1950's and 1960's.

(4) In particular the United Kingdom's share of world exports fell significantly.

(5) The strongest element of the accounts has been the invisible exports although the ability of this sector to support deficits elsewhere in the accounts has declined, largely because of heavy invisible payments by the Government.

(6) The post-war period saw a close connection between the Balance of Payments and the level of activity at home, leading to the stop-go cycle.

(7) Deflation and direct controls have generally been the means of eliminating a deficit, because of the reluctance to devalue within the present system.

(8) But in November 1967 a combination of poor trade figures and heavy speculation forced the Government to reduce the value of sterling from 2·80 dollars to 2·40 dollars.

(9) This combined with other measures eventually produced a substantial surplus in 1969.

(11) Suggested Further Reading

Committee on Invisible Exports, *Britain's Invisible Earnings* (W. M. Clarke), Skinner, London, 1967.

HIRSCH, F., *Money International*, Allen Lane The Penguin Press, London.

United Kingdom Balance of Payments (Annual), HMSO.

WELLS, S. J., *International Economics*, Allen & Unwin, London, 1969.

Exercises Set 7

1. Trace the history of the British Balance of Payments since the war pointing out the strengths and weaknesses.
2. How do you account for the changing area/commodity structure of Britain's exports?
3. Why does Britain now account for a much smaller proportion of world exports than she did twenty-five years ago?
4. 'The post-war difficulties of the British economy derived entirely from the rigidity of the exchange rate.' Comment.
5. 'The visible trade balance is rarely in surplus in the United Kingdom.' Is this due primarily to the failure of exporters?
6. Comment on the contribution made to the United Kingdom's Balance of Payments by her invisible exports.
7. What is the stop-go cycle? Comment on its operation during the 1950's and 1960's.
8. Why was it so difficult to deal with the Balance of Payments deficit that emerged in 1964?
9. Describe and evaluate the following as methods of achieving a Balance of Payments surplus: (*a*) deflation; (*b*) direct controls; (*c*) devaluation.
10. 'The Balance of Payments will cease to be a problem only when the domestic economy is on a sound footing.' What is the justification for such a statement?

CHAPTER EIGHT

THE FINANCE OF WORLD TRADE

(1) The Liquidity Problem

We have so far considered the Balance of Payments from the point of view of its general equilibrium and the way in which that equilibrium may be secured. We noted that in any given year it may be necessary to draw on our reserves of gold and foreign currency or to borrow from overseas authorities in order to make ends meet. (This, of course, is the official financing in Table 41.) It is to this problem of the finance of international trade that we now turn. This is generally referred to as the *international liquidity problem* and the problem stems from the fact that the volume of international trade has been rising more rapidly than the means of paying for it.

Figure 17 illustrates this. While the volume of world exports has shown a steady increase the volume of world reserves of various kinds hardly altered during the period 1958–68. However, just as the domestic economy needs an adequate supply of money to function effectively so does world trade rely upon the supply of liquidity if it is not to be hampered. Throughout the nineteenth century the means of settling international debts was gold and a country may still insist on being paid in this way. But the supply of gold has been inadequate to finance the growing volume of trade so paper currencies have been used instead, the recipients being confident that they can convert such currency into gold at any time by presenting it to the issuing government. Such currencies, notably the American dollar and sterling, are known as *reserve currencies.*

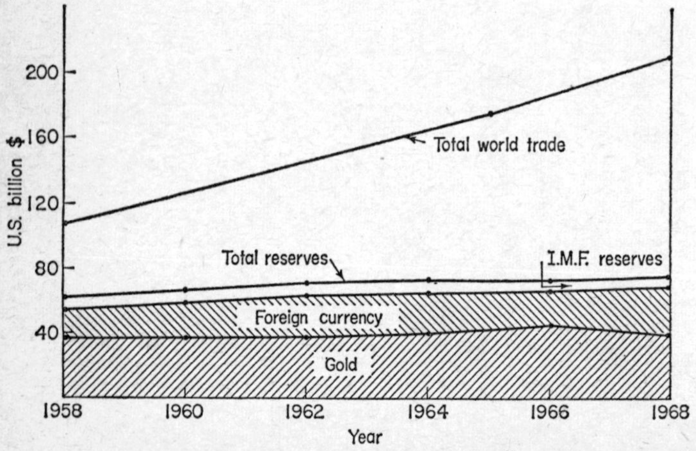

(*Source: Treasury Broadsheet*)

Fig. 17. Trends of world liquidity and trade

Confidence in reserve currencies is volatile and they are best regarded as a temporary feature of world payments which will eventually be replaced by an international paper currency. We must examine each of these means of payment—gold, reserve currency, and international paper in turn.

(2) Gold

For about thirty years either side of the turn of the century, the international payments system operated on the *gold standard* (see *Economics Made Simple*). This did not mean that all international payments were settled in gold (for sterling was already widely used for trading purposes), but each country was prepared to pay in gold and by keeping to the rules of the system ensured that its Balance of Payments was never in heavy deficit. The only way of ensuring this in those days of balanced budgets was by means of monetary deflation and the gold standard became associated with very high levels of unemployment. For this and a number of other reasons the gold standard was abandoned in 1931 and for a few years the international payments system relied upon free or *floating exchange rates* to adjust deficits and surpluses (see page 134). The experiment was not really successful and the result of wartime negotiations between the Allies was the present system of managed flexibility representing a partial return to gold.

In the last resort creditor countries can insist on being paid in gold, but we have already seen that gold as a proportion of world trade is falling, but there are those who believe that for the foreseeable future the liquidity problem can be solved only by increasing the amount of gold available. At one extreme of the liquidity spectrum are those who would like to see a return to the old gold standard and the discipline that it implied. The advocates of such a policy are a diminishing group motivated more by jealousy of the 'privileges' enjoyed by sterling and the dollar (see page 127) than by a genuine desire for the gold standard. Since other moves are afoot to reduce these privileges (and the responsibilities that go with them) we may perhaps leave the gold standard proper to the history books and look at other ways in which gold can help the liquidity problem.

Since the problem is that there is insufficient money to finance world trade one solution would be to increase the price of gold and so increase the purchasing power of reserves. Until recently the price of gold was fixed at 35 dollars per ounce, a rate established in 1935. To double the price would obviously double the purchasing power of the gold component of reserves and would seem a straightforward solution to the shortage. The advocates of an increase in the price point to certain benefits:

(*a*) The immediate rise in purchasing power. In fact an increase would be justified to restore purchasing power to its pre-war level.

(*b*) The increased supply of gold that would subsequently be forthcoming as gold producers found it more profitable to work what are at the moment marginal mines.

(*c*) The increased supply that would derive from dis-hoarding. In many countries (France and the Middle and Far East) the hoarding of gold by private individuals is widespread. Many would be persuaded to take their profits if the price were increased sufficiently and if it were clearly a once and for all move.

(*d*) A succession of currency crises involving the dollar and especially sterling have shown that the world does not have sufficient confidence in paper currencies and that therefore any rise in liquidity must for the time being come from gold.

Despite these apparent advantages the world monetary authorities in general and the Americans in particular have resisted any proposal for an increase in price. The main arguments that may be assembled in support of this attitude are:

(*a*) That an increase would tend to perpetuate a primitive system. It is argued that in the second half of the twentieth century we should be able to devise a monetary system which does not depend on man's ancient attachment to a specific metal. Paper currency is perfectly acceptable in domestic transactions and we should be moving towards a system where it is equally acceptable internationally. The argument seems to overlook the fact that it is not possible to legislate for confidence. If people or governments lack confidence they will not hold paper currency.

(*b*) The benefits of a revaluation of gold would be unequally distributed, the greatest benefits going to gold-producing countries (notably South Africa and Russia) and those with a large proportion of gold in their reserves. Those countries which have been prepared to hold their reserves in the form of reserve currencies, thereby economizing on gold and supporting the present system would derive least benefit. This is considered too arbitrary a method of increasing the world money supply.

(*c*) The increase in the price of gold would have an inflationary impact. A country suddenly finding that its reserves had increased, while prices initially remained constant, would be prepared to allow an emerging Balance of Payments deficit to go further before taking restrictive action in the form of deflation. If all countries pursued such a course the benefits of the increased purchasing power of gold would soon be eroded, necessitating a further revaluation.

(*d*) Such an increase is not necessary. World trade has been rising quite steadily at 6 per cent or 7 per cent a year with the price of gold fixed. When it becomes clear that world trade is failing to expand through lack of funds it will be time to consider increasing the price. This ignores the fact that in the post-war period it has been largely the growth of reserve currencies that has financed the increase and that this growth is unlikely to continue. In any case whatever reforms are likely to occur need to be instituted in advance of the crisis.

(*e*) The balance of the arguments seems to lie with those against increasing the price of gold. Certainly the official attitude has been that alternative sources of liquidity must be developed, though with gold remaining as the final support.

(3) Reserve Currencies

The development of sterling as a reserve currency dates from the British domination of world trade in the nineteenth century. Since Britain was the main source of manufactured goods, the main customer for raw materials, and the main source of investment funds, many countries, especially those in the Empire found it beneficial to keep their reserves (their means of settling international debts) in London. Any moneys received or payable could then pass through the appropriate bank account. The tendency was encouraged by the sophistication of the banking and financial institutions of London. The 'sterling balances' that were thus accumulated in London were as good as gold to the overseas countries since the Bank of England stood ready to convert them on demand.

The continued existence of a reserve currency depends entirely upon the confidence of holders that their paper can be converted, and we shall see that this requirement has put severe strains on the system in the post-war period. These countries which found it convenient and beneficial to hold sterling developed into the Sterling Area after the financial crisis of 1931.

The Sterling Area consists of the majority of Commonwealth countries and a few outsiders such as Iceland and from the 1930's to the post-war years followed a coherent and co-ordinated trading and commercial policy although there was no formal constitution until the outbreak of war. The gold reserves of the whole area were held in London, and individual member's currencies were fixed in terms of sterling (in contrast with the fluctuating rates elsewhere in the 1930's). In the war years the Sterling Area developed greater rigidity and of necessity became more inward-looking with strict control on the use of sterling and a rationing scheme to economize on dollars. The problems of the post-war years were little different. Every country urgently needed dollars to buy vital imports for war-damaged economies and controls on their use had to be maintained for a while, gradually being eliminated in the 1950's. The 1960's have seen a greater loosening of the ties of the Sterling Area. Overseas Sterling Area countries while maintaining their balances in London have not in general been adding to them, partly because of declining confidence on the pound and partly because of the greater diversification of their trade—especially with America. The greater political independence of the Commonwealth has also led to a loosening of economic ties with Britain.

Although the Sterling Area has been in decline over the last twenty years the pound has continued to play its part—albeit with increasing difficulty—as a reserve and trading currency, but the period has really been dominated by the dollar.

The Dollar Shortage. From the end of the First World War and more especially since 1945 the American dollar has challenged and surpassed sterling as a reserve and trading currency. As Britain dominated nineteenth-century trade so America dominates the twentieth century and it is on the basis of this great economic strength that the dollar has established its position. The difficulties experienced by Britain in the early post-war years served to emphasize the strength and desirability of the dollar and so confidence in, and demand for, the dollar rose.

We have already seen that the greatest absolute increase in world reserves in this period has come from the reserve currencies. The great danger of this process is that other countries can only acquire dollars and sterling if the United States and United Kingdom are prepared to supply them. In the event they have usually been only too happy to supply them to finance their rising overseas expenditure and deficits—for they are in fact settling their overseas debts simply by issuing paper money. Initially this causes them no problem, and it is equally acceptable to the recipients as long as they think they can change these paper promises into gold on demand. Such confidence, however, depends on the ratio between a country's gold reserves and its liabilities.

The ten years after the war saw an unprecedented demand for dollars. The American economy was in an insuperable position. Everything that Europe required was available in America (and virtually nowhere else) to those who had the means to pay—dollars. But Europe couldn't acquire the dollars through trade for they had nothing to offer the Americans. This was the so-called *dollar shortage*. The Americans themselves solved the problem through the Marshall Plan, a massive aid programme for Europe resulting in the outflow from America of sixteen billion dollars. Thus the dollar was triumphant and its desirability unlimited, especially in view of the pathetic attempt at making sterling *fully convertible* in 1947. The Government, harking back to the golden days, and borrowing almost four billion dollars from the Americans, declared the pound fully convertible in July 1947, indicating their readiness to turn sterling held by overseas residents and institutions into gold on demand. They were taken aback to find that everyone believed them and rushed to exchange their sterling for gold or dollars. Who wanted sterling anyway? The important thing was to acquire dollars to buy essential imports which were not available from Britain. After five weeks with the reserves rapidly disappearing, the pound was declared inconvertible, confidence in it was at its lowest ebb and the hopes of sterling regaining its former dominant position were lost forever. Not only that, the experience of Britain was a deterrent to any other country contemplating the move towards convertibility and it was 1958 before the major European currencies were fully convertible. This may sound a technicality, but it is important in that if a currency is fully convertible any central bank will accept it in the knowledge that it can pass it on to a third country and will not be confined to spending it in its country of origin.

In the 1950's the Americans did all they could to meet the demand for dollars, principally through military expenditure and what is euphemistically called economic aid. The American role as the world's policeman has kept up a continuing flow of dollars to countries being defended by American forces and of course the massive aid programmes had the same effect. The net result was a vast increase in the number of paper dollars outstanding and gradually there developed a disenchantment with the dollar.

Meanwhile the Sterling Balances were being troublesome. These balances which include all overseas bank balances held in London whether owned by official or unofficial bodies rose from about £600 million in 1938 to over £3,500 million at the end of the war, and although there have been fluctuations in the holdings of individual countries the total has been maintained at about this level while the gold and foreign currency reserves, the major short-term assets, were fluctuating around £900 million to £1,000 million. This ratio in itself seems adequate, but it is not sufficient to bear the strain of a weak Balance of Payments. Consequently as a Balance of Payments deficit develops and the ratio deteriorates either because the reserves are reduced or because short-term liabilities are increased, overseas confidence falls, withdrawals begin, and emergency measures in the form of high interest rates and restrictions at home, and extra support borrowing from abroad become necessary to protect the exchange rate (see page 118). By borrowing abroad a Government temporarily increases the reserve, but is really only storing up difficulties for the future. We see here the difficulty that Britain found itself in over devaluation in 1967. Its basic trading position was so weak that heavy Balance of Payments deficits were almost impossible to avoid unless the pound were devalued. But devaluation would cause greatest harm to overseas holders of sterling and was therefore ruled out on ethical or moral grounds. Consequently worse liabilities had to be incurred to forestall devaluation. Just as individuals' credit is limited so it is impossible for Governments to borrow indefinitely. As the difficulties increased in the 1960's the Sterling Balances became more difficult expecially that part that was privately held and the speculators were finally successful in 1967. Anticipating devaluation they were able to sell £100 to the Bank of England for approximately $278 (see page 117), wait for devaluation and buy back their £100 for only $240.

While few countries followed the devaluation the repercussions were widespread and the most important was the speculation against the dollar itself which led in 1968 to the two-tier system for gold which effectively separated the official market from the private.

(4) The Weakness of the System

So the 1960's saw the exposure of the world monetary system and its dependence on unstable reserve currencies. The world needed extra money, the authorities refused to increase the price of gold, were unable to agree on a new paper currency and were therefore thrown back on the reserve currencies and the United States and United Kingdom deficits as a source of liquidity. Sterling was quite unable to withstand the strains imposed upon it.

A viable reserve currency must be associated with certain characteristics: it must be of obviously stable value: its future as a reserve currency is limited if it constantly needs Government support because people are reluctant to hold it. Thus rapid inflation in the issuing country will not be desirable. Nor will large trading deficits be desirable for, though they will increase the amount of paper currency available to others, they necessarily reduce the confidence that new and existing holders can have in it. Furthermore, the greater the overseas commitments of the issuing country in relation to its economic strength the less suitable the currency for reserve purposes. These factors would seem to exclude sterling, but the things that have acted in its favour have been its historical standing, the unrivalled facilities of the City of London and the self-interest of overseas holders of sterling in not rocking the boat and inflicting losses on themselves.

Benefits to Britain. The reserve currency role allegedly was allowing privileges to Britain.

(i) The facility for settling international debts by issuing paper money is available only to reserve currency countries (which may be extended to include those such as Germany and Japan whose payments are very strong). While this is true in the short run, we have already noticed that it may really be storing up trouble for the future and in any case it is not a process that can continue indefinitely.

(ii) It is said that Britain benefits from the reserve and trading currency role bringing income to the City of London, but it is not clear that the trading functions of the pound depend on its reserve role. It seems certain that the short-run benefits to Britain have been offset by long-run disadvantages. The obsessive desire to maintain the exchange rate derives directly from the reserve currency function and maintaining that rate has necessitated the sacrifice of a variety of domestic goals, the stop-go cycle leading to slower growth and a lower standard of living.

Future of Reserve Currency. The sterling devaluation was followed in 1968 by a substantial move out of sterling by official holders (the 1967 withdrawals were largely unofficial). Such was the 1968 outflow that the monetary authorities were forced to conclude the Basle Agreement of September guaranteeing the gold content of overseas official sterling holdings in excess of 10 per cent of each country's total reserves. This must be seen as the beginning of the run-down of the reserve currency role, which has continued in more recent years as other solutions have been sought.

(5) The International Monetary Fund

The centre-piece of the present system of managed flexibility is the International Monetary Fund. Devised by J. M. Keynes and D. White, an American economist, but emerging closer to American than British ideals, the Fund was accepted by its forty founder members at Bretton Woods, USA, in 1944.

Exchange Rates. The system of managed flexibility required a member to declare the par value of its currency in terms of gold or the US dollar which was itself priced in terms of gold at 35 dollars per ounce. Once the rate was declared members had to ensure that the price in the foreign exchange market remained within 1 per cent of the par value. If Britain is running a Balance of Payments deficit the demand for sterling will be low (because few people want to buy British goods) and its price will fall away from its par of 2·40 dollars towards 2·38 dollars, but before it reaches 2·38 the Bank of England must intervene to buy sterling (thereby reducing the foreign exchange reserves) and therefore the Bank fixes the price somewhat above 2·38 dollars since no one will sell to other dealers at a lower price. The Bank of England sells pounds when the price approaches 2·42 dollars and thus fixes the ceiling. Changes in the par value are sanctioned only in cases of 'fundamental disequilibrium', a condition which is not defined but is usually fairly obvious. If a country finds it impossible to achieve a surplus despite severe domestic restraint the currency is almost certainly overvalued. On the other hand if a country cannot avoid surpluses, as was the case with Germany in the 1960's, its currency is probably undervalued and from a world point of view is just as much in need of change as an overvalued currency. Changes of less than 10 per cent need only be notified to the Fund, but greater changes require approval, though in the last resort there is little the Fund can do to prevent devaluations which it believes unjustified, but adjustments to the major currencies have been relatively few since 1949 when the overdue devaluation of sterling was followed by many other currencies.

The success of the Fund in maintaining stable exchange rates has led to increasing activity in its other role of providing currency to members in temporary Balance of Payments difficulties. (The greater the flexibility of exchange rates the lower the need for reserves as international prices are adjusted quickly through the changes in the rates, and the Balance of Payments accordingly moves towards equilibrium.)

Drawing Rights. The Fund may be regarded as a revolving pool of currency available to members in Balance of Payments difficulties. The 'borrowing' rights of a member are determined by its quota or contribution to the Fund, itself determined by a complex formula, but really depending on economic and political importance. Table 48 gives examples of quotas and shows how they have increased.

Table 48. International Monetary Fund Quotas

(millions of dollars)

	1945	1965	1971
United States	2,750	4,125	6,700
United Kingdom	1,300	1,950	2,800
France	450	787·5	1,500
West Germany	—	787·5	1,600
Canada	300	550	1,100
Japan	—	500	1,200
Australia	200	400	665
New Zealand	50	125	202
Kenya	—	25	48
Uganda	—	25	40

Source: IMF.

Twenty-five per cent of the quota is contributed in gold or US dollars and the remainder in local currency of the member. As a member draws foreign currency from the Fund it must deposit corresponding amounts of its own currency. Its drawing rights are limited to 25 per cent of its quota plus 'such a total amount as will increase the Fund's holdings of its currency to not more than 200 per cent of its quota'. Figure 18 illustrates the process.

The gold 'tranche' or slice is automatically available to a member. If this were not so its immediately available foreign reserve would be lower if it joined the Fund than if it remained outside. When this 25 per cent is withdrawn the Fund holds, for example, sterling equal to the extent of 100 per cent of the United Kingdom quota. Subsequent instalments may be drawn if the Balance of Payments deficit persists, although increasingly stringent conditions are likely to be attached to each drawing. Once the Fund holds 200 per cent of the quota in local currency a member's drawing rights are exhausted until either he repurchases sterling paying in a currency acceptable to the Fund, or another member draws sterling and reduces the Fund's holding below 200 per cent, the only exceptions being special arrangements for primary-producing countries. Currencies acceptable to the Fund in repayment are those where the Fund's holding has fallen below 75 per cent of quota through the drawings of other countries. This meant that until 1963 repayments were normally in dollars but since then other currencies have been used.

(6) The Fund in Action

Drawings. Figure 19 shows the use made of the Fund up to 1970. By the end of 1965 a total of $11,462 million had been advanced of which 42 per cent was in US dollars, 16 per cent in Deutschemarks, 11 per cent in French francs, and about 6 per cent in sterling. This distribution is in marked contrast to advances up to 1960. Of total drawings of $3,683 million, 87 per cent were in dollars and 8 per cent in sterling. The changing balance reflects, of course, the

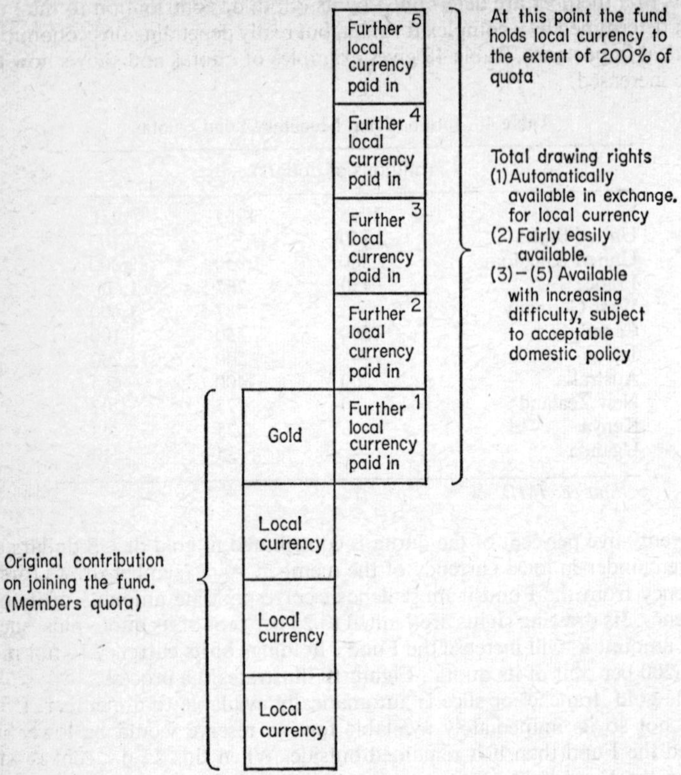

Fig. 18. Currency drawings from the IMF

achievement of convertibility in 1958 and the greater confidence in other currencies.

The United Kingdom's use of the Fund has been the most significant. It is noticeable that the year of greatest drawings coincides with the worst periods for the British Balance of Payments. Such extensive borrowing was the inevitable result of refusing to reduce the exchange value of sterling. The structure of the massive United Kingdom loans of 1964 and 1965 are shown in Table 49. The noteworthy point is the variety of currencies that were advanced, reflecting the willingness of our creditors to accept an increasing variety of currencies in settlement of our debts.

Standby Arrangements. Many of the advances have been made under standby arrangements whereby the Fund agrees to make currency available to a member should it be necessary over the following few months. Thus a country anticipating an outflow of currency for speculative reasons may make standby arrangements with the Fund, hoping that opening of such a line of credit will be sufficient to ward off the speculation and restore confidence.

The ability of the Fund to provide this and other finance was increased by the *General Arrangements to Borrow*. The main strain on the IMF resources is

Table 49. United Kingdom drawings from International Monetary Fund (December 1964–May 1965)
(millions of dollars)

	1964	1965
Austrian Schillings	28	—
Belgian Francs	57	82·5
Canadian Dollars	69	107·5
Danish Kroners	—	30
Deutsche Marks	273	310·5
French Francs	163	342·5
Italian Lire	23	182·5
Japanese Yen	54	77·5
Dutch Guilders	66	81·5
Spanish Pesetas	40	40
Swedish Kroners	27	37·5
US Dollars	200	200
	1,000	1,400

Source: IMF.

likely to occur when several currencies are under speculative attack at the same time, and when in effect the world payments system is threatened.

The General Arrangements to Borrow came into existence in 1962 when members of the 'group of ten' major industrial countries agreed to subscribe $6,000 million in the proportions shown in Table 50. The facility was first used to raise some of the $1,000 million credit for Britain in 1964. The procedure is that members advance currency to another member in difficulty by means of credits to the IMF. It is yet another example of the way in which the Fund has widened its activities over the years to develop the availability of liquidity, and to resist the attempts of speculators to bring down the system. An even more significant example is provided by the institution of Special Drawing Rights (see page 133).

Compensatory Finance. It has been said at times that the Fund is a rich

Table 50. General Arrangements to Borrow
(millions of dollars)

United States	2,000
West Germany	1,000
United Kingdom	1,000
France	550
Italy	550
Japan	250
Canada	200
Holland	200
Belgium	150
Sweden	100
	6,000

Source: IMF.

man's club, because it is of the greatest benefit to the industrial countries. But one way in which it has been of special assistance to developing countries has been in the provision of compensatory finance for those members dependent for foreign exchange on the export of one primary product. Fluctuations

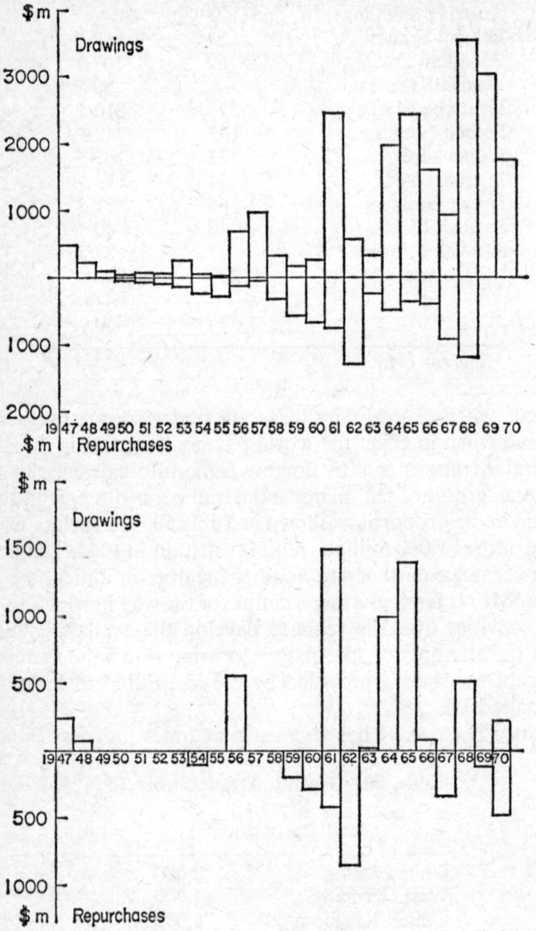

(*Source: International Monetary Fund*)

Fig. 19. IMF drawings (1946–70): total, top; UK, bottom

in the price of such products can cause great economic difficulties to such primary-producing countries. Although the difficulties may be eased by commodity marketing schemes of various kinds these are not infallible and since 1963 the Fund has been able to help.

The idea is simply that a country whose foreign exchange earnings are reduced through price fluctuations can apply to the IMF for the shortfall of currency, providing that it does not draw more than 50 per cent of its quota in compensatory finance. (A country's ordinary drawings are unrelated to and unaffected by compensatory drawings.) By 1969 some four billion dollars had been advanced under the scheme and further assistance to primary-producers was being planned in the form of finance for 'buffer stocks' as a means of reducing price fluctuations in primary-produce markets.

(7) **Special Drawing Rights**

The strains on the IMF system exemplified by the difficulties of sterling and the dollar, and the strains likely to develop if Britain and America move into persistent Balance of Payments surplus, so depriving the rest of the world of currency, each intensified the need for reform. The contribution of the Fund to the development of world trade through the provision of credit to members does not disguise the fact that it has not in any way been a world central bank with control over the supply of international money akin to the control of the Bank of England over the British money supply. Lord Keynes had proposed that the IMF should be a clearing union through which member countries would settle their debts with each other in terms of 'Bancor' units. The scheme, at the time too adventurous for the Americans, was shelved but the SDR scheme bears a great resemblance to it.

Three instalments of credit totalling $9,500 million in 1970, 1971, and 1972 were credited to each member in proportion to their quotas. Unlike the ordinary drawing rights the SDR's are automatically available to members and are regarded by them as part of their reserves. The SDR's exist only in the books of the Fund and can thus be transferred only between members. They cannot be used in trade for the purchase of goods and services, but may be transferred to other members in exchange for foreign currencies. The success of this 'paper gold' depends on the willingness of surplus countries to accept it and provide their currency in exchange—an obligation which ceases once a member's holding of SDR's exceeds 300 per cent of its allocation.

Thus if Britain has a deficit with Germany and is short of Deutschemarks she could (with IMF approval) transfer part of her SDR's to Germany in exchange for marks which are then available for British traders to obtain in exchange for sterling so as to settle their debts with their German creditors.

As yet SDR's form but a small proportion of world reserves and their immediate purpose is not to replace gold or the reserve currencies, but to supplement them. As the international role of sterling declines, however, it is foreseen that the use of SDR's will become more widespread though the possibility of 'paper gold' eliminating real gold from the system is more remote. A major criticism of the scheme is that since the SDR's are allocated in proportion to quotas the greatest benefits go to the rich industrial countries. While it is not the main purpose of the IMF to solve the problems of the underdeveloped countries, the proposal has been made either that a different allocation should be devised or that the rich countries should transfer foreign currency to the World Bank equal to a small percentage of their allocations of Special Drawing Rights. However, this is a minor matter compared with the landmark that SDR's represent. No longer does the world monetary system depend solely upon arbitrary increases in purchasing power dictated by the output of gold-mines and the Balance of Payments deficits of the USA and Britain. Henceforth the opportunity exists to adjust the supply of money to the growth of trade. (Easier said than done as domestic experience shows.)

Special Drawing Rights have become an accepted part of the international currency system though there are many obstacles to the full-scale adoption of the new medium as the principal international currency.

(8) More Flexible Exchange Rates

Upheavals in the international economy in the early 1970's proved too much for the managed flexibility system with the result that greater flexibility has been introduced in international payments. In the extreme form of completely free exchange rates Balance of Payments difficulties as we know them, in the form of a shortage of foreign currency, would be eliminated. As a country developed a deficit in its payments the demand for its currency would fall and the exchange rate would depreciate, making its goods more attractive to overseas buyers and imports more expensive. The price mechanism of the foreign exchange market would ensure that equilibrium in the demand and supply for currency was achieved, although it might require a very large depreciation. The main advantage claimed for such a system is that it leaves Governments free to pursue domestic economic aims, allowing the exchange rate to look after the Balance of Payments—an attractive proposition. It has certainly been British experience that the domestic aim of full employment is incompatible with a Balance of Payments surplus under the present system of more or less fixed rates.

Objections to Free Rates. While the opinion of economists is divided on the merits of flexible exchange rates that of bankers and finance ministers is almost universally hostile to drastic alterations to the present system. The objections to free rates may be summarized as follows:

(*a*) The discipline of a fixed exchange rate is necessary as an incentive to control inflation. There are, of course, other reasons for controlling inflation but the Balance of Payments is most important.

(*b*) Free rates provide an additional hazard in international trade. With fixed rates exporters can be confident that a payment from an American customer of $240 will be worth £100 when it arrives in a few weeks' time. No such confidence can exist with freely fluctuating rates and if by the time he receives payment the rate is 3 dollars to the pound our exporter will receive only £80 unless he has already taken precautions in the foreign exchange market. In the circumstances it would not be surprising if a few marginal exporters turned to less hazardous activities.

(*c*) The system would encourage speculation. This criticism may be countered to some extent, but not completely by pointing to the one-way speculation encouraged by the present system. At least under fluctuating rates the speculators may lose. Under managed flexibility there was no possibility of sterling being revalued in 1964–7: the worst that could happen to the speculators was that they would have to buy back their pounds at the same price as they sold them.

(*d*) A related point is that capital movement may have a destabilizing effect on the exchange rate. Thus heavy overseas investment by United Kingdom residents would depreciate the rate and give British traders a temporary competitive advantage as the overseas price of their exports was reduced.

(*e*) Depreciation and appreciation of currency depends on the elasticity of demand being high and responsive in the short run. There are, however, good reasons to think that elasticity may be fairly low in the short run.

(*f*) Completely free exchange rates would in any case be completely impractical and Governments would have to intervene to some extent.

(*g*) Moreover, there is very little wrong with the present system. The degree of flexibility could be achieved by a more frequent alteration of rates than has occurred to date.

Compromise Solutions. Since Governments have shown themselves reluctant to resort to devaluation and since completely free exchange rates may be ruled out various compromises have been proposed.

(*a*) The most likely to be adopted is to allow currencies to fluctuate within wider bands than the 1 per cent either side of par that is currently permitted. Mr. R. Jenkins observed at the IMF annual meeting in 1969 that a 2 per cent range either side of parity might be useful but that a 5 per cent margin either side would be excessive. Any increase in the bands would reduce the dependence on reserves but only in the case of completely free rates would the need for reserves disappear.

(*b*) An alternative is the so-called crawling-peg, where an overall annual adjustment of 2–3 per cent is allowed, perhaps by one-sixth of 1 per cent per month, but this does not seem to attract much support in official circles, and we come back to the fact that anything these systems might achieve could equally well be achieved by proper use of the managed flexibility system.

(9) Eurodollars

It is appropriate at this stage to mention the recent rapid development of Eurodollars, even though they do not form part of any country's official reserves. Eurodollars are dollars which are held in commercial banks outside the USA and which are available for relending by those banks for trading purposes. The market for such dollars is centred in Europe rather than the USA for technical reasons, but mainly because the interest rates available to depositors are higher than in America.

The growth of the business, reflecting the importance of the dollar as a trading currency has been rapid. Between 1957 and 1970 the deposits of foreign currency in UK banks rose from £100 million to almost £14,000 million.

(10) Summary of Chapter Eight

(1) International debts may be settled in gold, certain generally accepted currencies or, more recently Special Drawing Rights. The difficulty is that various forms of liquidity have not kept pace with the growth of trade.

(2) One solution would be to increase the price of gold but on balance this is considered a reactionary move.

(3) The reserve currencies have been important in financing trade since the war but are really a symbol of the inherent weakness of the system.

(4) The International Monetary Fund has been able to provide extra currency to members with Balance of Payments difficulties.

(5) The latest development is the introduction of Special Drawing Rights, a credit facility transferable between members of the IMF which gives some hope that the world money supply might be more carefully controlled in future.

(6) The alternative to the creation of extra liquidity is more flexible exchange rates.

(7) The Eurodollar market has developed to channel dollars for trading purposes in appropriate directions.

(11) Suggested Further Reading

HARROD, R., *Reforming the World's Money*, Macmillan, London, 1965.
HIRSCH, F., *Money International*, Allen Lane The Penguin Press, London.
IMF and IBRD, *Finance and Development* (Quarterly).
SCAMMELL, W. M., *International Monetary Policy*, Macmillan, London, 1962.

Exercises Set 8

1. What is the international liquidity problem? How would it be alleviated by the use of more flexible exchange rates?

2. Consider the merits of doubling the official price of gold to solve the liquidity problem.

3. What are reserve currencies? Would you regard the running of a reserve currency as a privilege or a burden to the United Kingdom?

4. Assess the contribution made by the IMF towards the solution of post-war financial problems.

5. 'Special Drawing Rights represent the most important development in the international payments system since the war.' Comment, explaining the circumstances which necessitated their introduction

6. 'The inherent weakness of the post-war international monetary system has been its dependence on the Balance of Payments deficits of the USA and UK.' Explain.

7. 'International money must have intrinsic value: therefore we need more gold.' Comment.

8. Explain the rights and obligations of a member of the International Monetary Fund.

9. Why do the international monetary authorities resist the introduction of more flexible exchange rates?

10. 'We are quite happy to print paper money for our domestic use, but we will not accept paper money in exchange for our exports.' (Finance Minister.) Comment and explain.

CHAPTER NINE

FREE TRADE AND THE EUROPEAN TRADING GROUPS

(1) Introduction

The theory of comparative costs demonstrates that under conditions of free trade specialization will occur, leading to the optimum use of resources and gains for all nations. For most of the nineteenth century world trade was dominated by Britain within framework of free trade, which was to the mutual benefit of all concerned—Britain acquiring food and raw materials, the suppliers of which received a wide range of manufactured goods from the workshop of the world. The period between the two world wars was one of exceptional economic difficulty and was marked in international trade by the erection of tariff barriers and quota restrictions by all nations designed to protect home industry by restricting the import of goods which could be produced domestically. Restrictions were intensified during the Second World War but since the war the trend has been reversed—albeit slowly—partly through the work of the General Agreement on Tariffs and Trade and partly through the formation of free-trade blocs such as the European Economic Community and the European Free Trade Area. Before considering these bodies we examine some of the reasons used for putting obstacles in the way of free trade.

(2) The Case for Restrictions

Restrictions fall into two groups: *tariffs* which are in effect an *ad valorem* tax imposed on goods as then enter the country, producing revenue for the Government (even if this is not their main purpose) and providing a disincentive in the form of higher prices to consumers. The amount of such goods imported then depends on the demand for them. *Quota restrictions* on the other hand set a limit to the quantity admitted and allow the price to find its own level in the market. Revenue to the Government will be derived from the sale perhaps by auction of permits to those wishing to supply the goods. While such restrictions are not so widespread as tariff barriers their effect is ultimately the same—the reduction of trade and output.

Employment Arguments. A major reason for the growth of tariffs in the 1930's was the desire of Governments to eliminate unemployment at home. The higher the tariff the more difficult for imported goods to compete. Such protective measures are understandable because of the mountainous unemployment prevailing at the time. Consumers probably have to pay more for goods than would be necessary in the absence of the tariff but the Government may believe that the extra cost is worthwhile if unemployment is reduced. The danger is that the protected industry becomes accustomed to the barrier, lobbies against its removal, and uses it to disguise its own inefficiency.

Infant industry tariffs are viewed more sympathetically than most where the efficiency of an industry is dependent on great economies of scale as in steel production or motor manufacture, newly developing industries are unable to compete with those fully established. A protected home market is the least that is required to facilitate the growth to maturity. Since such tariffs are mainly the prerogative of the primary-producing countries it is frequently argued that they would be unnecessary if those countries concentrated on producing their primary products, and importing manufactures. However, it is only through the development of the secondary and tertiary sectors of the economy that the primary producers can eventually become self-sufficient and make the best use of their resources. Even if there are difficulties in removing the tariff once the infant has matured the prohibition of such tariffs would cause even greater problems for the primary producers whose growth is discussed in Chapter Ten.

Balance of Payments weaknesses frequently leads to the introduction of tariff barriers. The United Kingdom imposed an import surcharge in 1964 for this reason and later introduced an import deposit scheme requiring the deposit with the Customs of half the price of the imports before they could be released. Such measures (and quota restrictions) can lead to a surplus and thus achieve their aim, but the surplus will conceal a prospective deficit and the erection of the barrier will deny home industry the benefit of competition needed as a spur to efficiency. Furthermore, such tariffs would be unnecessary if the authorities took a more flexible attitude towards exchange rates. The use of import duties and export subsidies for Balance of Payments reasons is a substitute for devaluation.

Political and social justifications are sometimes put forward in defence of tariffs. Most industrial countries, for example, offer some kind of protection to their agricultural sector because they do not want to be completely dependent on imported supplies which could be cut off during military or other crises. The United Kingdom coal industry has enjoyed a long period of protection against foreign competition for several reasons including the need to maintain supplies of what was until recently the nation's only available native fuel.

Whatever the motive for imposing the tariff or quota restriction it must be recognized that the effect is to transfer resources to the protected industry at the expense of other industries in the economy, and to reduce the size of competing industries overseas. And in imposing such tariffs Governments must balance the gains to one sector of the economy or economic activity against the losses to others.

(3) The General Agreement on Tariffs and Trade

GATT was intended as a temporary measure to supervise international trading practices while the *International Trade Organization* was being established, but since the powers could not agree on the nature and purpose of ITO, GATT has become a permanent feature of the world economy, pursuing the liberalization of world trade and attempting in particular to eliminate quantitative restrictions on trade. GATT is in effect a bargaining shop: conferences are held periodically where members reduce tariffs on a reciprocal basis but without discrimination between members. Of the six conferences held so far, the most important was that spread over a series of meetings at Geneva from 1964 to 1967, and known as the Kennedy Round.

The agreements reached within the Kennedy Round like those at earlier conferences were all primarily concerned with manufactured goods, the industrial countries being unable to bring themselves to reduce the protection afforded to agriculture. It was agreed to reduce many industrial tariffs by over 50 per cent and the average cut was between 30 and 40 per cent spread over a five-year period. The effects of such cuts are difficult to predict and depend partly on the respective elasticities of demand for traded goods and partly on the reaction of domestic industries to the extra competition.

Earlier moves towards trade liberalization within GATT and outside it had facilitated the formation of the European Economic Community in 1957.

(4) European Economic Community

Although the movement towards European unity has a long history it was not until the end of the Second World War that any positive steps towards union were taken. Then an amalgam of political and economic forces led first to the establishment of the Organization for European Economic Co-operation in 1948, the Council of Europe in 1949 and, most significant, the European Coal and Steel Community in 1951, the latter being the brainchild of the Frenchmen Jean Monnet and Robert Schuman. The Community was, in effect, a common market in coal and steel products with no discrimination between members. The members were later to form the EEC—France, Germany, Italy, Belgium, Holland, and Luxemburg, the last three having already formed a customs union (Benelux) in 1948. Britain at this stage preferred to stay outside the ECSC, a decision reflecting partly a distrust of the supranational authority vested in the ECSC and partly the lack of commitment to the European idea. In 1954 Britain did in fact acquire associate membership of the ECSC but by this time events were moving quickly on the European mainland. The Six were moving towards the creation of a full customs union between themselves. The United Kingdom torn between the Commonwealth and pretension to world power on the one hand and the European idea on the other could not bring itself to accept the implications of full membership of a customs union and withdrew from the negotiations at Messina which led up to the Treaty of Rome in 1957.

The United Kingdom would have been prepared to join the Six in the creation of a free-trade area in 1957 but the Six were already looking beyond such a loose form of organization, where relationships with non members are left to the discretion of individual members. The Six were anxious to form a Customs Union where members not only undertake to reduce trade barriers between themselves but also agree to adopt a common policy towards non-members through the application of a common external tariff. In addition they agree to harmonize various aspects of domestic policy.

It was not until 1973 that the United Kingdom, accompanied by Denmark and the Irish Republic, joined the Community, bringing the membership to nine.

The Treaty of Rome 1957

The decision to establish a common market was embodied in the Treaty of Rome which also laid down the framework of institutions that were to form the basis of the customs union. The most important are:

(*a*) *The Council of Ministers* comprising one member from each state and responsible for the co-ordination of policy within the Community. There is a weighted vote: Germany, France, Italy, the United Kingdom have 10 votes each; Belgium and Holland, 5 each; Denmark and Ireland, 3 each; and Luxemburg 1. Since 41 votes are required for a majority it is impossible for the four largest countries to dictate to the others—a safeguard for the smaller members. In practice the Council seeks unanimity on all major decisions, since it is difficult to impose majority decisions on dissenting members.

(*b*) *The European Commission* has thirteen members, who are representative of the interests of the Community: they do not represent nor take instructions from member Governments. The Commission is the central body of the Community: it is responsible for seeing that the provisions of the Treaty are carried out and represents the Community in negotiations with third countries; perhaps most important is its function in making proposals to the Council.

(*c*) *The Assembly* comprising delegates from the Parliaments of members has general supervisory powers over the Commission with the right to question it on policy. If the EEC moves closer to political union the Assembly will doubtless assume a more important role and will have to be elected on the basis of universal suffrage.

(*d*) *The Court of Justice* has the task of adjudicating on disputes between members over the interpretation and implementation of the Treaty.

(*e*) *Other Institutions.* The running of the Community and the formulation of policy necessitates a great network of specialist committees and institutions each backed by a huge and growing secretariat at the Community headquarters in Brussels.

The Aims and Achievements of the Community

While there were clearly important political motives in forming the EEC the immediate aims were essentially economic. Obviously the most important task was the removal of the trade barriers between members. To avoid too severe an impact on the structure of members' economies this was to be achieved by a series of 10 per cent reductions on the 1957 tariff culminating in 1970, but confidence of members was such that trade was free of orthodox barriers by the middle of 1968.

As tariffs were reduced the importance of non-tariff barriers became increasingly apparent; for example even if there are no tariffs imposed on motor-cars it is possible to restrict imports of them by demanding that they meet very rigid technical specifications. Government purchasing policies, and the attitudes of publicly owned industry can also limit the freedom of trade, and such matters still need to be resolved by the Community, presumably through the establishment of Community standards to replace national standards.

The establishment of the Common External Tariff proceeded alongside the elimination of internal tariffs and this, too, was completed ahead of schedule in 1968. Since then the existence of the Union has been emphasized by the fact that all revenue from the CET is paid into the Community Budget rather than that of an individual member.

Thus the short-term objective—the establishment of the Customs Union itself had been accomplished except in respect of the new members. The next step is for the members to work out common policies for taxation, social security, transport and other matters.

We have already noted that Community members should have adopted a form of value added taxation by 1972 with a view to subsequent harmonization of fiscal policy. Plans are being laid for the introduction of a common currency by 1980, an achievement that would represent an important landmark in the formation of a United States of Europe. Committees are at work on various other aspects of policy, but most attention has been focused on the establishment of the Common Agricultural Policy, a matter of great importance whenever the position of Britain within the EEC is discussed.

The Common Agricultural Policy

In the United Kingdom agriculture has long been protected through a system of deficiency payments equivalent to the difference between the market price and the target price which is felt to give producers a fair return on capital invested. This support to agriculture cost the British taxpayer approximately £270 million in 1972.

In the EEC support for the farmers is provided in a different way partly because the British system would be too arduous for the taxpayer since even now over 10 per cent of the EEC work force are employed on the land as opposed to less than 3 per cent in the United Kingdom. The Community experienced great difficulty in establishing the policy, largely because of a clash of interests between France and the other members, but after long negotiations the policy was operative in 1968. The provisions of the scheme vary according to the commodity but the basic framework is illustrated by the arrangements for wheat.

(i) A target price is established by reference to the price in the area which produces the smallest proportion of its own requirements (Duisburg, Germany). Related to this main target price are others for other areas which differ only to take account of transport costs.

(ii) An intervention price is set 5 per cent to 7 per cent below the target price, and if market price falls to this level the agricultural authorities have to intervene and keep prices up by buying surplus supplies.

(iii) The threshold price is the price of imported grain once it has paid the import levy which is designed to raise the price of imports to the level of the target price once they reach their destination.

Farmers are thus guaranteed a price between the intervention price and the target price, and are fully protected against foreign competition. The finance of intervention is provided by the European Agricultural Guidance and Guarantee Fund which is itself financed by the levies imposed on imports and the contributions of members. The Fund also has an important role in encouraging the modernization of agriculture through the amalgamation of holdings (which are small even by British standards) and the introduction of new techniques.

The system of support for all products is similar to that for wheat, though in many cases there is no intervention: farmers are protected by frequent adjustments to the threshold price to keep out foreign competition. In almost every case the effect of the policy is to encourage overproduction of commodities.

(5) The European Free Trade Area

Alongside the EEC the European Free Trade Area has been developing and before we consider relations between the United Kingdom and the EEC it is appropriate to examine the structure and achievements of EFTA.

The formation of the EEC signified an important division in the ranks of the OEEC countries. The danger that the EEC might develop into an inward-looking organization, at the expense of the rest of Europe, was a real one. An attempt was made by those left outside of the EEC to form a European Free Trade Area embracing the whole membership of the OEEC, but this proved unacceptable to the Six.

Accordingly in November 1959 seven countries came together through the *Convention of Stockholm* to form the European Free Trade Association which came into operation the following year. The founder-members were Austria, Denmark, Norway, Portugal, Sweden, Switzerland, and the United Kingdom; in 1961 Finland became an associate member and in 1970 Iceland a full member. Denmark, Ireland and the UK left in 1972.

The Free Trade Area is a much looser form than the customs union, but the immediate objective of both is the same—the abolition of trade restrictions between members. By the end of 1966 the EFTA countries had fully established conditions of free trade in industrial goods (but not in agricultural products most of which do not come under the EFTA convention). In the case of new members special time-tables for tariff reductions are established.

The greatest problem facing members of a free-trade area is to ensure that only goods originating in the area should be freely traded. For example, if two countries A and B form a free-trade area and both import cameras from C, A imposing no import duty and B imposing 25 per cent duty, there would be an incentive for the producers in C to export to B via A if all goods entering B from A were exempt from duty. To avoid this abuse (which does not arise in a customs union) the EFTA countries have established rules of origin to determine which goods shall qualify for area treatment.

The Rules of Origin

These are designed to ensure that only goods originating in the area or undergoing certain qualifying processes in member countries benefit from the tariff reductions. The whole character of a free-trade area depends upon the rigidity of its rules of origin. In EFTA there are three grounds which need to be satisfied for goods to qualify for area treatment:

(*a*) They must have been consigned from one member country to another.
(*b*) Then they must meet one of the following requirements:

(i) they must have been produced entirely within EFTA countries; or
(ii) they must have undergone certain specified productive processes within EFTA countries; or
(iii) 50 per cent of the value of the goods as measured by their export price must have been added within EFTA.

(*c*) Finally, the goods must not have been subject to drawback when exported (i.e. the exporters must not have reclaimed duty paid on imported components embodied in the exports).

Very few goods qualify for area treatment on the grounds of being wholly produced in EFTA. The majority seek exemption under the process rules which cover about 90 per cent of industrial goods.

The process rules are very complicated frequently relating to particular chemical processes, but are necessary to preserve the character of the area.

If rigid definitions of the processes that have to be performed within the area are not adopted abuse of the tariff concessions to members becomes widespread. For example it might become necessary to establish a process rule for books. The EFTA authorities must decide which processes in the production of a book must be performed in EFTA. At one extreme they could say that the qualifying process is the manufacture of paper, so that any books incorporating paper imported from Canada would not qualify. A more moderate rule would stipulate that the printing had to occur in EFTA, and an even more moderate requirement would be that the binding should be the qualifying process. The same principle applies to the percentage rule: the lower the proportion of the value that has to be added in the area the easier it is for goods embodying components manufactured outside the area to qualify for area treatment. It is indeed the tightness of the rules that determine the success of the area in increasing trade between members. The greater the obstacles placed in the way of non-EFTA components the smaller the proportion of trade that can benefit from the dismantling of tariff barriers between members.

The EFTA countries, like those in the EEC, have found that the abolition of tariffs and quota restrictions has increased the significance of non-tariff barriers to trade, and their 'rules of competition' dealing with Government assistance, purchasing policies in the public sector, private sector restrictive practices, and the dumping of exports are designed to prevent discrimination. (Dumping is the practice of selling goods overseas at prices lower than that at home, often below the cost of production.)

The United Kingdom and EFTA

EFTA was dominated by the United Kingdom: over half of the total population of the Association was British; in 1969 total EFTA exports amounted to $38,245 millions of which 17,515 were from the United Kingdom, who was responsible for a similar proportion of the area's imports. The impact on United Kingdom trade with the other members has been favourable: between 1959 and 1968 her exports to the area grew at an annual rate of 7·3 per cent against a rate of 4·9 per cent for exports as a whole; the comparable figures for imports were 8·6 per cent and 5·8 per cent.

There has been a more favourable impact for other members: intra-EFTA exports rose at 10·5 per cent per year while EFTA's exports to the rest of the world rose at only 4·6 per cent. But significantly British trade with EEC countries rose at a faster rate than that with EFTA: exports at an average rate of 8·1 per cent and imports at 10·1 per cent.

The impression is that while the United Kingdom did derive significant benefits from her membership of the Association her main industrial competitors are to be found elsewhere. The possibilities opened up by direct access to the EEC market led successive British Governments to apply for membership of the Community and for membership to be effected in 1973.

(6) The Case for British Membership of the EEC

The main argument in favour of British membership of the EEC is probably the political one that a united Europe is an essential part of the world balance of power and perhaps of world peace. But the political arguments are not our main concern here and it is to the possible economic benefits of membership that we must give our attention.

(*a*) *The achievements of the EEC.* The pro-marketeers point out that the rate of economic growth within the Community is much greater than in Britain alone. Between 1963 and 1973 the combined Gross Domestic Product of the Six rose at approximately 5·0 per cent per year while that of Britain grew by only 2·9 per cent per year. The faster rate of growth affects almost every aspect of economic life: fast growth permits improving living standards; slow growth prevents them.

In the first ten years real wages are calculated to have risen by 20 per cent in the United Kingdom but by 41 per cent in France and 75 per cent in the Netherlands. The value added to materials by each worker is shown in Table 51. Clearly the efficiency and productivity of European workers has been rising more rapidly.

Table 51. Industrial Efficiency

	Gross Value Added per worker (dollars)		
	1962	1968	Percentage change
Belgium	2,800	4,400	57
France	3,800	6,100	60
Germany	3,100	4,800	55
Italy	1,900	3,200	68
Netherlands	2,900	5,300	83
EEC	2,900	4,700	62
United Kingdom	2,700	3,400	26

Source: EEC.

Many other indicators tell the same story. Britain was gradually falling behind the Community countries in economic performance and in standards of living. The pro-marketeers believe that the effect of joining the market should be to increase Britain's rate of economic growth for a variety of reasons.

(*b*) *Economies of Scale.* Membership of the EEC has given Britain's industry direct access to a home market of about 250 million people as opposed to the 100 million provided by EFTA. Such a market could enable much longer runs of production, the wider spreading of overhead costs and, perhaps, steadier prices than are available outside the market.

(*c*) *Competition.* Although the effect of the Kennedy Round had been to reduce tariffs between the United Kingdom and the EEC, they were still at such a level as to inhibit trade, and to offer shelter to inefficient industries. By entering the market United Kingdom industry could be exposed to more competition which must lead to a more positive approach from both sides of industry. Already the EEC provided Britain's most important export market and the United Kingdom denied herself opportunities by remaining outside.

(*d*) The increasingly technological nature of many industries necessitates not only a large market but frequently a supply of capital beyond the scope of most individual nations. By joining with Europe Britain could more easily participate in projects such as Concorde, space research, computer development, and nuclear research. While it is true that arrangements in such fields can and have been made without joining the Common Market, such projects would benefit from a united European approach.

While the case for British entry rested on arguments of this kind it needs to be recognized that no one can prove that entry will have a beneficial effect on the United Kingdom economy. Many of the benefits to be derived from membership are probably not yet apparent to the original members: although growth has been spectacular since 1958 we should remember that the true Common Market has been fully operative only since 1968 when internal tariff barriers finally disappeared and the common external tariff was established. It is still too early to gauge the full economic effects of the extra competition and the economies of scale. Thus the advocates of British entry are hard put to quantify the benefits available. They would argue, however, that by the time the full economic benefits of membership had become clear the gap between the United Kingdom and the original six members would have been too large to close. For this reason membership as an act of faith was essential to them by 1972.

(7) The Case against British Membership

The Price of Food. A great deal of emphasis has been placed upon the high price of food in the Common Market. The system of support that is used within the market means that the consumer rather than the taxpayer subsidizes the farmer. It has been estimated that entry has raised the cost of living by perhaps 2 per cent on account of high food prices. This is much less than the rise that is attributable to the general rise in world price of food caused by a number of factors. And in April 1971 the British Government began to introduce levies on some imported food which can only lead to higher prices in the United Kingdom and a narrowing of the gap between British and European prices, a tendency that is reinforced by the more rapid inflation in Britain than Europe.

The Balance of Payments. It has been estimated that one of the costs of entry could be a deterioration of, perhaps, £1,000 million per annum in the Balance of Payments. The precise figure depends on assumptions about the change in our exports to and imports from the EEC, the loss of other export markets partly because of the ending of preferential Commonwealth tariffs, and partly because of higher costs at home, and the extent of Britain's contribution to the agricultural fund. While it may be argued against this that growth that would follow from entry could finance the deficit, or that the Balance of Payments impact could be modified by changing the exchange rate, a potential extra deficit of £1,000 million must constitute a serious disadvantage to entry.

The Commonwealth. Many feel that Britain would have done better by maintaining loyalty to the Commonwealth than by entering the EEC. There are likely to be more difficulties for the Commonwealth countries than Britain as Britain has entered. The West Indian economy is very heavily dependent on the export of sugar and bananas to the United Kingdom. But the EEC countries import hardly any sugar and acquire bananas from their former African territories. Special arrangements have had to be made in such circumstances. In fact most of the former dependent territories of EEC members qualify for associate membership and direct access to the market under the Yaoundé Agreement.

For Britain to turn to the Commonwealth rather than Europe would be to swim against the tide of world trade: whether she joined the market or not the bulk of world trade will be in industrial goods and for the foreseeable future the principal market will be Europe. Commonwealth countries are moreover making their own trading arrangements—Australia looks increasingly to Japan and the USA for markets for example; East African countries have established their own market. The most serious problem is that of New Zealand who depends upon Britain for a market for over 30 per cent of her exports. The majority of these could be effectively excluded as Britain became a member of the EEC unless special terms were negotiated as New Zealand, an independent dominion, does not qualify for associate membership under the Yaoundé Agreement.

The problem of the Commonwealth draws attention to one aspect of free-trade areas and customs unions that is frequently ignored. The aim of the group is to create more trade between its members and both the EEC and EFTA have succeeded in this. This trade creation must be balanced against the loss of trade that would have otherwise occurred with non-members—trade diversion. The effect of the trade grouping is sometimes to encourage members to buy from relatively inefficient high-cost members, goods that they previously acquired from non-members. From a world point of view this clearly results in a less than optimum use of resources.

Sectional interests could be damaged in the United Kingdom. As tariffs are dismantled and competition increased, structural unemployment could rise in declining industries. Labour will need retraining before being absorbed into the expanding industries. But this should be the whole point of joining the market, and represents one of the short-term costs payable to gain long-term benefits.

Loss of Sovereignty. Many people argue that membership of the Common Market must involve considerable loss of economic sovereignty. In so far as the common agricultural policy, the eventual harmonization of taxes, the introduction of common currency will all limit the freedom of the British Government, it is true that some power will be lost. It should, however, be remembered that all major decisions still need British concurrence and loss of sovereignty involved need not therefore be very great, particularly as the political development of the Community is by no means so advanced as the economic development. Nor should it be forgotten that in the second half of the 1960's Britain's economic sovereignty was necessarily impaired by our external debts. The days of economic nationalism are past.

Alternatives are Available. It may be argued that membership of the EEC is superfluous for Britain. An extension of EFTA, perhaps, into a North Atlantic Free Trade Area, some versions of which would include Japan and Australia as well as North America, would give Britain the larger domestic market it needs as well as plentiful competition. Allied to an ending of sterling's reserve currency role and perhaps a more flexible exchange rate policy this might induce a better economic performance in Britain. Such associations are, however, probably too loose to have the kind of effect that successive Goverments have been hoping for in drafting their applications to join the EEC.

But there is a further important consideration: while it is true that the rate of growth of the six countries is faster than that of the United Kingdom it does not necessarily follow that the faster rate of growth is the result of their membership of the Community. In the years before the formation of the market the members' economies were growing at a faster rate than the United Kingdom; and since the formation of the market some non-members have grown more rapidly than the members. There is no clear evidence that membership will automatically shower economic benefits on the United Kingdom.

The arguments over British membership are thus inconclusive. All that can be said with any degree of certainty is that the members of the Community have enjoyed a much healthier economic life than the United Kingdom since the war, and that unless her performance can be improved within the market there is a danger of the United Kingdom becoming the poor man of Europe.

(8) The View from the EEC

British entry to the EEC is not viewed without concern by the members of the Community. In 1967 and 1969 the European Commission published its views on the applications of the United Kingdom, Ireland, Denmark, and Norway to join the Common Market. It is made quite clear that any prospective member must not only accept the provisions and aims of the Treaty of Rome, but also the implications of the policies already agreed by the members: and negotiations must be about transitional arrangements, and not an attempt to modify the existing institutions of the Community. For example, 'the Commission believes that the negotiations must not jeopardize the essentials of the common agricultural policy; the problems raised for the new members by the need to adapt themselves to this policy must be solved through the appropriate transitional measures'.

In the case of the United Kingdom the Commission was especially worried in 1967 about the weakness of the Balance of Payments and the international role of sterling. The improvement from 1969 onwards allayed the fears about the debilitating effects of the payments weakness, while the satisfactory development of Special Drawing Rights suggested that suitable arrangements might be negotiated as to the international role of sterling.

(9) Other Trading Groups

It would be misleading to suggest that the industrial countries of Europe are the only ones to have established trading blocs. In the communist bloc, the Council for Mutual Economic Aid (Comecon), in South America, the Latin American Free Trade Association, in the West Indies, the Caribbean Free Trade Association, in East Africa, the East African Community, are representative of the attempts of other countries to secure the benefits available from extensive free trade. Except for the first they indicate one of the responses of the less-developed countries to the problems of economic growth. As such they are dealt with in the following chapter.

(10) Summary of Chapter Nine

(1) The theory of comparative costs predicts that conditions of free trade will lead to an optimum use of resources.

(2) Free trade was the characteristic feature of nineteenth-century British trade but in the twentieth century, especially between 1918 and 1945, tariff

barriers and other obstacles were erected for many reasons, political, social, and economic.

(3) The General Agreement on Tariffs and Trade has organized a series of conferences with a view to cutting the level of tariffs. The most important was the Kennedy Round involving cuts of an average of 30–40 per cent, to be completed by the beginning of 1972.

(4) The development of trading blocs such as the EEC and EFTA has resulted in the abolition of tariffs between members and a significant growth of trade. We must remember that the trade diversion effects are also important.

(5) The EEC is a customs union, a much tighter form than EFTA. EEC members are not free to decide their own policies towards non-members.

(6) Although the United Kingdom felt unable to join the EEC at the outset several subsequent applications for membership have been made.

(7) The economic arguments for and against membership seem to depend on the balance between fairly clear short-term costs and possible, but by no means proven, long-term benefits.

(8) Many less-developed countries have developed their own trading groups to take advantage of the benefits of broader free trade.

(11) Suggested Further Reading

DENIAU, J. F., *The Common Market*, Barrie & Rockliff, London, 1961.

European Free Trade Association, *Annual Reports*, Geneva.

General Agreements on Tariffs and Trade, *Annual Reports*, Geneva.

Statistical Office of the EEC, *The Common Market: 10 years on*, Brussels, 1968.

SWANN, D., *The Economics of the Common Market*, Penguin, London, 1970.

Exercises Set 9

1. 'The law of comparative costs shows that there is no economic case for the imposition of tariffs.' Discuss.
2. What economic benefits might the UK derive from membership of the EEC?
3. Compare the problems confronting the authorities of a customs' union with those confronting the members of a free-trade area.
4. How do you account for the fact that the price of food is higher in EEC countries than in the UK?
5. 'There are frequently very good reasons for countries imposing restrictions on international trade.' Comment.
6. What would be the economic advantages and disadvantages of the UK developing trading links with the Commonwealth rather than Europe?
7. What are the advantages and disadvantages of British membership of the Common Market from the point of view of existing members?
8. Assess the contribution of GATT to the growth of world trade since the war.
9. How do free-trade areas create trade? How do they destroy trade? Are they necessarily advantageous?
10. Discuss with examples the contention that the character of a free-trade area is determined by its rules of origin.

CHAPTER TEN

THE THIRD WORLD: THE UNDERDEVELOPED COUNTRIES

(1) Introduction

The 1950's and 1960's witnessed a great increase in the interest in the problems of economic growth. Improved communications led to a growing awareness on the part of the poorer countries of the great gap between their living standards and those of the industrialized world. The political independence of the emerging nations increased the demands from their people for greater economic independence and material benefits. On the other hand the wealthy industrial countries felt the need to help the poor for several reasons, partly to ease the pressure on new governments abroad, partly to win their political loyalty, partly a genuine desire to see the recipient countries achieve economic independence. While the achievement of economic independence should be the main aim of international aid, its direction and effectiveness is frequently limited by political considerations, especially in the case of bilateral aid from one country to another. However the World Bank and other international institutions acting as channels for multilateral aid, reduce the political aspects of economic assistance and concentrate on its effectiveness in inducing development.

The debates that surround this subject are complicated and often acrimonious: the desirability of aid, the institutional framework of aid, the types of aid, the effectiveness of aid, and even the purpose of aid are all called into question. In this chapter we look briefly at some of the more important aspects of the problems of the underdeveloped countries and some possible solutions to them.

(2) The Extent of the Problem

Table 52 gives some indication of the differences that exist between the industrialized countries and the rest. While recognizing the difficulties implicit in this kind of international comparison, and allowing for the widest margin of error it is clear that with many industrial countries increasing their *per capita* income at around 3 per cent per year and many poorer countries achieving much less than 2 per cent the gap between them must be increasing. The most pressing problems are in South Asia where *per capita* income increased by about $\frac{1}{2}$ per cent per annum during the 1960's, not enough to make any difference at all to most inhabitants.

Such figures are only the symptoms of the disease. A closer examination reveals some of the underlying causes of the trouble.

(3) Population Growth

The Pearson Commission, reporting to the World Bank on aid and the developing countries, said 'No other phenomenon casts a darker shadow over the prospects for international development than the staggering growth of population. . . . It is clear that there can be no serious social and economic planning unless the ominous implications of uncontrolled population growth are understood and acted upon.'

Fig. 20 gives an indication of the problem.

Table 52. Population and Gross National Product per head

	Population (000's) (1968)	GNP per head (US dollars)	Annual Growth Rates 1961–8	
			Population	GNP per head
EUROPE				
Sweden	7,918	2,620	0·7	3·2
France	49,920	2,130	1·1	3·7
West Germany	60,165	1,970	1·0	3·4
United Kingdom	55,283	1,790	0·7	2·0
Portugal	9,465	460	0·9	5·0
NORTH AND CENTRAL AMERICA				
United States	201,152	3,980	1·4	3·4
Trinidad and Tobago	1,021	870	2·6	4·4
Jamaica	1,908	460	2·0	0·8
Mexico	47,627	930	3·5	3·4
AFRICA				
South Africa	19,781	650	2·3	3·7
Nigeria	62,650	70	2·4	−0·3
Tanzania	12,508	80	2·5	1·2
Kenya	10,209	130	2·9	1·4
Uganda	8,133	110	2·5	1·1
ASIA				
India	523,893	100	2·5	1·0
Japan	101,090	1,190	1·0	9·9
Singapore	1,988	700	2·5	3·8
Philippines	35,883	180	3·4	0·8
Hong Kong	3,927	710	3·1	8·1
SOUTH AMERICA				
Venezuela	9,686	950	3·5	1·4
Brazil	88,209	250	3·0	1·6
Bolivia	4,680	150	2·6	1·8
OCEANIA				
Australia	12,031	2,070	2·0	2·4
New Zealand	2,828	2,000	2·2	1·7
Fiji	505	330	3·1	0·6

Source: World Bank 1970.

In the post-war period death-rates have fallen rapidly while birth-rates have been slow to follow. Though the population explosion is not a problem confined to the developing countries it is in countries such as Mexico, Malaysia, and India that growth is most severe. The fall in mortality rates is attributable to better standards of medicine which have eliminated former scourges and better standards of diet and hygiene which have increased the resistance of man to disease. Most important has been the reduction in the infant mortality rate: prolonging the expectation of life from, say, fifty to sixty years does not

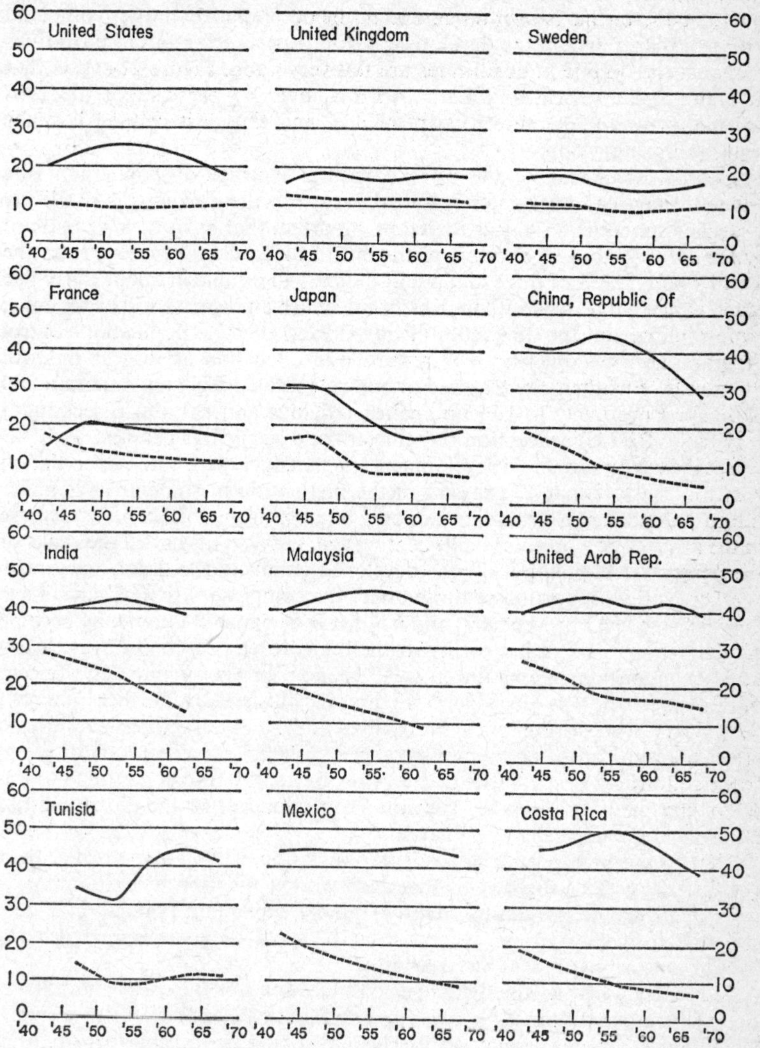

(*Source: World Bank*)

Fig. 20. Birth- and death-rates per '000 population for selected areas have serious cumulative affects on the population; but saving the lives of infants, and raising them to maturity enables them to exert a permanent effect on the population. Even so the IMR (which measures infant deaths per 1,000 life births) is over a hundred in the developing countries compared with less than thirty in the developed. The prospects for a fall in birth-rates to match the decline in death-rates are not very good. Figure 21 shows that in South Asia, Africa, and Latin America over 40 per cent of the 1968 population was under fifteen years of age, and thus just coming into the child-producing group.

In such circumstances the rate of natural increase of population (the difference between birth-rates and death-rates) in these regions is not likely to decline spontaneously. It is therefore important that birth-rates be reduced by the introduction of effective birth-control methods. At present rates the world's population of three and a half billion will double in about thirty-five years, while in the areas with high birth-rates such an increase will occur much more rapidly. But the difficulties of introducing effective population-control programmes are immense: it is a matter of education as well as finance; thousands of workers are required to implement the policy; and international authorities are likely to run up against religious and cultural objections if they try to foist contraception on reluctant and suspicious peoples.

Yet the key to economic development lies in reducing the rate of population growth. The fact that 40 per cent of the population of some areas is under fifteen years of age is important not only because of the forthcoming increase in the number of women of child-bearing age, but also they swell the ranks of the dependent population. In the developed countries the dependency ratio is taken as the proportion of those under the compulsory school-leaving age and over the age of retirement, and while it is true that children may become productive workers rather earlier in the underdeveloped countries it clearly imposes a considerable strain on weak economies when almost 50 per cent of the population is dependent. Figure 21 illustrates a further potential difficulty: the proportion of over sixty-fives in the underdeveloped countries is lower than in Europe and America reflecting the lower expectation of life in those countries. As standards of medicine, hygiene, and diet continue to improve and the life expectancy rises the proportion in this age-group will rise and so will the dependent population.

The significance of the dependent population is that the greater their number the greater the surplus that each worker must produce to maintain *per capita* income. Necessarily with a rapidly expanding population a high proportion of the national income must be spent on consumption, leaving insufficient for investment and growth.

Accordingly neither the difficulties of education nor the sheer enormity of the problem should be used as an excuse for the postponement of a major programme of population control. The aim should be to achieve a situation in which couples just replace themselves, thus giving long-run stability to the population. But this has not yet been achieved even in developed economies with the widespread availability of contraceptive methods. It has been calculated by the World Bank that if the developed countries reached this replacement position by the year 2000 and the developing by 2050 world population would not be stabilized until 2120 by which time it would be about 15 billion, or over four times its present level.

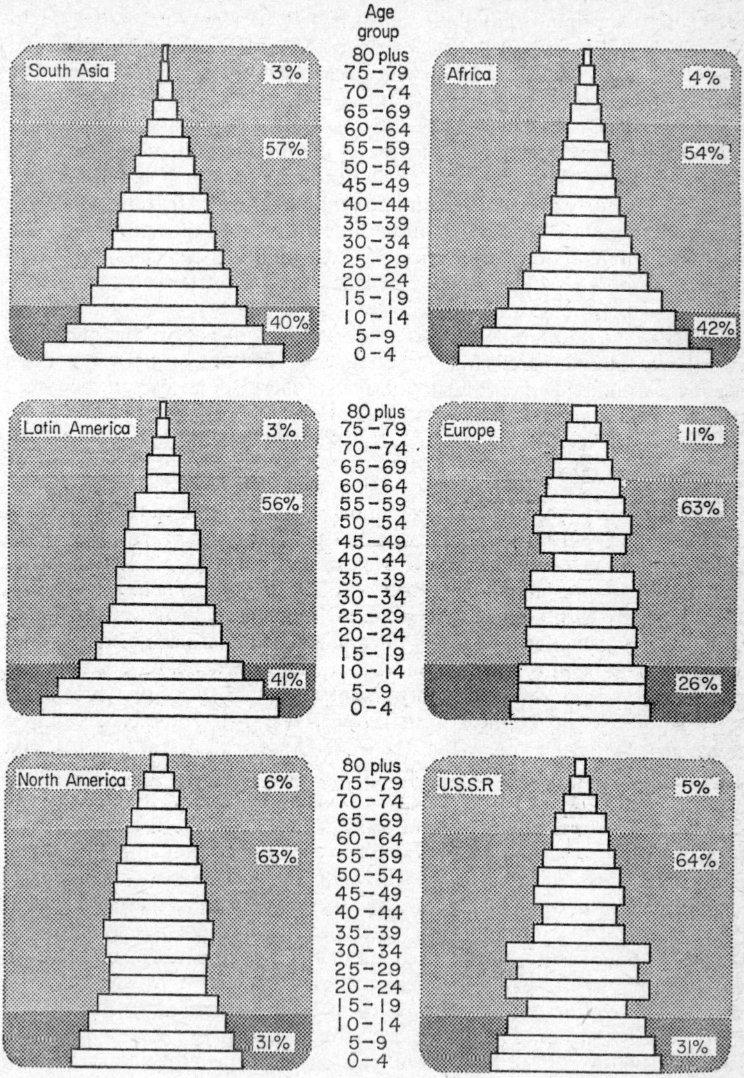

(*Source: World Bank*)

Fig. 21. Age-structure of population of selected areas

The Optimum Population

Many demographers discuss the population of a country in relation to the concept of the optimum population, which may be regarded as that population which will afford a country the highest Gross National Product and Gross National Product per head, given the supply of other resources. The optimum population is thus likely to be easier to talk about than assess; the optimum level at one time will be too great at another, and too small at another. As improved technology increases the productivity of labour so the optimum will rise. While it is easy to point to countries such as India whose population is clearly above the optimum and Canada or Australia which are clearly underpopulated it is much more difficult to assess the appropriate size for the United Kingdom or France. We can only suggest a range within which the optimum is likely to lie. Nor is it merely a matter of size—the age and sex-structure are also of importance.

As most of the developing countries have populations above the optimum, and as those populations are likely to go on rising for many years yet, policies concentrate on improving productivity so as to increase the level of the Gross National Product per head.

(4) The Aims of Aid

It is only in very recent years that emphasis has been placed on the control of population. The traditional type of assistance has been geared to 'westernizing' the recipient countries. The European and North American countries underwent their agrarian and industrial revolutions in the nineteenth century, a period which witnessed a vast increase in national products attributed mainly to the productive investment of capital. The underdeveloped countries of the twentieth century need to undergo a similar process to close the gap between rich and poor and to reduce the political and social pressures likely to be generated by economic dissatisfaction. This, then, is the broad aim, to increase *per capita* income. While there are those who argue that this is a matter for the countries concerned and that since aid can at best have only a marginal effect it is not worthwhile, the Governments of East and West are both committed to the continuation of assistance. The aim for the 1970's is that *per capita* income should rise at 6 per cent per annum. But this global target is quite insufficient in itself. The allocation of the extra income is of overriding importance. While there is a desperate need to increase the level of consumption there is probably a greater need to increase investment. This merely begs the question of the direction of the investment. The emphasis in the British Industrial Revolution was on clearly productive private enterprise investment; investment in what we know as social capital was of secondary importance. This order of priority reflects the spontaneity of economic growth in the late eighteenth and nineteenth centuries. Today the inducement of economic growth is far from spontaneous, and it therefore raises awkward questions for would-be developers.

(*a*) *The Primary Sector*. The theory of comparative costs suggests that the developing countries should concentrate on the production of primary products. In some cases, notably that of the petroleum-producing countries, there can be little doubt of the benefit of this. In others, such as countries concentrating on the production of food products or agricultural raw materials there is more doubt. The demand for such products is inelastic with respect to both price and income and they do not therefore present great opportunities for expansion. Further, the proper development of agriculture with more capital-intensive production would lead to much greater unemployment of labour as the extent of disguised unemployment became more apparent. So development of the primary sector alone would itself create difficulties, and these would not be diminished by the growing consciousness in the developing countries that it is in the secondary and tertiary sectors that the real trimmings of wealth and a high standard of living are to be found. While they do not reject the idea of agricultural efficiency—indeed its overwhelming importance is acknowledged—the developing countries seek more.

(*b*) *The Secondary Sector.* The expanding industrial sector is the aim. But investment outside the agricultural sector tends to be low, and thus the opportunities for employment are low. There have been instances in the past of a donor country encouraging industrial investment and a recipient country acquiescing because of the prestige value of perhaps a steelworks, only for the plant to stand idle for lack of labour or raw materials. While such cases may be exceptional they indicate the care that is necessary in developing the industrial sector. The fostering of a manufacturing sector is desirable to absorb labour released from a developing agrarian sector—similar to the process that occurred in the British Industrial Revolution.

(*c*) *The Infrastructure.* But there is obviously a further problem. If agriculture is to become more capital-intensive, if an industrial sector is to be developed, then a large number of subsidiary services must be available. A more efficient agriculture requires a wider market for the disposal of surplus output, so an effective network of communications must be established; it requires a better-educated farmer so schools must be improved. A rural labour force needs much training before it is amenable to factory life, and so on. A wide variety of skills and knowledge need to be built up. In fact the effective development of the primary and secondary sectors presupposes the existence of an efficient tertiary sector, and so an increasing emphasis has been placed upon the development of the infrastructure of the developing countries' economies: communications, education, hospitals, housing, banking, and financial services are seen as the prerequisites of growth.

Thus the aim has become that of the balanced development of recipient economies with interlocking advances in each sector. There is a danger though of the problem being seen in only economic terms. It is impossible to cram the equivalent of the British Industrial Revolution into twenty-five or thirty years. Even the attempt must be seen as an effort to change centuries of history and as such it must create many sociological and political problems. The position of the developers is clearly delicate: an absence of aid is likely to lead to resentment among the political leaders in developing countries; excessive aid may lead to bewilderment among the population of these countries.

(5) The Types of Aid

The developed countries can offer assistance to the developing in a number of ways.

(*a*) *Financial Aid.* The most obvious form of aid is the provision of foreign currency by the donor country. (In this section we are concerned mainly with bilateral aid.) In its extreme form such aid would be provided completely without obligation on the recipient country. While this would enable the recipient to spend it on what it regards as the most desirable project it raises certain difficulties for the donor. If the recipient is so ungrateful as to spend the grant other than with the donor country, it represents a permanent drain on the latter's Balance of Payments. It is, therefore, the practice of donor countries to 'tie' their aid in two ways. First, the aid is given on condition that it is spent in the donor country. Second, the aid is usually tied to a particular project, again to be supplied from the donor country. The tying of aid in this way like any protective measure inevitably diverts resources from optimum uses and forces the recipient countries to buy from high-cost producers. This has led to a great deal of cynicism about the motives of the donors. (The World Bank has estimated that recipient countries would gain by 10–15 per cent if all tied aid were untied.) However the anxiety of, for example, the United Kingdom Government to minimize the harmful Balance of Payment effects of aid during the period from 1964 to 1969 was understandable if not wholly excusable.

It is not just for Balance of Payments reasons that donors make a practice of tying aid. It is a convenient way of winning export orders; it is of political value to donors to be associated with prestigious projects; it may even be a form of retaliation if other countries are tying aid; it may have a marginal effect on employment in the donor country, though a corollary of this is that it may be inflationary if full employment exists in the donor country; it may in the long run lead to expanded markets for the donor countries. None of these, however, would seem to provide a major motive for tying aid; indeed as far as the Balance of Payments is concerned, the gain is most unlikely to be as great as the aid that is tied—even if all of the aid were untied it is likely that some orders would be placed with the donor.

It may be, then, that the tying of aid started for Balance of Payments reasons and has become self-perpetuating for no particular reason other than the fact that everyone else does it. The higher costs of tied aid constitute an important argument for channelling more aid through the multilateral channels (see page 158).

(*b*) *Commodity Aid* is perhaps the least useful form of aid to the developing countries but the most convenient for the donor. For humanitarian reasons such aid is important: population growth has so completely outstripped agricultural productivity that people in many developing areas now eat less well than they did fifteen to twenty years ago. Food aid can help to fill the gap while the so-called Green Revolution is underway (see page 160). But from a long-term point of view the very availability of such aid not only acts as a disincentive to increase agricultural output and productivity in developing countries, but also postpones the incidence of Malthusian crises. (In his *Essay on Population* Thomas Malthus argued that the tendency of population to outstrip the supply of food was corrected, for the poor, at least, by periodic calamities such as epidemics, plagues, or famine.) Commodity aid is moreover the least flexible form of aid; the recipient has the choice of accepting it or rejecting it. Only if an equivalent amount of financial assistance would have been spent on this particular commodity does it constitute a proper substitute for financial assistance. One merit, however, is that the gift of food may release scarce foreign exchange for other purposes.

For the donor countries commodity aid has certain attractions. It does not involve the expenditure of foreign exchange (though some foreign exchange earnings are foregone if the gift could have been marketed either in the recipient country or elsewhere). But, while imposing little direct burden on the Balance of Payments commodity aid is an important acknowledgement of the existence of the problems of the underdeveloped. A further advantage to the donor is that commodity aid disposes of embarrassing agricultural surpluses which must otherwise be stored or destroyed.

(c) *Technical Aid* is available in two forms. First in the form of skilled personnel recruited in and paid by the donor country and working in the recipient country. Economic development requires a whole range of specialists in planning and implementing programmes, but they are not readily available in the underdeveloped country. This is thus an important feature of the development process. It is sometimes said that technical aid in this form like other kinds of tied aid is more useful to the donor than the recipient. Clearly if there is a surplus of engineers or agricultural economists in the donor country a convenient way to keep them occupied is to recruit them for service overseas, but if economic development is to be encouraged the recipient countries must accept that until they reach the stage where they can produce their own specialists in sufficient numbers they will have to make use of brains from elsewhere. And if they wish to make the best use of other forms of aid then technical assistance becomes vital.

An alternative form of technical assistance is the provision of scholarships in the developed countries for students from the developing areas. Where domestic resources are insufficient to provide a comprehensive system of further and higher education the availability of training in industrial countries for accountants, engineers, scientists, and teachers, financed by such bodies as the British Council can make a significant contribution to the development process, as well as furthering international understanding.

Trade may be regarded as another form of aid. This is discussed in section 9 of this chapter.

(6) The Institutions of International Aid

Most of the developed countries have their own specialist authorities sponsoring aid in various forms. In the United Kingdom Overseas Development was accorded a Ministry of its own in 1964, but the administration of aid is now under the auspices of the Foreign Office. In addition the Commonwealth Development Corporation, empowered to borrow up to £160 million, contributes towards the development of dependent and newly independent Commonwealth countries. The British Council while primarily concerned with the promotion of the English language is also involved in the provision of scholarships for overseas students. A variety of private institutions such as Oxfam and the Save the Children Fund are also involved in the mobilization of funds for international development. In the European Economic Community the European Development Fund, financed by all members, is responsible for the disposal of assistance. All over the developed world agencies of various kinds are working towards a common end.

The most important and influential of these is the World Bank or the International Bank for Reconstruction and Development, created alongside the International Monetary Fund at the Bretton Woods Conference in 1944.

(7) The World Bank

Structure. Just as the Allies appreciated during the Second World War that the pre-war systems of Balance of Payments adjustment would need modification on the resumption of peace, so they were aware that the reconstruction of war-damaged Europe and the development of backward economies would entail the mobilization of capital well beyond the scope of private investors. It was to deal with the latter problem that the World Bank was formed. Membership of the Bank (which is not really a bank, but an important channel for investment) is open to all Governments and by 1970 stood at 113. All members must pay a subscription to the Bank which depends roughly on their economic importance. One per cent of the subscription is payable in gold and is at the immediate disposal of the Bank authorities; 9 per cent is payable in a member's local currency and may be used only with the prior permission of the member; and the remaining 90 per cent may be called by the Bank only to meet obligations arising out of its loans or guarantees. In June 1970 subscriptions totalled $23,158·8 million. The control of the Bank is vested in the Board of Governors with one representative from each member, but it meets only once a year. Real control lies with the Executive Directors, one chosen by each of the five largest stockholders and the remaining fifteen elected by other members.

Lending Policy. We noticed earlier that bilateral aid is open to the criticism that it is often politically motivated and that it is tied to particular projects and countries. World Bank assistance is tied in that it must normally be for a specific project. This is to ensure that funds are used for the most productive purposes and that the Bank and the borrower are both clear as to the direction of expenditure. The absence of the specific project rule could easily result in prestige expenditure which had little impact on economic development.

World Bank lending is not tied to particular countries. Aid may be spent in any member country (or Switzerland) and thus has an advantage over the bulk of bilateral aid. But while there is greater freedom in this respect there is probably greater restriction in actually obtaining World Bank approval and assistance. Once a project is submitted to the Bank it becomes subject to the most stringent investigation. The Bank must be satisfied on many points before approval is forthcoming:

(i) Creditworthiness: since repayments must be made in foreign currency the Bank must be satisfied that a borrower is in a position to earn sufficient foreign currency and that a borrower's existing external debt is not too high. In some countries the service payments on external public debt already amounts to a high proportion of foreign currency earned by exporting goods and services: thus in Tunisia recently 24 per cent of export earnings was absorbed, and in Mexico 26·8 per cent. It may be that in such cases the Bank while agreeing on the desirability of a project would be unable to help. In such a case the member would be referred to the International Development Association (see below). In fact both Mexico and Tunisia received IBRD assistance.

(ii) Economic appraisal. The assessment of a project requires a close knowledge of the economy into which it is to be fitted. The Bank maintains a continuous watch on the performance of those economies where it has or is likely to have funds committed.

(iii) The project itself is subject to the most careful scrutiny under six different headings: economic, technical, managerial, organizational, commercial, and financial. Not only must it be shown that a project has high economic priority and is technically sound but the Bank needs assurances that adequate local or imported managerial ability is available, and that procurement will be on a commercial basis. Most important, since the Bank never finances the whole of a project, it needs evidence that the remaining funds are available elsewhere.

The policy of close appraisal does not end once a loan is agreed. The Bank maintains a close supervision of any project it is financing to ensure that funds are not misused—indeed funds are only made available as expenditure is incurred.

No wonder some countries have been deterred! But remember that in relation to demand the funds are severely limited, that the Bank has an obligation to secure significant development, and that it is really disbursing other people's money. Moreover, the careful economic and project appraisal by the Bank will often be to the advantage of the recipient in revealing avenues of development hitherto unconsidered.

The length of a loan and the terms of repayment depends on the project, and is generally related to the estimated useful life of the project as well as the borrower's other commitments. Interest charges are kept as low as possible, but are obviously related to the rate at which the Bank itself has to borrow. This brings us to the means of finance.

Finance. The World Bank is not intended to supersede other channels of aid. The bulk of the money it makes available to members has been raised through the sale of its bonds on the world's capital markets. The absolutely sound status of the Bank gives these bonds gilt-edge status, which enables the Bank to relend to developing countries at rates well below those they would themselves have to pay in the markets. Table 53 gives an indication of the sources of World Bank funds, emphasising the importance of the dollar. Table 54 shows the accelerating rate of World Bank borrowing.

Table 53. World Bank Borrowings

Currency of issue	No. of issues	Original amount ($m)	Outstanding amount ($m)	No. of outstanding issues
US Dollars	68	5,553·1	2,665·9	35
Belgian Francs	1	10·0	10·0	1
Canadian Dollars	7	124·9	89·1	5
Deutsche Mark	24	1,016·6	707·4	18
Italian Lire	1	24·0	24·0	1
Kuwaiti Dinars	1	42·0	21·0	1
Netherlands Guilders	5	58·0	41·6	5
Pounds Sterling	3	48·0	33·8	3
Swedish Kronor	1	14·5	14·4	1
Swiss Francs	22	339·1	195·2	13
	133	7,230·2	3,802·4	83

Source: World Bank.

Thus the existence of the Bank ensures that funds, both public and private, which would otherwise be withheld from international investment because of the risks are made available to developing countries for a wide variety of projects. Before we consider the allocation of funds let us briefly look at the subsidiaries of the World Bank.

Table 54. Gross Borrowing by World Bank

1966	729 million dollars
1967	735 ,, ,,
1968	1,224 ,, ,,
1969	4,302 ,, ,,
1970	4,921 ,, ,,

Source: World Bank.

The International Development Association was established in 1960 to provide aid to developing countries that could not meet the stringent requirements of the basic World Bank scheme. Loans are for up to fifty years, interest free, with repayments to begin after ten years. There is a service charge of ¾ per cent per year. The IDA is financed mainly by the Governments of richer members and while lending on much different terms it otherwise follows much the same lines as the World Bank in its appraisal and support of projects. The scale of operations is much smaller than the Bank: by 1970 just over $2,800 million had been made available by the IDA.

The International Finance Corporation. When the World Bank lends to private enterprise it always requires a guarantee from the Government of the country concerned. Such a guarantee has not always been forthcoming and so it became clear in the early work of the Bank that there was an important gap in the assistance available. Accordingly, the IFC was established in 1956 with the role of assisting productive private enterprise in developing countries, by providing both equity and loan capital. The role of the IFC may be expected to become more important as the developing economies expand and the scope for private investment grows. The capital of the Corporation subscribed by members entirely in gold or US dollars amounted to $106·5 million by 1969. The whole of this is available for lending and together with other credits available to it, the IFC had advanced almost $500 million by the end of 1970.

The Application of Funds. Table 55 shows the main activities which the World Bank funds were used to support.

It is noticeable that a relatively small proportion of loans has been for industrial development. Emphasis has been on the primary sector and especially on development of the infrastructure when the return on capital is likely to be very long term and unattractive to private investors. A brief examination of the Bank's activities in 1969/70 gives some idea of the range of activities.

The Bank in 1970. In 1969/70 $413 million was lent for agricultural purposes compared with an average of $124·2 million in 1964–8. The development of high-yield seeds and the improvement of financial institutions in developing countries has increased the scope for investment in this sector. The finance of irrigation projects was especially important, and the support of institutions to foster the Green Revolution has increased. ('The Green Revolution' is the

Table 55. World Bank and IDA Loans (31 November 1969) by purpose

Purposes	IBRD loans (dollars millions)	IDA loans (dollars millions)
Reconstruction	497	—
Electric power	4,264	142·8
Transportation	3,993	783·6
Telecommunications	193	120·8
Agriculture	1,234	406·5
Industry	1,974	46·1
Imports	552	580·0
Water supply	109	37·6
Education projects	98	162·1
Project preparation	1	12·5
IFC	200	—
Total	13,115	2,292·0

Source: World Bank and IDA.

term applied to the vastly increased yields available through the development of new seeds and the application of modern technology to primitive agriculture.)

A relatively new area of interest for the Bank is in what it refers to as agro-industries such as vegetable processing, marketing facilities, and fisheries.

Table 55 indicates a relatively low priority for education projects, but the Bank began lending for education projects in 1962. Clearly where resources for education are limited they need to be carefully used. The Bank authorities accordingly finance those sectors of education likely to contribute most directly to economic development. The emphasis is on technical and vocational education rather than a traditional academic education. For example, in 1970 the IDA made available to Pakistan a credit of $8 million for a University of Engineering and Technology; and $6·1 million to Kenya for the development of agricultural education; Zambia received a Bank loan of $5·3 million for expansion of Engineering and Education faculties at the University of Zambia; Sierra Leone received $3 million from IDA for the development of agricultural, commercial, scientific, and industrial education in secondary schools.

Public services have always been one of the main targets for Bank aid. Effective transport, communications, and power supplies are essential to economic development, and approximately 60 per cent of Bank and IDA aid is devoted to the infrastructure. In 1970 Nigeria received $25 million for the development of roads, ports, and railways. Of a total of $660·8 million devoted to transport in 1970, $401·4 million was for roads, $168·8 million for railways, $48·1 million for ports, and $42·5 million for pipe-lines. The largest single loan was of $100 million to Brazil for road development, but other beneficiaries for road development included the Central African Republic, Kenya, Mali, Rwanda, Tanzania, and Uganda.

Malawi was one of the countries to benefit from loans for the development of electricity. It is interesting that the assistance was to provide the foreign exchange costs of generating equipment and to further the training of local personnel. The loan also provides an example of a project partly financed by the IBRD and other authorities: the problems of aid co-ordination are important and have only recently received the attention they deserve.

In these and other areas the Bank and its associates were also active in the fields of telecommunications (in the East African Community for example) and in the development of industry.

New areas of activity are developing all the time. Much of the emphasis now placed upon population growth is attributable to the Bank's work and they have established a separate division to lead their work in this area. In 1970 the Bank made its first loan to finance a family-planning programme to Jamaica. The growing awareness of developing countries of the importance of tourism has resulted in the commitment of funds especially by the IFC.

In every sector and in every continent the World Bank attacks the problems of underdevelopment. That it is an uphill struggle is no reason for abandoning it. The world must be made aware of the need for more aid.

(8) The Amount of Aid

Table 56. Flow of Financial Resources to Developing Countries and Multilateral Institutions (1964 and 1972)

	1964 (billion dollars)	1972 (billion dollars)
Total	9·14	17·7
Total Official	5·94	9·9
Total Private	3·20	7·8
Total as percentage of GNP	0·75	0·9
Total Official as percentage of GNP	0·49	0·4
Total Private as percentage of GNP	0·26	0·5

Source: IBRD.

It is politically wise to make pronouncements in favour of aid, and doubtless most political leaders in the developed economies would like to transfer a greater proportion of resources to overseas development. Unfortunately this may not have the impact upon the electorate that equivalent domestic expenditure may have. Despite all the brave talk the target of the Development Decade of 1961–70 of 1 per cent of the GNP being devoted to aid was not reached by the developed countries as a whole. Much of this should not really be regarded as aid since it is commercially motivated. In 1970 the President of the World Bank Mr. Robert MacNamara set the target that 0·7 per cent of resources should be devoted to aid in the form of public sector development assistance.

The contrast that he drew between two aspects of expenditure needs no comment: in 1970, $7 billion was spent on aid by public bodies, in the same year $180 billion was spent on defence.

(9) Trade and the Balance of Payments

The Problems. We noted earlier that trade may be regarded as a form of aid. Indeed the United Nations Conference on Trade and Development (UNCTAD) an association of the underdeveloped members of the UN, exists for the purpose of transferring the emphasis in international development from the traditional forms of aid to the opening up of trading opportunities.

For the last fifteen years world trade has expanded at a steady rate. The main growth, however, has been in the export of manufactured goods. The developing countries have therefore largely been excluded from the expansion, since less than a quarter of their exports are manufactured goods. Increasingly they are producing these goods but there are considerable difficulties in their way when they try to market them in the developed countries, not the least being the protective attitudes adopted by industrial countries towards their own industry.

Perhaps as important as the amount of trade are the *terms of trade*. As we saw in Chapter Seven the terms of trade show the relation between import prices and export prices over a number of years. An index of import prices and an index of export prices are drawn up for the base year, each being given the value 100. The terms of trade are measured by the formula

$$\frac{\text{Index of Import Prices}}{\text{Index of Export Prices}} \times 100 = 100$$

If in subsequent years the prices of exports rise relative to those of imports the terms of trade fall below 100, indicating a favourable movement in the terms of trade: a given volume of exports will now finance a greater volume of imports. A deterioration in the terms of trade means that a greater volume of exports is necessary to pay for a given volume of imports.

The terms of trade of the developing countries were at their most favourable in 1951 when the Korean War forced up the prices of all important commodities. This was followed by decline in the 1950's which has continued after a temporary improvement. In the 1970's an expansion in the demand for primary products resulted in a sharp rise in the price of the developing countries' exports. A parallel rise in the prices of their manufactured imports means that their terms of trade have not shown the same improvement. Thus a declining proportion of world trade and modestly improving terms of trade are characteristic of the developing world, yet they need an increasing amount of foreign exchange to survive their rising overseas debts. How can the problem be overcome?

Solutions. The development of trade is essentially a long-term problem, but there are interim measures that could be beneficial in the short run:

(*a*) The developed countries could adopt a more liberal attitude to the import of primary and manufactured goods from the underdeveloped even if they do compete with domestic industry. This could only be to the long-term benefit of all concerned.

(*b*) Dependence on primary-product exports leads to fluctuations in foreign exchange earnings. The IMF helps to overcome this through compensatory finance (see page 131) but the most important development has been the institution of commodity marketing schemes to even out fluctuations in supply and market price. There are already in existence schemes for coffee, olive-oil, sugar, tin, and wheat, and UNCTAD is anxious to see other products covered, but commodity agreements run up against the difficulty of securing agreement among member countries and producers since they frequently necessitate export quotas which may reduce exports (even though through controlling supply they increase long-run earnings).

(*c*) The industrial countries of Europe have derived great benefit from the formation of trading groups. One way in which the less-developed countries can expand their trade is to form similar groups to increase trade between themselves. An example is the East African Community created by Kenya, Tanzania, and Uganda in 1967. Long before the establishment of the EAC there was co-operation between these countries, though the greater industrial development of Kenya caused sufficient resentment for Tanzania and Uganda to adopt certain protective measures in 1965. Protracted negotiations, however, led to the inauguration of the EAC in December 1967, with the object of strengthening and regulating economic relations between members. The main attraction of such co-operation is surely the economies of scale available. The populations of Kenya, Tanzania, and Uganda in 1968 were respectively 10 million, 12½ million, and 8 million, so they now have a home market of 30 million instead of at most 12½ million. Co-operation over infrastructure especially in communication and power is likely to yield further economies. While it is too early to assess the affects of the formation of the community (it is not in fact a full common market) it is perhaps significant that several neighbouring states have expressed an interest in joining. In 1971 about 75 per cent of developing countries' exports went to the developed countries. The formation of trading groups might increase the proportion going to developing countries.

(*d*) Tourism is one form of trade that does promise to grow quickly. The development of air travel, increasing leisure in the developed countries, overcrowding in traditional holiday areas, have all led to a search for new holiday centres. In 1950 there were about 2¼ million visitors to the developing countries; in 1971, 18 million. Receipts rose from $0·5 billion to $4 billion.

The demand for international travel is likely to continue to grow. It is one area in which the developing countries have unique advantages over the developed and where they can provide a service for which the elasticity of demand is high. It is an area where they can generate considerable foreign currency earnings in a relatively short period, pending the growth of other sectors of the economy.

(10) Conclusions

There is clearly much more to the economics of development than can be covered in one chapter of a book. We have looked at a few of the difficulties; there are many more: the Balance of Payments; the relation between sectors; the difficulties of financing education projects; the high cost of industrial products in developing countries. High levels of consumption in the less-developed countries reduce savings and make aid imperative. It is the responsibility of the developed countries to make it available. The situation in which one-tenth of the world's population own nine-tenths of its wealth cannot be tolerated indefinitely. If developed countries cannot alter their priorities themselves, sooner or later they will be forced to do so.

(11) Summary of Chapter Ten

(1) The post-war period has seen a great upsurge in interest in the problems of the less-developed countries.

(2) There are great differences in the *per capita* incomes of the richest and

the poorest (3,980 dollars per head in the USA and 70 dollars in Burma for example).

(3) Moreover the gap between the rich and the poor is growing, largely because of the population explosion in the poor countries.

(4) The population explosion has been caused by a large fall in death-rates, attributable to improvements in medicine, hygiene, and food supply, without a corresponding fall in birth-rates.

(5) Economic aid aimed at securing faster economic growth, and eventually self-sufficiency, must seek balanced growth, expanding the infrastructure as well as the primary and secondary sectors.

(6) Aid may be in the form of financial assistance, commodity aid, or technical aid.

(7) Each country has its own institutions for channelling aid effectively.

(8) The International Bank for Reconstruction and Development (the World Bank) is the major multilateral aid institution. It brings assistance on all fronts, borrowing money on very good terms in the world's capital markets and relending to developing countries, subject to a very careful appraisal of projects.

(9) The International Development Association and the International Finance Corporation are both offshoots of the World Bank, the former specializing in long-term interest-free loans, and the latter in the development of the private sector of underdeveloped economies.

(10) Despite the ostensible concern of Governments about the problem of development, 'aid' (very broadly defined) amounted to no more than 0·72 per cent of the GNP of developed countries in 1969.

(11) An alternative to aid is trade, but once again the developed countries do less than they might to facilitate the growth of exports from the underdeveloped countries.

(12) The best hopes for developing trade lie in the formation of trading groups, the introduction of commodity agreements and the development of one important invisible export—tourism.

(12) Suggested Further Reading

IBRD, *Annual Report*, Washington

IMF and IBRD *Finance and Development* (Quarterly), Washington.

STAMP, L.D., *Our Developing World*, Faber & Faber, London, 1968.

Exercises Set 10

1. In what ways do the problems of the underdeveloped countries differ from those of the advanced countries?

2. 'The key to the problem of the less-developed countries is the control of population growth.' Why?

3. Consider the effect of the age structure of a population on the economic development of a country.

4 Assess the relative usefulness of various forms of aid available to the underdeveloped countries.

5. 'The purpose of aid is to develop the export markets of the industrial countries.' Comment.

6. Describe the structure of the World Bank and its affiliates. Why are such institutions necessary?

7.

Country	GNP per head (US dollars)
United Kingdom	1,790
Tanzania	80

'The average citizen in the United Kingdom is more than twenty-two times better off than the average person in Tanzania.' Comment.

8. 'Bilateral aid is political; multilateral aid is economic.' Discuss.

9. What considerations should determine whether aid is devoted to the development of the primary, secondary, or tertiary sectors of underdeveloped economies?

10. 'Malthus was right.' What evidence is available to support this statement?

CHAPTER ELEVEN

MONOPOLY AND RESTRICTIVE PRACTICES

(1) The Theoretical Argument

The textbook monopolists are literally the sole sellers of a particular commodity for which there is no substitute and since this is the case they are in a position to reduce output and raise prices as long as demand is inelastic. In this way they are able to maximize their profits and they do so by charging a higher price and producing a lower output than would their counterparts in a perfectly competitive industry.

In practice, certainly in capitalist economies, such monopolists do not exist: for while it may be true that the National Coal Board have a monopoly in the mining of coal in the United Kingdom, they do not have a monopoly in the provision of fuel: they must compete with the producers of electricity, oil, and gas, and even if the production and marketing of all fuel in the United Kingdom were handed over to one giant firm, consumers may still spend their income on something other than fuel: in this respect all goods are substitutes, and all firms are competing for the consumers' money. The perfect monopolist would be a firm with which consumers had to spend their incomes.

Thus in the nineteenth century, factory-owners paid wages in the form of tokens. An employer's tokens were accepted only in a local store itself operated by the factory-owner. The workers had to spend their money with him. He was a true monopolist.

Despite the extinction of such monopolists Governments have become increasingly interested in and concerned about two aspects of monopoly:

(*a*) The accumulation of capital by one firm which puts it into a dominant market position. Dominance may be achieved by forcing competitors out of business, or by taking them over.

(*b*) The extent to which a group of firms in a given industry collaborate to fix prices or output or otherwise to restrict the freedom of action of members.

In practice it has been the latter group that has been of major concern to United Kingdom Governments. Since the war a considerable amount of legislation has provided a framework within which the Government has imposed restraints on monopolistic and restrictive practices. Before looking at the legislation we turn to the theoretical case against the monopolist.

(2) Monopoly Pricing

The monopolist, seeking to maximize profits, will equate marginal cost and marginal revenue and produce a quantity OQ, charging whatever the market will bear, in this case OP. Since the average cost (including normal profits) of this output is OC and average revenue OP there are abnormal profits (monopoly rent) of CPAB. Moreover, since average costs are still falling when output is OQ, the industry is operating at less than optimum size (when average cost is at a minimum) and there is excess capacity in the industry.

In these circumstances various possibilities present themselves to a Government wishing to control monopolies.

(*a*) A tax equivalent to the monopoly rent could be levied to prevent the shareholders gaining at the expense of consumers, although it would do nothing to increase output, and the level of tax might be difficult to fix.

(*b*) The Government might compel the division of industry into smaller units to introduce some competition. But this is a very arbitrary procedure and one in which the loss of economies of scale might well offset any gains from extra competition.

(*c*) Price controls. If the Government could stipulate the price of the product it would achieve more for the consumer. For example, if the price were fixed by law at OF, whatever the output, FG would become the marginal revenue curve and output would expand to OH as the producer equated marginal cost

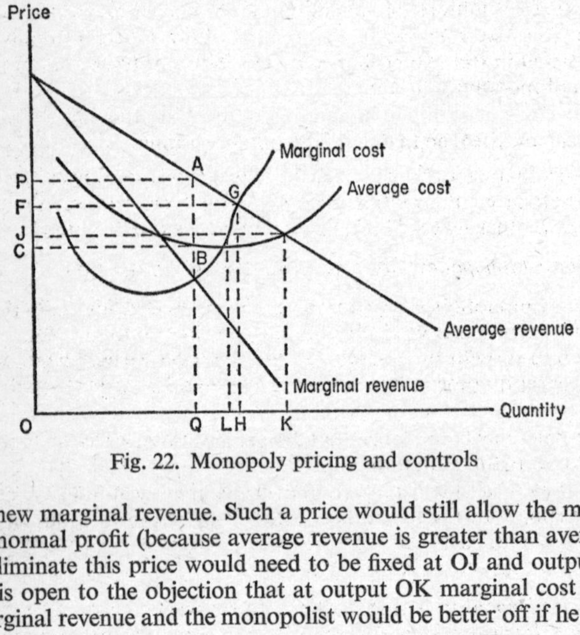

Fig. 22. Monopoly pricing and controls

and the new marginal revenue. Such a price would still allow the monopolist some abnormal profit (because average revenue is greater than average cost) and to eliminate this price would need to be fixed at OJ and output at OK, but this is open to the objection that at output OK marginal cost is greater than marginal revenue and the monopolist would be better off if he restricted output to OL.

In practice the sole producer is not the problem. Most of the difficulties arise over groups of firms co-ordinating policies.

(3) Cartels

Such groups are known as cartels and there are many ways open to them to reduce competition between themselves and to prevent new firms entering the industry.

One of the most popular schemes was that for fixing minimum prices in an imperfectly competitive industry. The danger here, of course, is that prices will be fixed to allow the marginal (least efficient) firm to survive and thus to increase the abnormal profits of intra-marginal firms. The alternative for the firms especially in the face of shrinking markets and excess capacity would be a period of cut-throat competition with no certain winner.

The effect of such an agreement is to allow firms to continue to operate below optimum output, retaining excess capacity and resources which could be more usefully employed elsewhere in the economy.

A group of firms may also shelter from competition by dividing the market between them either on a commodity or a geographic basis; or they may keep out new competitors if they control the supply of an essential raw material or by exerting pressure on distributors not to handle the newcomer's product.

Thus to summarize the case against monopolies:

(*a*) They charge higher prices and restrict their output so appropriating excess profits for their shareholders.

(*b*) They distort the allocation of resources by preserving excess capacity in the industry which would be more productive elsewhere, and by restricting entry they inhibit the development of new techniques. In practice, though, there are a variety of constraints on the monopolist and the cartel which prevent excessive exploitation, but let us examine in more detail the sources of monopoly power.

(4) The Sources of Monopoly and Economies of Scale

While the characteristic monopoly today derives its power from technological factors or great accumulations of capital there remain many examples established in other ways. The following types may be identified:

(*a*) *Natural Monopolies.* There are two distinct categories:

(i) Natural monopolies dependent on the geological and climatic factors. Thus South Africa has virtually a monopoly in diamonds, and Canada in nickel. Countries with other mineral deposits have varying degrees of monopoly power, as do those with the climate suitable for the growth of particular crops.

(ii) Industries in which competition would clearly be wasteful are frequently referred to as natural monopolies. The cost of gas or electricity would be increased if two or three concerns each with their own distributive system were competing for sales in the same street. The history of public transport is full of examples of such natural monopolies and in practice many such monopolies fall within our third category of statutory monopolies.

(*b*) *Local Monopolies.* Inadequate or expensive transport costs result in a multitude of local monopolies—usually with higher prices than more competitive sectors of the market. Thus local village stores enjoy a degree of monopoly power.

(*c*) *Statutory Monopolies.* Parliament has from time to time established machinery to enable individuals to enjoy monopoly power, or has itself created monopolies. Thus inventors are empowered to patent their creations, authors to copyright their work, and producers to register their trademarks.

Like all monopolies these statutory monopolies have their critics. In particular it is objected that the patent system reduces competition. The original idea was to afford protection to individual inventors, but the majority of inventions today are patented by industrial concerns, not individuals. However, it does not seem unreasonable that a company employing an expensive research team should enjoy at least a temporary return on its investment.

More noticeable statutory monopolies are the Public Corporations. Occasionally (for example in the supply of water in the United Kingdom) a monopoly is granted to a private or public joint-stock company: the principal consideration being to keep overhead costs to a minimum. Alternatively, but rarely these days, a whole industry is taken into public ownership as a giant monopoly (see Chapter Twelve), or special organizations such as the agricultural marketing boards are created by the Government.

(*d*) *Technological Monopolies.* As the accumulation of capital has transformed the capitalist economies, it has become one of the accepted contentions of economics that large-scale operations are more efficient than small-scale. Certainly it is indisputable that certain elements of costs per unit of production will fall as output rises, resulting in economies of scale.

(i) Fixed costs per unit of output will fall. The costs of setting up machinery are the same for long runs of production as for small. In some cases they are so high as to preclude small runs altogether.

(ii) Capital costs per unit tend to fall as size increases. The justification for super-tankers at sea and the move to increase the maximum size of lorries derives partly from the fact that the capacity of such containers increases more than proportionately to the surface area. Thus a 50 per cent increase in capacity does not involve a 50 per cent increase in costs.

(iii) Moreover the crew of the super-tanker does not increase in proportion to its capacity—a further saving. Similar economies are available in many fields of production: in bread production an increase in oven size does not normally require a similar increase in labour. There is thus a saving in variable costs as well as overheads—especially as fuel consumption does not rise in proportion to output or capacity. Other reasons for expecting unit costs to fall include:

(iv) Efficiency of labour: as output rises labour is likely to become proficient in particular tasks. The whole basis of specialization and the division of labour is that certain costs per unit of production fall.

(v) Stocks of raw materials and finished products to meet fluctuating markets can be minimized. As the market becomes larger it usually becomes more predictable (especially if there is little competition) and a given absolute change in demand is a smaller proportion of output. Less capital need be tied up in stocks.

(vi) Administrative or managerial economies. The economies above are mainly production economies. With many contemporary mergers the emphasis has been on the administrative economies deriving from the large organization. Large organizations can make the best use of managerial ability; clerical costs will be lower: the processing of an order for 100,000 units will cost nothing more than that of an order for 1,000. The large organization can more effectively employ specialists in accountancy, marketing, and other aspects of modern management.

(vii) Economies in distribution are of importance to large firms. Indeed the greatest increases in productivity have occurred in this area in recent years.

(viii) Research costs can be borne more easily by large firms than small firms, and monopolization of an industry will eliminate a great deal of duplication of research.

The benefits of economies of scale are not the preserve of monopolists but they are an important source of monopoly power. The economies of mass-production enjoyed by the major motor manufacturers make it impossible for a newcomer to enter the industry.

(5) Diseconomies

Although all these economies may be identified there is a limit to the benefits to be derived from size.

(*a*) In the first place there is no point in using large units of machinery merely because they are more efficient if they are not going to be used to capacity. Hence the practice of buying computer time rather than computers.

(*b*) As size increases so do difficulties after a certain point. The super-tanker cannot use normal docking facilities, the Jumbo jet necessitates great expenditure on runways and hangars. As the size and complexity of plant and machinery increases so do maintenance costs. This increase may effect any capital savings achieved through purchasing one large instead of two smaller machines.

(*c*) The problems of organization, communication, and decision-making are greater in, for example, the nationalized industries than in a small private company, and indeed the British Transport Commission with over 900,000 employees was so unwieldy that it had to be abolished.

Increasingly in recent years doubts have been cast on the efficiency of the large firm. Many researchers have suggested that the biggest firms in the United Kingdom are less efficient (in terms of the return on capital) than somewhat smaller firms.

Generalization on the effect of size and economies of scale is impossible: undoubtedly savings are available, and the Labour Government went to the length of establishing the Industrial Reorganization Corporation to exploit such economies, while at the same time maintaining the monopolies legislation to safeguard the consumers.

(6) Mergers

While many firms reach great size as a result of the natural growth of their markets over a period of years, many others have reached their present size by a process of amalgamation with their competitors, their suppliers, their customers, or more recently, with firms in an entirely different field.

Horizontal mergers are those involving two or more firms engaged in the same stage of production: the merger between the National Provincial and Westminster Banks to form National Westminster was a horizontal merger.

Vertical mergers may be illogically, either *backward* when a company engaged in a prior process is taken over (for example, a motor manufacturer taking over a car-body producer), or *forward* when a customer is taken over to secure retail or other outlets (for example, brewers acquiring public-houses).

Diversifying or conglomerate mergers are those where the companies involved operate in completely unrelated fields. In recent years, for example, the cigarette manufacturers have acquired interests in the food and cosmetics industries, as a safeguard against a future decline in demand for their main product.

Reverse mergers or take-overs occur where the smaller of two firms makes a successful bid for the larger.

Of course mergers in an advanced economy do not usually fit neatly into such well-defined groups. For example the basically horizontal merger between British Leyland and the British Motor Corporation also contained many vertical elements.

Motives for Mergers. The majority of mergers occur quietly almost without public discussion. The implications of merger activity are discussed mainly in connection with heavily publicized and frequently disputed take-overs. The principal arguments put forward in support of mergers include:

(*a*) The merger will lead to economies of scale and a better use of scarce resources especially where there is a heavy commitment to research. This will benefit the consumer and the national economy.

(*b*) The merger will allow greater competitiveness in export markets; or will allow more effective competition with imports—there were many such defensive mergers in the 1930's.

(*c*) The merger is necessary to safeguard essential raw material supplies or retail outlets and will benefit the consumer by eliminating profits at some stages.

(*d*) The (conglomerate) merger is beneficial because the victim company is inefficiently run and the bidder can make better use of the capital.

Among the less publicized motives are the following:

(*e*) Shareholders of either or both companies will enjoy a higher income.

(*f*) The new company will have greater control over the market.

(*g*) The bidder hopes to acquire cheaply liquid capital tied up in some firms, or to realize under-utilized capital by the sale of sites acquired through take-overs—an especially attractive proposition in the 1950's before the introduction of capital gains taxes.

(*h*) The merger is a means of quick entry to new fields of activity.

(*i*) It is not unknown for highly profitable companies to take over loss-making companies for the purposes of reducing their tax liability.

Dangers of Mergers

Against the frequently projected benefits of rationalization must be set the following doubts and dangers:

(*a*) The merger may lead to an undesirable reduction in competition. This is not a danger that is confined to horizontal mergers: in the BMC take-over of Pressed Steel the Board of Trade required assurances that the new owners of Pressed Steel would not discriminate against other motor manufacturers in the supply of bodies.

(*b*) There may be a divergence between the private costs to the firms and the social costs. As firms grow in size their importance to towns and even regions grows as well. The closure of a large plant in the reorganization following a merger may cause serious redundancy and unemployment, which create further problems for commercial life in the area.

(*c*) In conglomerate mergers it may be impossible for top management (however efficient) to maintain control of all sectors. Moreover the techniques involved in management of one industry may not be suitable in others.

(*d*) Take-overs may result in large-scale capital gains to shareholders—for doing nothing.

(*e*) Diseconomies may result—the optimum size may be exceeded. And the rationalization may be a long while in producing the desired effects.

(*f*) To an increasing degree mergers are being financed not by cash but by an issue of company shares. While this has not yet reached dangerous proportions in this country it is considered a potential difficulty.

Mergers and the Public Interest. The finance and technique of mergers is a very complicated business as is the task of forecasting the economic effects of any particular amalgamation. It has proved necessary to set up two bodies to supervise the merger fever of recent years. The *Monopolies Commission* has the duty of investigating important projected mergers and reporting on their economic effect to the Government. The Government's attitude to mergers is perhaps revealed by the fact that of well over 300 referrable mergers since the legislation of 1965 only 13 mergers had in fact been referred by December 1970. (For a full discussion of the Monopolies Commission see page 174.)

The City Panel on Take-overs exists to see fair play in the mechanics of take-overs and has established a code of behaviour to this end in an effort to prevent unfair discrimination between groups of shareholders.

The Extent of Mergers. Table 57 shows mergers occurring since 1969.

Table 57. Acquisition of Independent Companies

	No. Acquiring	No. Acquired	Value (£m)
1969	593	742	961
1970	484	608	954
1971	498	620	745
1972	710	931	2,337
1973	722	949	1,055
1974	306	366	451

Source: Department of Trade and Industry.

Table 58 shows the extent to which mergers were financed through the issue of company securities rather than by paying cash.

We must turn now to the attempts of post-war Governments to prevent abuses by monopolists and cartels.

(7) Monopolies and Restrictive Practices Act 1948

The immediate post-war reaction to the mass of monopolistic practices that had developed in the face of shrinking markets before the war was to investigate each on its merits. In 1948 the Monopolies Commission was established to examine and report on cases referred to it by the Government. There were two categories of monopoly:

(*a*) Situations where at least one-third of the goods of any description supplied in the United Kingdom were in the hands of one body or two or more connected bodies.

Table 58. How Mergers were Financed

	Total Expenditure (£m)	Total Cash (£m)	Issue of Shares (£m)
1969	1,069	296	773
1970	1,122	251	871
1971	911	285	626
1972	2,532	493	2,039
1973	1,304	691	613
1974	508	347	161

Source: Department of Trade and Industry.

(*b*) General cases where the Commission was asked to investigate practices brought to light by previous inquiries and thought to be widely used to restrict competition. The only such inquiry, perhaps the most important of all, was that into collective discrimination (see page 175).

For a variety of reasons the Government had encouraged interference with the free play of the market in the inter-war years and the tendency towards co-operation (though not monopolistic abuse) but it was now felt that the mass of restrictions could inhibit the post-war recovery of the economy, that obstacles to competition and efficiency might deprive the United Kingdom of industrial leadership. But as no one knew the extent nor even the nature of many restrictive practices and no attempt had ever been made to quantify their effects on prices, output, and quality, there could be no banning of specific practices: each situation must be judged on its merits and assessed in the light of the public interest.

The public interest is not directly defined in the Act but the Commission was in effect required to take into account the broad aims of economic policy, especially the need to encourage efficiency and the proper use of resources and to ensure an adequate supply of goods and services. It was left to the Commission itself to decide which practices were incompatible with these objectives and to make recommendations to the Government as to the elimination of the abuse: the Commission itself had no executive powers; it was established as a tribunal and had no judicial powers.

The first report of the Commission dealt with the supply of dental goods and the summary below gives an idea of the way in which the public interest was interpreted.

The Supply of Dental Goods. 'Dental goods' included almost all equipment and materials used in dentistry, 90 per cent of which were supplied by the Association of Dental Manufacturers and Traders who imposed a variety of obligations and requirements on their members, including the collective enforcement of resale price maintenance and the collective boycott of non-members. In addition the dominant firm The Amalgamated Dental Company was technically in a monopoly position, supplying as it did almost 50 per cent of the home market, and a greater proportion of exports.

The effects of the restrictive practices in the industry were to prevent price competition (since prices were maintained); to impose undue rigidity on the trade since entry was carefully controlled: this, of course, would prevent innovation.

The *Commission*'s objections were particularly directed at the collective enforcement of boycotts which could effectively exclude anyone from the industry. Moreover while recognizing the high standards maintained by the Amalgamated Dental Company the Commission did feel that their prices were too high and that their monopoly position contributed to this.

As a result of the report the Minister of Health made an order in 1951 which rendered unlawful the collective enforcement of resale prices in dental goods, and those practices which restricted the number of suppliers of dental goods.

This was the only occasion when the Government did in fact implement the findings of the Commission by a statutory order.

It was, however, already clear that the Commission was interested in the *collective* enforcement of restrictions and prior to 1956 received twenty references (other than the general reference on Collective Discrimination), in each of which the concern with collective practices in ostensibly competitive industries was maintained, though the Commission was not in general asked to investigate the major concentrations of economic and industrial power in the economy.

(8) Collective Discrimination

The main practices objected to included:

(*a*) The deliberate limitation of the capacity of an industry.
(*b*) The imposition of quotas on output.
(*c*) Exclusive dealing—to prevent new firms entering an industry.
(*d*) Aggregated rebates to compel loyalty to a supplier or group of suppliers.

The existence of such practices was likely to result in higher prices and lower outputs than was desirable but in particular they imposed a rigidity on the industry that would inhibit its growth.

The Commission's report on Collective Discrimination (1955) confirmed the prevalence of these restrictions and others (notably resale price maintenance) and found that in general they were against the public interest, while recognizing their necessity in particular circumstances. The principal dangers observed included:

(*a*) The rigidity mentioned above.
(*b*) The creation of privileged groups of buyers or sellers to the detriment of the public.
(*c*) These, and the practice of allowing aggregated rebates, reduced competition. (Aggregate rebates depend on total purchases from a group of suppliers and may be fixed so high on marginal purchases as to make it virtually impossible to buy outside the group.)

The belief of the Commission in the virtues of competition is clear—but unfortunately largely unsubstantiated, the arguments being based on theoretical concepts rather than on a wealth of empirical evidence.

Justification for Restrictive Practices. The Trade Associations (for it was normally through these that the collective agreements were administered) put up many ingenious arguments in support of their agreements, most of them doomed to failure before the Commission's belief in competition.

(*a*) The manufacturers of Rainwater Goods justified the charging of common minimum delivered prices on the grounds that it put all producers on a common footing irrespective of their geographical position in relation to the market.

(*b*) Collective resale price maintenance was supported by many associations on the grounds that it ensured adequate profit margins in the face of intense competition at the retail stage.

(*c*) The Timber Trade Federation had an approved list of agents and importers who entered into exclusive dealing arrangements. Justification was on the grounds that there were sufficient dealers to ensure competition, that only those with appropriate experience were admitted and that prices would not be lower if the system were abolished.

The reader should consider these contentions carefully assessing the economic implications of each.

(9) The Restrictive Trade Practices Act 1956

The importance of the 1948 Act lay not so much in what it achieved as what it revealed. But the accumulation of evidence of restrictive practices, the gradually strengthening economy and finally the report of 1955 persuaded the Government to move from its deliberately neutral position of 1948 to adopt a more hostile attitude in 1956. The Act which still provides the framework of monopoly policy is divided into three sections.

(*a*) *The Restrictive Practices Court*. The starting-point for the new procedure was to demand the registration of agreements which limited the freedom of two or more parties as to prices, output, quality methods of manufacture or classes of buyers or sellers. The Court is thus not primarily concerned with the large monopoly firm.

It is the duty of the Registrar to bring cases before the Restrictive Practices Court, which comprises a combination of legal and lay members. The onus is then on the parties to the agreement to show that it should be upheld by the Court by demonstrating that it is in the public interest.

The Public Interest. If the agreement is to survive the parties must convince the Court that it meets one or more of seven gateways, stipulated in the Act as constituting the public interest. Briefly the gateways open to the respondents are:

(i) That the agreement is necessary to protect the public against injury.

(ii) That the restriction is necessary to counteract restrictive measures taken by another person not party to the agreement.

(iii) That the removal of the agreement would deprive the public of specific and substantial benefits.

(iv) That the agreement is necessary to enable the parties to negotiate fair terms with a monopolist or monopsonist.

(v) That the removal of the agreement would be likely to have a serious and persistent adverse effect on the general level of unemployment in an area or an industry.

(vi) That the removal of the restriction would cause a reduction in the volume or earnings of the export business either in relation to United Kingdom export or the exports of the industry concerned.

(vii) That the restriction is necessary to maintain some other agreement upheld by the Court.

Even if the respondents are able to persuade the Court that their agreement meets one or more of the gateways they have the further obstacle of showing that the benefits accruing to the public through the restriction are not outweighed by any detriments that ensue from the restriction.

The Impact of the Court. The gateways did not seem to leave much room for agreements to meet the public interest, and the early cases before the Court confirmed this. Thus in the first case it was found that the agreement of the Chemists' Federation to sell proprietary medicine only through registered chemists was against the public interest, even though the Federation argued that the agreement was necessary in the interest of the health of the public (gateway i) and to protect dispensing chemists in country districts (gateway iii).

The Yarn Spinners Association sought to justify their minimum price scheme under gateways iii and v. An impressive list of 'particular benefits' was presented, and the Association argued that 20 per cent of cotton-workers would be unemployed within twelve months if the agreement were terminated. The Court found that any benefits under gateway iii were outweighed by the higher prices which prevailed because of the agreement; and while the Association's arguments on unemployment were accepted the Court still found that the agreement was against the public interest in view of some of the disadvantages, including the waste of national resources through the maintenance of excess capacity in the industry.

The Watertube Boilermakers Association and the Black Bolt and Nuts Association each had their agreements upheld by the Court.

By 30 June 1969 the Register contained 2,660 agreements of which 2,370 had been terminated, the majority of them without recourse to the Court. Thus ostensibly the 1956 Act has made an important contribution towards increasing competition in the British economy. But in practice it has been very difficult to legislate competition into existence and there are many economists who feel that where a formal agreement is terminated, by the Court or the parties, it is frequently replaced by a less formal but equally effective information agreement. As a result of the Registrar's comments on such agreements their registration was provided for in the Restrictive Trade Practices Act of 1968.

(*b*) *Resale Price Maintenance.* The development of Resale Price Maintenance in the United Kingdom can be traced back to the pharmaceutical industry in the late nineteenth century when independent retailers persuaded manufacturers to insert price maintenance changes into contracts to protect the independent from price competition from the developing multiples who relied on small profit margins and a quick turnover. Initially reluctant, the suppliers soon became strong advocates of price maintenance as they realized it preserved a large number of retail outlets—especially important where impulse buying is widespread. Furthermore, the preservation of retail profit margins ensured that retailers were able to provide the appropriate degree of service before, during, and after sales.

The public also benefited from RPM in that the absence of price competition allowed manufacturers to concentrate on the quality of their product. If markets are fiercely competitive there is always a temptation to reduce price and quality at the same time.

In 1949 the Lloyd-Jacob Committee recommended the abolition of resale price maintenance but it was not until 1956 that the first steps were taken. By then, particularly in the grocery trade, the disadvantages of the practice were apparent:

(i) By preventing price competition it inhibited the development of new types of retail outlets. Conversely it allowed the continued existence of relatively inefficient small retailers. Table 59 shows the changing balance between various types of retail outlet since 1950.

Table 59. Retail Outlets (1957–71)

	1957		1961	
	Number	Turnover (£000's)	Number	Turnover (£000's)
Total	577,405	7,587,154	577,307	8,918,860
Co-operative Societies	28,945	904,796	29,396	959,339
Multiple Retailers	59,105	1,883,809	63,299	2,580,073
Independent Retailers	489,355	4,798,548	480,612	5,379,448

	1966		1971	
	Number	Turnover (£000's)	Number	Turnover (£000's)
Total	504,412	11,131,816	485,346	15,217,963
Co-operative Societies	26,684	1,015,938	15,343	1,117,463
Multiple Retailers	73,852	3,837,244	67,479	6,061,363
Independent Retailers	403,876	6,278,634	402,524	8,039,137

Source: Annual Abstract of Statistics.

(ii) Consumers were compelled to pay the same price irrespective of the amount of service they were buying with the goods.

(iii) As a result there was excess capacity in the retail trades.

The 1956 Act prohibited Collective Resale Price Maintenance, but specifically upheld individual resale price maintenance. (This was because the 1955 report was concerned with collective discrimination. Moreover there were many who believed it wrong to interfere with the right of individual suppliers to fix the retail price of their goods.)

Increasing avoidance of resale price maintenance (through the use of trading-stamps, co-operative society dividends, special discounts to members of certain groups, 'free' gifts, inflated trade-in prices and other devices) and an increasing belief in the virtues of competition led to the outright abolition of resale price maintenance in the *Resale Prices Act 1964*, except for those classes of goods registered with the Registrar of Restrictive Practices. It was the duty of the Registrar to bring such cases before the Court where those wishing to maintain prices had to show by meeting any of five gateways that the practice was in the public interest.

The gateways were:

(i) That the quality or variety of goods would be reduced.
(ii) That the number of retail outlets would be reduced.
(iii) That retail prices would rise.
(iv) That goods would be sold under conditions endangering health.
(v) That services provided with or after sales would deteriorate.

Even if a gateway is met it is still necessary to show that the harm to the public that would follow the abolition of RPM would be greater than that inflicted by RPM itself.

Only three cases have been heard under the Act. Manufacturers of confectionery sought exemption under gateways i, ii, iii, and v, with the main emphasis on the effects of abolition on the number of outlets. Manufacturers of branded footwear claimed exemption under gateways i, iii, and iv. In neither case was the Court persuaded that the public interest would be upheld by allowing RPM to continue. The manufacturers of pharmaceutical drugs, however, were successful in their claim that it would be against the public interest to abolish RPM on their products.

The attitude of the Court persuaded the majority of suppliers that the legal costs of preparing a case, not to mention the adverse publicity involved, outweighed the remote chance of an exemption order being granted and the practice was gradually abandoned, only to be replaced in many fields by a system of recommended prices. The growth of this practice led the Monopolies Commission to recommend that the Government take powers to bar the practice of recommended prices in particular cases where investigation shows the practice to be against the public interest.

(*c*) *The Monopolies Commission.* The central role of the Monopolies Commission was clearly taken over by the Restrictive Practices Court and after 1956 it was confined to a more limited area including investigations into single-firm monopolies (using the 33⅓ per cent criterion) and the conduct of general inquiries such as that into collective discrimination.

(10) Monopolies and Mergers Act 1965

The 1956 Act established a framework for appraisal of monopoly situations once they had developed but the Government had no powers to prevent industrial concentration which might lead to monopoly power. The Monopolies and Mergers Act filled the gap.

Where a merger would result in a group controlling one-third of the market supply or would involve the transfer of assets of £5 million the Board of Trade was empowered to delay the merger for six months pending a Monopolies Commission investigation into its likely effect on the public interest. In the event of an adverse report the Board of Trade was given powers to prevent the merger proceeding.

The reports under this arrangement are necessarily produced under considerable pressure and some economists have been rather critical of this aspect of the Commission's work. In particular in an examination of nine reports on projected mergers Mr. A. Sutherland has drawn attention to some apparent inconsistencies. However, in defence of the Commission it may be said that each case has to be considered on its merits and that there is no question of 'case law' being built up. Perhaps it is the system that is wrong. One other area in which inconsistency has sometimes been alleged is in the actual process of referral to the Commission: in 1969 110 proposed mergers were notified to the Government but only four were referred to the Commission.

(11) The Fair Trading Act 1973

In 1973 the Fair Trading Act tidied up the whole field of monopoly legislation. The existing framework of the Restrictive Practices Court and the Monopolies Commission was retained but the criterion for a monopoly was altered to a market share of 25%.

In addition, the Act contained many provisions for the protection of consumers from various abuses. To supervise the implementation of the Acts, provision of a Director General of Fair Trading was instituted and the early indications are that he will have a vigorous effect on trading practices.

The Industrial Reorganization Corporation

While the bulk of legislation has been designed to reduce monopoly power, the Labour Government conducted useful experiments in 1966 with the establishment of the Industrial Reorganization Corporation, designed to encourage rationalization and concentration in those sectors of the economy where it was needed. The IRC was criticized on two grounds: to some it was simply a means of back-door nationalization. It was provided by £150 million of public money with which to facilitate change in the private sector by loans or by the acquisition of equities. A number of important mergers were thus facilitated by public funds without public acquisition.

In 1970 the IRC was dismantled by the Conservative Government before its work could be properly assessed. However, the proposals in 1975 to create a new catalyst to industrial efficiency resulted in the establishment of the National Enterprise Board, armed with powers and considerable public funds to acquire a stake in British industry.

Fears of backdoor nationalisation were renewed. But at times of low industrial investment and poor economic growth it is to be expected that Governments will seek new means of securing improvements.

(12) Summary of Chapter Eleven

(1) Monopoly price tends to be higher and output lower than competitive price and output. Cartels may be particularly harmful in restricting competition.

(2) Monopoly power may derive from legislation, possession of unique natural facilities, or the accumulation of capital.

(3) Such accumulation of capital leads to economies of scale but the point at which economies become diseconomies is difficult to decide.

(4) Mergers—horizontal, vertical and diversifying may lead to monopoly power.

(5) The Government have found it necessary to reduce restrictive practices (practices which restrict competition) by legislation, the centrepiece of which is the Restrictive Practices Act of 1956.

(6) The philosophy underlying the legislation has always been that each

case must be considered on its merits—though the onus is on the parties to an agreement to show that it is in the public interest.

(13) Suggested Further Reading

ALLEN, G. C., *Monopoly and Restrictive Practices*, Allen & Unwin, London, 1968.

Institute of Economic Affairs, *Retail Price Maintenance*, Hobart Paper No. 1, 1964.

Reports of the Monopolies Commission, HMSO.

Reports of Registrar of Restrictive Practices, HMSO.

SUTHERLAND, A., *The Monopolies Commission in Action*, Cambridge, 1969.

TOWNSEND, H., *Scale, Innovation, Merger and Monopoly*, Pergamon Press, London, 1968.

Exercises Set 11

1. Explain and comment on the theoretical arguments against monopoly.
2. Assess the changing attitude of post-war British Government to monopoly and restrictive practices.
3. Why have there been so many mergers since the war?
4. How does the Government seek to safeguard the public interest through its monopoly policy?
5. 'Since monopolies derive from economies of scale they should be encouraged.' Comment.
6. Study the financial columns of the National Press and compile a list of mergers currently under negotiation.
7. Why do mergers occur?
8. 'Restrictive practices are designed to preserve inefficiency.' Comment.
9. To what extent did the establishment of the Industrial Reorganization Corporation represent a reversal of Government policy?
10. 'The Government's policy has been anti-restrictive practices rather than anti-monopoly.' Discuss.

CHAPTER TWELVE

THE NATIONALIZED INDUSTRIES

(1) Introduction

The origins of public-ownership lie deep in socialist theory. In the United Kingdom such ownership has developed mainly in the form of the Public Corporation, a distinct form, clearly not in the private sector and yet not directly under ministerial control. The Public Corporations cover a wide range of activities from broadcasting to manufacturing, but we shall focus our attention on the main nationalized industries—supplying coal, electricity, and gas, and providing rail and air transport. The importance of the Public Corporations may be gauged from the fact that their combined average fixed-capital formation for the years 1967–9 was £1,587 million per year out of a national total of £7,351 million per year, and they were responsible during those years for over one-third of total investment in plant and machinery, and for the generation of almost one-fifth of the Gross National Product.

There is no single factor that explains why such an important sector of the economy should be in public hands, but in most cases a mixture of political and economic forces were at work.

(2) Motives for Nationalization

Natural Monopolies. We observed in Chapter Eleven that there are many industries where competition would be wasteful and lead to higher prices through the duplication of capital. Such are electricity and gas supply, which have always been subject to strict public control to prevent exploitation of the public, and in the interests of public safety.

The Commanding Heights Argument. It is sometimes argued that an industry vital to the effective running of the economy should be under public rather than private control. The White Paper on the Nationalization of the Steel Industry, for example, noted that 'Conflict between the requirements of private enterprise, with its responsibilities to its shareholders, and the requirements of the public interest has arisen in the past and is in the nature of things, likely to recur in future so long as the industry is in private hands.' Matters such as the timing of new investment and the scale and location of new plant may cause conflict.

Strategic Arguments. Where an industry is vital to national security it is frequently in public hands. Thus the exploitation of nuclear energy has always been a Government responsibility in the United Kingdom and the troubles of Rolls-Royce in 1971 led to the nationalization of its aero-engine division because Western air defences depend on the Rolls-Royce products.

Rationalization and Development. Economies of scale available in the generation of electricity and the manufacture of gas were contributory factors to the nationalization of those industries which were in any case accustomed to public control. The British Transport Commission symbolized the dream of an effectively co-ordinated transport system covering the whole country—a dream still unfulfilled. In the case of the railways and the coal industry their condition was so poor by the end of the war that only the Government could have found the capital necessary to revive them.

Macro-economic Policy. In the early post-war years it was argued that to achieve its macro-economic aims the Government required control of a substantial sector of the economy. Counter-cyclical policies might then be implemented via that sector: when private sector investment was falling public investment could be increased; as activity in the private sector rose public investment could be curtailed. In practice such a policy is impracticable: public investment is not an alternative to private investment but is complementary to it; moreover investment planning and execution involve a long and continuous programme which cannot be turned on and off like a tap; and even if it could the difficulty of forecasting the change in investment required would be overwhelming.

Political Arguments. Many believe that public-ownership is its own justification, and that all the means of production and distribution should accordingly be nationalized. This was certainly an important factor in 1945–51, the first opportunity the Labour Party had had to implement its theories of public-ownership.

(3) The Public Corporation

The Public Corporation represents a quite distinct legal form, clearly outside the private sector but yet not directly controlled by a Minister of the Crown in its day-to-day business. The Corporations are each established by an Act of Parliament which lays down their duties and their structure; the boards of such Corporations are appointed by the Government; there are no shareholders but the Boards are accountable to Parliament. The broad policy of the Corporations is laid down by the appropriate Minister, but the day-to-day running of the industry is a matter for the Board, though there have been many clear instances of Government intervention in, for example, wage settlements.

The Public Corporation is a twentieth-century development, representing in the case of the nationalized industries an attempt to balance commercial and capitalist motives against the public interest. This dual aim of providing a public service and achieving economic efficiency was a source of confusion to the industries for a number of years.

(4) The Dilemma between Service and Profit

Most of the nationalized industries were taken into public ownership by the post-war Labour Government. The structure and development of these industries varied considerably but they were all expected to achieve roughly the same results. Taking one year with another the industries were expected to be able to pay their way in the sense of covering their costs and accumulating reserves. In general during the 1950's the results of Public Corporations were disappointing as Table 60 indicates.

The return on capital in the private sector was considerably above that in the nationalized industries, who were frequently accused of the inefficient use of resources. But at least some of the deficiency could be attributed to the very fact that they were nationalized industries, subject to a greater measure of price control than the private sector, operating in fields where the return on

Table 60. Net Income as a percentage of net Assets

	1957	1958	1959
Manufacturing and distribution	19·3	18·3	19·0
Iron and steel (55 companies)	20·3	17·9	17·4
National Coal Board	10·9	9·8	8·3
Gas Council and Boards	8·8	7·8	7·8
Electricity (BEA, CEA, EC, and Boards)	9·6	10·6	10·7
South of Scotland Electricity Board	10·1	9·2	9·5
North of Scotland Hydro-Electric and Board	4·9	5·1	5·4
British Transport Commission	2·4	1·0	2·3
British European Airways	17·4	13·3	16·7
British Overseas Airways Corporation	6·7	6·4	12·7
Post Office	12·2	12·6	13·2

Source: Financial and Economic Obligations of Nationalized Industries 1961.

capital was traditionally low even when privately owned, and required in many cases to provide services at a price that no private concern would consider.

The greatest danger of allowing public enterprise to operate in this way is that it upsets the balance between private and public sectors. To take an extreme and hypothetical case, if electricity is supplied free to all consumers the demand for electricity increases enormously since it is now a better bargain than other fuels, and resources are sucked into the electricity supply industry at the expense of gas and oil—because the consumer has no way of comparing the real cost of electricity and other fuels. Equally if public enterprise is able to sell its products at artificially low prices because it does not require such a high return on capital then the public sector is enlarged at the expense of the private sector and the consumers of public sector goods and services are subsidized at the expense of the taxpayers (and the two groups do not coincide).

The problem went deeper. Since the Corporations were earning an inadequate return on capital (partly because they had been given little indication of the ways in which investment projects should be evaluated) they were unable to accumulate funds to finance the expansion demanded because of their low prices. The result was that in the period from 1954 to 1959 the capital formation (investment) of the Public Corporations exceeded their savings by £2,220 million. This had to be found by the Government either by increasing taxation (so that consumers, often wealthy, were subsidized by taxpayers) or borrowing in the capital markets thus forcing up interest rates and increasing the costs of the private sector.

These problems became increasingly apparent in the 1950's when it seemed as if maximization of output was the main aim of many of the Corporations. Consequently the Government undertook a review of the nationalized industries which led to a change of policy in 1961.

(5) 'Financial and Economic Obligations' 1961 and 1967

The changes were announced in a White Paper, *The Financial and Economic Obligations of the Nationalized Industries*, which proposed greater financial stringency for the future. On the Revenue Account there was to be an obligation to ensure that deficits were offset by surpluses over a five-year period, as opposed to an indefinite period which had become accepted practice; depreciation was to be provided for on a replacement cost, rather than historical cost basis (that is greater reserves have to be established as a new machine will be more expensive than was the one it is replacing); in an effort to secure greater efficiency each industry was to be given a specific target return on capital in the light of its own prospects: the electricity boards had on average to achieve a gross return of 4 per cent and the gas boards of 10·2 per cent (before charging depreciation). In the case of British Railways the target was to break even as soon as possible.

The new framework marked a change in emphasis in the policies of the nationalized industries, with a greater emphasis on commercial efficiency, but there were still deficiencies, some of which were dealt with by a further White Paper *A Review of Economic and Financial Objectives* in 1967. Investment criteria were tightened to ensure that funds employed by the nationalized industries were properly used: in future investment projects had to meet a 'test rate of discount' of 8 per cent: if the prospective yield was lower than this projects could only proceed if there were compelling social reasons. (The test rate was raised to 10 per cent in 1969.) The timing of investment was still to be a matter for discussion with the Government, to avoid pressure on the capital market which might result from the heavy bunching of projects.

Pricing policy was also reviewed in the White Paper. The basic system in the public sector was that of average costing. A Corporation would make an estimate of total costs and divide them equally between the units sold. This leads to a great deal of cross-subsidization of one group of consumers by another. For example, if a letter sent from one part of London to another costs 8½p, and a letter sent from London to Aberdeen costs 8½p it is likely that the senders of long-distance letters are subsidized by the senders of local letters. (This problem is discussed more fully on page 189.) The White Paper advocated that in future prices charged should more closely reflect the costs imposed, so that consumers who impose the greatest costs on a Public Corporation should pay the highest prices.

The good intentions came to nothing. Governments found good political reasons to prevent the public corporations from increasing their prices to a commercial level. In the early 1970's the deficits continued, thus demanding further subsidies from the taxpayer and increasing Government expenditure.

In the autumn of 1974 there was a further reversal of policy. In future the Public Corporations were to charge the full economic price for their goods and services. The Government was no longer prepared to offer open-ended subsidies. The result was rapid price rises in 1975. In some cases prices almost doubled in less than two years. The subsidy from taxpayers to consumers was at an end: in effect, the price rises were a substitute for extra taxation. It is too early to judge the effects of the new policy, but we may examine responses to earlier policy changes.

(6) Fuel and Power

The case for the nationalization of the coal industry in 1946 was almost unanswerable. For the whole of the inter-war period the industry, controlled by hundreds of independent groups, had been in difficulty as more convenient fuels began to supersede coal. Gas and electricity had always been subject to close public supervision and it was not perhaps illogical that they should be taken into public-ownership to secure the economies of scale that were undoubtedly available.

(*a*) *Problems of Organization and Control.* The size of the nationalized industries imposes considerable problems of organization, which have been dealt with in different ways in different industries. All of them are controlled by a board or council whose chairman and members are appointed by the Government, for their experience and suitability for the job. The organizational structure below board level varies from industry to industry, according to the degree of centralization thought desirable. Much of the criticism of the Public Corporations derives from their highly complex structure and the difficulty of 'getting things done'. None are so aware of this as the leaders of the nationalized industries and their political masters, and as a result of investigations such as those of the Herbert Committee (on electricity) and the Fleck Report (on the coal industry) patterns thought appropriate to each industry have been evolved.

Each of the Corporations is responsible to a particular minister, who normally has the right of appointment and dismissal of Board members, emphasizing the overall political aspect of the Corporations, a feature which may militate against effective management—and which may also militate against the recruitment of suitable management personnel.

The Board of a private sector company is accountable to its shareholders who have the right to examine the accounts and if necessary remove the Board from office. There are no shareholders in Public Corporations, but their function in this respect is assumed by Parliament. An annual report has to be submitted to Parliament and the Corporations may be subjected to investigations notably by the Select Committee on Nationalized Industries, which over the years has established an expertise which has enabled Parliament to make a more rational assessment of the performance of the industries than before. However, interesting as the problems of organization and accountability are, they take us beyond the scope of this book. We must return to the recent economic performance of the industries.

The Coal Industry. Table 61 indicates some of the problems confronting the coal industry since nationalization.

In the early 1950's there was a gentle expansion in the demand for coal, which reached its peak of 229 million tons in 1954 and 1955. Since then there

Table 61. Coal Supply and Consumption
(million tons)

	1949	1960	1972
Total supply	215·2	201·2	124·1
Total consumption	214·4	202·2	122·7
of which			
Electricity supply	30·0	51·9	65·6
Gas supply	25·3	22·6	0·6
Railways	14·3	8·9	0·1
Iron and Steel	8·2	3·8	0·3
Large industrial consumers	30·1	27·9	9·9
Domestic	29·2	29·1	14·3

Source: Annual Abstract of Statistics.

has been a progressive decline in demand and output. The table indicates some of the reasons: although the demand from the electricity supply industry continued to grow demand from other major industries fell away. This was partly because of the more efficient use of coal itself, but mainly because large industries were not expanding or were using other fuels. The change in demand from the railways and iron and steel industries was accentuated by the gradual change-over to convenience fuels for domestic heating.

During the period there has been a corresponding decline in the labour force in the industry; from a peak of 724,000 wage-earners in 1948 the payroll fell to 699,000 in 1958 and more rapidly to 268,000 in 1972–73; correspondingly, productivity rose from 22·0 cwt per man-shift in 1948 to 45·7 cwt in 1972–73.

However, the future is a brighter one for the industry. The decline that occurred in the 1960's was slowed down by the Government's placing of an embargo on coal imports, and import duty on fuel oils, as well as encouraging public authorities to burn coal rather than other fuels, and on occasions directing the electricity industry to maintain coal-fired power-stations rather than convert to other types. The prospect now is that the industry will enjoy a new lease of life as a result of the enormous increase in the price of petroleum products and the Balance of Payments problems that this implies.

Electricity. The decline of the coal industry has been matched by the expansion of the electricity supply industry. Table 62 shows the way in which sales have increased since the war.

Table 62. The Demand for Electricity (1949–72)
(million kilowatt hours)

	1949	1959	1972
Total of which	40,919	90,504	206,370
Domestic and farm premises	13,657	30,487	88,821
Domestic and commercial premises*	—	1,336	2,833
Shops, offices, and other commercial premises	5,035	11,501	32,164
Factory and other industrial premises	20,445	44,695	78,486
Public lighting	335	855	1,822
Traction	1,447	1,630	2,244

* Premises used for domestic and commercial purposes having a combined tariff.

Source: Annual Abstract of Statistics.

Sales have increased on all fronts, though most rapidly for domestic purposes. The convenience, instant availability, and cleanliness of electricity are obvious explanations of their expansion.

One of the great problems for the electricity supply industry is that of pricing. Electricity has to be produced when it is required. Figure 23 shows when it was required during 1968–9. There are two aspects of electricity pricing in England and Wales which derive from the structure of the industry. (The organization is different in Scotland.) In England and Wales the Central Electricity Generating Board has responsibility for generating electricity which it then sells on the Bulk Supply Tariff to the twelve area boards who

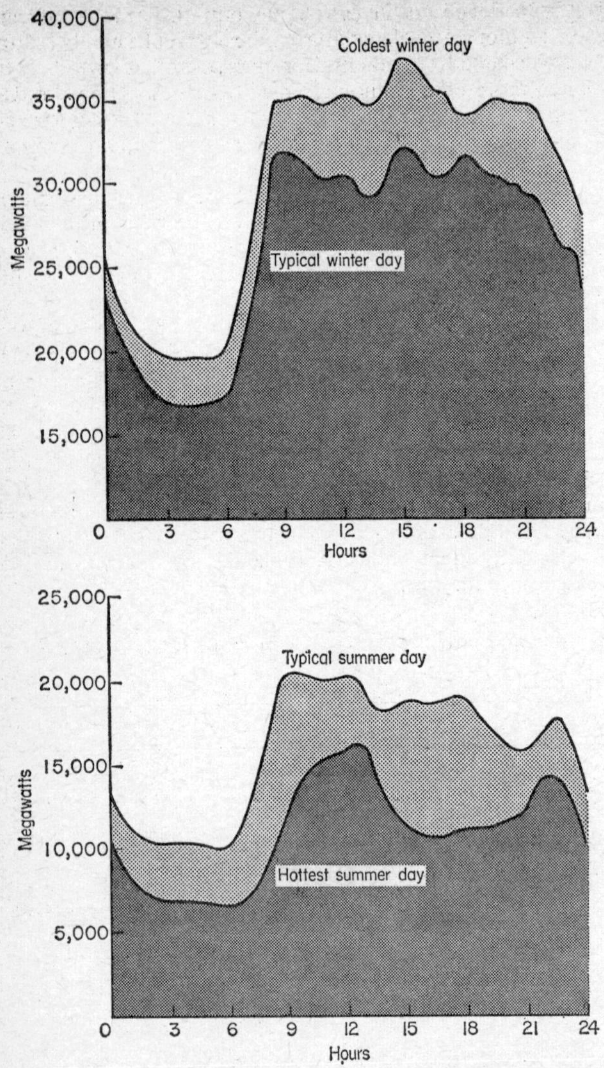

(*Source: Central Electricity Generating Board*)

Fig. 23. Summer and winter demand for electricity

are responsible for the retail distribution of the product.The Bulk Supply Tariff is rather complicated and the principles underlying electricity pricing can be equally appreciated from the retail side.

Since electricity cannot be stored the industry must have sufficient generating capacity to meet peak demand on the coldest winter's day (see Figure 23). For most of the year a large part of the generating capacity will be unused. The load factor in the industry was 51·9 per cent in 1969, the best ever achieved. (The load factor is the amount of electricity sent out during the year expressed as a percentage of the amount that would have been sent out if generation had been at its peak level throughout the year.)

The consumers who determine the capacity of the industry are thus those who insist on using electricity at the peak period on the coldest day of the year. But as the diagram shows there are regular daily peaks throughout the year.

When determining prices there are two theoretical extremes that could be adopted. First the principle of average costing outlined on page 185. While this has the obvious merit of simplicity it means that the fixed costs incurred by the industry in order to meet peak demands are allocated among consumers in general—including those who take their electricity at off-peak hours, and who are thus utilizing equipment that would otherwise stand idle. There is an even greater injustice in this than is apparent at first sight. The power-stations on the National Grid system are graded in order of efficiency. When the demand for electricity is low only the high-grade very efficient units will be generating. As demand grows less efficient units are brought into use so that the average cost of peak-hour electricity is greater than that supplied off-peak.

The basic system of charging for electricity does not make allowance for this. Each domestic consumer pays a fixed charge plus so much per unit of electricity consumed. While this reduces the average cost of electricity to him as he increases his consumption it makes no difference to him or his costs whether he takes his electricity entirely at peak hours or entirely off-peak. The price charged does not reflect the costs he imposes on the system, which brings us to the other theoretical extreme.

It is technically possible not only to measure the consumer's intake of electricity, but also to time this intake, and it would presumably be possible to determine the amount of electricity consumed by a particular consumer at any time on any day in the year. He could then be charged (retrospectively) according to whether he consumed the bulk of his electricity at peak hours in the winter or on summer afternoons. But, of course, it would be hopelessly complicated and expensive to administer such a metering system.

The electricity boards compromise. The most publicized scheme is that of the 'White Meter', whereby domestic consumers buying electricity for storage heaters are charged a lower rate for units taken between 9 p.m. and 5 a.m. than for daytime consumption. Not only does this more closely reflect the cost of the electricity supplied but in helping to spread the load it reduces the overall average cost of electricity and reduces the overall capacity required in the industry.

Similar considerations apply to railway charges and the student should assess for himself the implications of charging according to the costs imposed for rush-hour commuters and mid-morning shoppers travelling by train.

The Gas Industry. The gas industry shared in the expansion enjoyed by the electricity industry, but while sales of electricity rose by over 300 per cent gas sales rose by just over 200 per cent (see Table 63).

Unlike electricity, sales of gas were fairly constant in the 1950's and did not exceed 3,000 million therms until 1965, since when there has been a rapid expansion, and it is forecast that demand will rise to over 13,000 million therms by 1975. The most important development in the industry has been the

Table 63. Gas Sales in Great Britain (1949–72)
(million therms)

	1949	1959	1972
Total	2,241	2,515	9,757
of which			
Domestic	1,352	1,266	4,489
Industrial	517	794	4,278
Commercial	276	387	878
Public administration	47	40	111
Public lighting	49	28	1

Source: Annual Abstract of Statistics.

discovery and utilization of natural gas. It is estimated that by 1975 more than 90 per cent of total gas supplied in the United Kingdom will be natural gas.

Like the electricity industry the gas boards have to cope with seasonal and daily peaks, but they do have the advantage that they can store their product.

A Policy for Fuel. One of the benefits of having the bulk of the fuel industry in the public sector should be that it facilitates the effective planning of the total fuel industry. One of the benefits of the oil crisis in 1973 is likely to be a great re-appraisal of the role of each of the energy industries and, it is hoped, the development of an integrated energy policy for the United Kingdom.

In another field, that of surface transport, the dreams of a co-ordinated system are somewhat older.

(7) Transport

The history of road and rail transport in the public sector is really one of the changing legislative background. There could be little disputing the need for the nationalization of the railways in 1947, though the proposal to take over road haulage produced a sharper reaction. Probably no industry has been subjected to more public abuse than the railways since nationalization, yet it is abuse that derives largely from the confusion in the mind of the public between the railways as a public service and the railways as a paying industry. The very people who complain when the railways announce a deficit also denounce any reduction in services or alteration of prices designed to reduce the deficit. However, before considering some of the economic difficulties faced by the railways since the war, let us briefly review the transport legislation of the period.

(*a*) *The Transport Act 1947.* The almost unrestricted development of road transport until 1933 and the difficulties that had ensued for the railway companies persuaded the post-war Labour Government that only an integrated system could lead to an efficient, adequate, economical, and properly co-ordinated system of public inland transport. Accordingly the 1947 Act established the British Transport Commission, whose six executives were to be responsible for the integration of the system: the railway executive, the road-haulage executive, the road passenger transport executive, the docks and inland waterways executive, the London transport executive, and the British transport hotels executive.

(*b*) *The Transport Act 1953* increased competition in road haulage by providing for its denationalization though the Road Haulage Disposals Board was unable to sell back to private enterprise some of the larger units, which were retained in the public sector.

The railway executive was abolished and replaced by six area boards each with considerable policy-making powers. At the same time the railways were given somewhat greater freedom over their charges—a first move away from average costing and non-discrimination. The British Transport Commission remained to supervise the whole of public sector transport until 1962 when the Conservatives introduced their second Transport Act.

(*c*) *The Transport Act 1962* set up five bodies to replace the British Transport Commission: the British Railways Board, the London Transport Board, the British Transport Docks Board, the British Waterways Board, and the Transport Holding Company, the latter assuming among other things responsibility for road transport services. The most important economic aspect of this decentralizing act was that it gave the boards much greater freedom over prices and provision of services than they had enjoyed hitherto. Thus the attempt at integration begun in 1947 was now abandoned. The Conservatives sought an answer through competition between road and rail.

(*d*) *The Transport Act 1968*. The search for the right framework continued: on the railways a return to an integrated system: planning not competition. The 1968 Act drew a distinction between passenger transport which was to remain the main responsibility of British Rail (with the Government financing socially necessary uneconomic lines) and freight which became the responsibility of the new National Freight Corporation—integrating road and rail, a possibility that has become more practicable thanks to containerization. An effort to reverse the trend towards road transport for freight (see Table 64) has been made and wherever possible the NFC uses rail rather than road. Road passenger transport became the responsibility of the National Bus Company, superseding the Transport Holding Company.

The Traffic. So much for the legislation. Let us examine some of the economic developments in inland transport.

Table 64. Goods Traffic in the United Kingdom (1959 and 1972)

	Million tons		Thousand million ton miles	
	1959	1972	1959	1972
Rail	234	175	17·7	14·2
Road	1,146	1,698	28·1	51·4
Coastal shipping	43	47	9·5	13·0
Inland waterways	9	5	0·1	0·1
Pipe-lines	3	51	0·1	1·9

Source: Annual Abstract of Statistics.

The move from railways towards the roads which had been a feature of the inter-war period continued in the 1950's and as the table shows persisted through the 1970's, though it may now be that the trend is beginning to be reversed. The greater flexibility and convenience of road freight outweighed any advantages of speed that the railways might enjoy once the journey had begun. The trend was even more distinct in passenger transport where the post-war epidemic of car-ownership has severely reduced the traffic available to the railways.

Table 65. Passenger Transport in the United Kingdom (1959 and 1972)

	Thousand million passenger miles 1959	1972
Air	0·4	1·3
Rail	25·5	21·1
Road (public service vehicles)	44·1	34·2
Road (private transport)	82·1	222·2
Total	152·1	278·8

Source: Annual Abstract of Statistics.

During the period from 1959 to 1972 the number of private cars rose steadily from 4,966,000 to 12,740,000. In the face of such trends successive Governments have sought to make the railways viable. The greatest difficulty was that until 1963 no one knew which of the services provided by British Railways was economic and which was uneconomic. However, in 1963 the Beeching Report, *The Re-Shaping of British Railways* was presented.

The Beeching Report. Dr. Beeching became Chairman of the British Railways Board in 1961, charged by the Government with the task of making the railways pay. A detailed survey revealed some startling figures: one-third of the track mileage carried 1 per cent of the traffic; one-half of the mileage accounted for only 5 per cent of traffic. Similar conditions were revealed in many other parts of the business. Beeching's solution was prescribed by his mandate: if services could not be made to pay their way they must be eliminated. This would involve the closure of many rural services and stations; commuters' fares should be increased to meet the heavy costs of buying rolling-stock which was used only at peak hours; as for freight a system of liner trains was needed to exploit the advantages that British Rail had but did not use.

The change of Government in 1964 meant that many of these proposals were unacceptable and that others were delayed. But some services have been eliminated, the route mileage has been reduced by about 30 per cent, partly by the elimination of duplicate lines, partly by the elimination of uneconomic services, and freightliner services have been introduced. Soon after its election the Conservative Government withdrew the subsidy to certain commuter services, insisting that the cost of the services should be borne by the users, a policy certain to encourage still more of them to use their cars. While this will not of itself be of any assistance to the railways, it might encourage the development of a more rational system of road pricing which could reverse the flow of passengers to the roads.

(8) Conclusions

The post-war period has seen a change of emphasis in the Public Corporations, which is reflected not only in those that we have been looking at but also in the others such as steel and the Post Office.

The emphasis is now on efficiency and a proper balance between the public and private sectors and most important on the attempt to allocate costs to the consumers who impose them.

(9) Summary of Chapter Twelve

(1) A combination of economic and political motives have led to the nationalization of many industries in the United Kingdom.

(2) The Public Corporation with a degree of autonomy is yet responsible and accountable to the Government.

(3) In the early post-war years the Corporations had a dual aim—the provision of an adequate service and the efficient use of their resources.

(4) The White Papers of 1961 and 1967 clarified the position by setting more rigorous economic targets.

(5) The size of the Corporations imposes considerable problems of organization.

(6) The coal industry has suffered from a continuous decline in the demand for its product which is likely to continue.

(7) But the demand for gas and electricity has continued to expand.

(8) One of the major problems especially in electricity and railways is the allocation of costs to consumers.

(9) In transport there has been a fluctuating background attributable to the different views of the political parties on planning and competition.

(10) Suggested Further Reading

REID, L. G. and ALLEN, K., *Nationalised Industries*, Penguin, London, 1970.

The Annual Reports of the individual industries, HMSO.

The Financial and Economic Obligations of the Nationalized Industries, (Cmnd 1337), HMSO, 1961.

TIVEY, L., *Nationalisation in British Industry*, Jonathan Cape, London, 1966.

Exercises Set 12

1. Why has the Government found it necessary to nationalize certain industries?
2. In what respects do the problems facing the nationalized industries differ from those facing firms in the private sector?
3. Why is the return on capital employed lower for the Public Corporations than for large Joint Stock Companies?
4. What are the economic arguments for and against the nationalization of the motor vehicle manufacturing industry?
5. What are the difficulties of using the Public Corporations as instruments of general economic policy?
6. If electricity costs 2p per unit to produce between 6 a.m. and 8 a.m., but 1p at any other time what are the arguments for and against charging all consumers the same price?
7. What is the economic case for providing 'free' public transport to London commuters?
8. 'Public control does not necessitate public ownership.' Why nationalize?
9. 'We must nationalize this industry because it cannot make a profit in the private sector.' (Politician.) Discuss the economic implications of this statement.
10. Describe and assess the changing framework within which the nationalized industries have been required to operate.

CHAPTER THIRTEEN

LOCATION OF INDUSTRY

(1) Introduction

The factors influencing the location of industry have long been of interest to economists, but only in fairly recent times have Governments taken a close interest in the problem. In the United Kingdom, for example, it was not until 1934 that any serious effort was made to attract industry to particular areas. Since then, and especially since 1944, a complex framework has been established to secure a balanced distribution of industry and a reduction in regional unemployment. But before examining this policy let us consider the location decision for the firm in the absence of Government intervention.

(2) Tied Industries

Some industries have little choice of location. Coal-mines and chalk quarries are tied to their raw materials. The same is true to varying degrees of most extractive industries: agricultural location for example depends on climatic and geological factors.

There is little that can be done to influence the location of such industries, but it is not only in respect of these that raw materials are important. In many cases where there is a choice of location the nature of raw materials may be the deciding factor in the location decision.

(3) Fuel and Raw Materials

The present distribution of heavy industry in the United Kingdom still reflects the pattern established in the nineteenth century when all industry was dependent on coal as the major source of power. The choice was often between siting the plant on the coalfield and bringing in other raw materials, or moving towards the other raw materials and transporting the coal at considerable expense. Thus the pottery industry is found in Staffordshire despite the necessity of importing other materials from other parts of the country.

As it happens coalfield locations were further encouraged by the local presence of other vital materials—iron ore and tin for metal industries, suitable soft water for textile industries, and so on. The concentration of basic industries on the coalfields naturally had multiplier effects, attracting subsidiary trades and consumer industries, as well as population to provide the labour force.

At the end of the nineteenth century there was a close correlation between the location of the coalfields and the distribution of population. The principal exception to the pattern being London which retained its commercial dominance and continued to support a large population.

The pulling power exerted by raw materials depends upon several factors:

(*a*) The extent to which they lose weight during manufacture.
(*b*) Their bulk in relation to their value.
(*c*) The nature of the finished product and its bulk in relation to its value.

The difficulty of transporting coal is that it is only used once and that in proportion to its value transport costs are likely to be high. Moreover it involves the transport of waste. Similar considerations apply to low-grade ore. It is often cheaper to smelt it where it is found rather than pay for the transport of a large amount of waste though iron ore is imported from Australia. The importance of transport costs in this respect is illustrated by the coastal location of large steelworks which avoids the inland transportation of imported ore.

On the other hand where raw materials (or components) are of little bulk and relatively high value they exercise little control over location: diamonds can be processed almost anywhere; the cost of transporting transistors does not determine the location of radio assembly, sparking-plugs have no influence over the location of motor manufacture.

(4) External Economies of Scale

The concentration of industry on the coalfields became a self-perpetuating process in the nineteenth century as *acquired advantages* were added to the *natural advantages* of the areas. The industrial areas developed communications more rapidly than other parts, the supply of industrial labour grew, marketing facilities developed, all exercising an important influence. It was not of course that industry was attracted from elsewhere, but simply that the atmosphere of coalfields was more conducive to growth and industrial development.

These were the factors that dictated the locational pattern in the nineteenth century, and clearly the important considerations were on the supply side. But by the end of the century other influences were already at work, and as the twentieth century progressed it became clear that the pattern was gradually changing in favour of the South-East and Midlands, attracted by the great market represented by London. In addition to changes in the conditions of supply, market and demand factors had become important. The one factor of overriding importance was the release of industry from the stranglehold of the coalfields through the use of electricity, gas, and oil.

(5) Electricity, Gas, and Oil

The increasing availability and industrial application of electricity in the twentieth century, while itself dependent on coal, provided industry with a highly mobile and convenient form of energy especially after the establishment of the National Grid in the 1930's. Together with the use of other convenient fuels this has more or less removed the question of fuel supply from the location decision. Locations can be decided by other factors in the certain knowledge that the required energy will be available. This has not of course resulted in a mass migration of industry from the coalfields. The heavy capital commitment of industry, and the external economies established over a long period have resulted in *industrial inertia* preserving the old pattern to a great extent. But new industries have been able to turn their backs on the coalfields and their locations have been determined largely by market factors.

(6) Markets

The nineteenth-century industries were frequently fortunate in that their markets as well as their materials were on their doorsteps or where they relied on exports effective transport linked them to not too distant ports. Modern industry is fortunate in that its raw materials are frequently not expensive to transport and it can therefore look to its markets. Frequently modern products will be assembled from components drawn from a number of areas, and frequently the finished product will be more bulky than the components to transport (for example it is easier to transport steel sheets than finished washing-machines). If this is the case then a market location may be preferred. There is also an increasing number of *footloose industries* whose locations, especially in such a small country as Britain, make little difference to their prosperity. These have tended to opt for market locations in the South-East.

The switch to markets was encouraged by the commercial advantages of being near London which had continued to grow as a commercial centre and a population centre while other areas developed industrially. This tendency to move towards London and the South-East, strong in any case, was encouraged by the difficulties experienced in the coalfields in the 1920's and especially in the 1930's.

(7) Transport

The expense of transporting coal was the most important determinant of location in the nineteenth century, and even today no location decision can be removed from transport facilities. As transport improves so location becomes more flexible. The development of container transport is yet too young to have had any discernible effects on location but the cheap transport of perhaps thousands of units of a product will widen the location possibilities and might be expected in the long run to facilitate the solution of the problems of regional unemployment.

(8) Structural and Regional Unemployment

The trade cycle had its most devastating effects in the United Kingdom and the rest of the capitalist world during the 1930's. Indeed the average rate of unemployment was approaching 14 per cent for the whole of the inter-war period, and it was thus a period of general economic difficulty. But in many areas the situation was made even more serious by a combination of *structural and regional unemployment* within the general or *cyclical unemployment* that would have occurred anyway.

Structural unemployment is a continual process, the inevitable result of economic change. Industries and sectors of industry that seem to constitute a vital part of the economy at one period are superseded by others. An indication of broad structural change is given by Table 11 in Chapter Three.

Structural unemployment occurs because of a permanent change in the pattern of demand. Provided the change in the pattern is a gradual process it will cause few problems and need hardly be noticed outside the industries in which it occurs, but when it strikes suddenly its impact can be marked and it may have serious consequences.

Regional unemployment is related to, and often caused by, structural unemployment and is of course highly localized. In the 1930's the coal, textile, and shipbuilding industries all experienced structural changes in demand. Excess capacity in the world shipping industry, combined with a reduction in the proportion of world trade carried in British ships, reduced the demand for new ships and caused severe unemployment in the shipbuilding and allied industries. In the period from 1927 to 1936 unemployment in shipbuilding averaged over 40 per cent. The textile industry and coal industry had their own problems as other countries began to produce more of their own textiles, and consumers began to use other fuels. As unemployment rose in such industries which are of course very localized other businesses in the region suffered and a negative multiplier was underway causing unemployment to rise to 60 per cent in places such as Merthyr Tydfil and Jarrow in 1934.

(9) Government Policy

Although the Government did not yet formally accept responsibility for the maintenance of full employment, it was in the circumstances bound to act. There were broadly two alternatives:

(*a*) *Migration of Labour*. If one accepts the argument that businessmen, left to themselves, will settle in optimum or most profitable locations there may be substance in the further argument that labour should be moved to the jobs available in other areas. It is not, however, a policy that has enjoyed much Government support. Some attempts were made in the 1920's to induce or bribe labour away from depressed areas, but in general human and social considerations have suggested that the policy is undesirable. Any migration does imply an initial waste of social capital (housing, roads, public utilities, etc.) in the areas of emigration and a corresponding burden in areas of immigration.

(*b*) *Movement of Industry*. Consequently the Government has relied mainly upon a policy of inducing and pushing industry into the areas of high unemployment. Before considering the merits of such a policy let us look briefly at the course the policy has taken since its inception in 1934.

(i) *The Special Areas Acts 1934 and 1937*

(*a*) Assistance was made available to those families prepared to migrate.

(*b*) Two million pounds was made available in 1934 to Local Authorities instituting public works schemes to improve amenities.

(*c*) In the amending act of 1937 assistance in the form of low rents and tax concessions was made available to firms moving to the special areas.

(ii) *The Barlow Commission* (Royal Commission on the Distribution of the Industrial Population) reporting in 1939 laid the onus for eliminating pockets of high unemployment clearly on the Government. The outbreak of war prevented the implementation of their proposals but they were reinforced by Lord Beveridge in *Full Employment in a Free Society* published in 1944, as a result of which the Government formally accepted its responsibility for the maintenance of full employment and for securing a proper distribution of industry to secure full employment in the regions.

(iii) *The Distribution of Industry Act 1945*

(*a*) The special areas were to be enlarged into Development Areas of which there were eleven by 1953.

(*b*) Government Trading Estates were established with factories available at low rents.

(*c*) Grants and loans were made available to Local Authorities for the improvement of the infrastructure and social capital.

(iv) *Town and Country Planning Act 1947*. This was important to the location policy since it instituted Industrial Development Certificates issued by the Board of Trade which were required for any industrial development over 5,000 square feet. Thus to the incentives offered by the Distribution of Industry Act was added a negative control by which the Government could prod firms into moving into the Development Areas.

(v) The rise in unemployment in 1957 and 1958 led to a change of policy in that the *Distribution of Industry Act 1958* extended the assistance available under the 1945 Act to services as well as manufacturing and in some cases was available outside the designated Development Areas, where unemployment was generally above 4 per cent.

(vi) All the post-war legislation was brought together in the *Local Employment Act of 1960*. Development Areas were replaced by Development Districts where unemployment was high and persistent. The issue of IDC's became more stringent now being required for developments exceeding 3,000 square feet.

(vii) *The Industrial Development Act 1966* introduced a system of capital grants to induce firms into the areas of high unemployment; now renamed Development Areas. Firms received a grant equal to 40 per cent of capital costs in those areas but only 20 per cent outside.

(viii) Furthermore in 1967 the *Regional Employment Premium* was introduced allowing employers to draw a premium of 30*s*. per week in respect of every adult male employee in respect of whom the Selective Employment Tax was payable, and half as much for women and boys.

(ix) In 1970 the so-called *grey areas or intermediate areas* were established to mitigate the effects of the Development Area incentives on the areas outside the boundaries, the intention being to avoid the emergence of more areas of high unemployment.

(x) By 1970 within the legislation, building grants of up to 35 per cent were available where sufficient employment was offered, and in the Development Areas higher tax allowances were granted for such building and there is often some preference in the allocation of Government contracts.

In the *Special Development Areas*, established in 1967 and seriously affected by colliery closures, some rent-free factories (for five years) are available. And in its general policy the Labour Government did take special account of regional factors—for example in directing aluminium smelting works to Development Areas. (Figure 27 shows the location of the Development Areas in 1970.)

(xi) And finally in 1970 the new Conservative Government abolished the 1966 grant system and introduced instead a system of tax allowances and depreciation allowances.

(10) The Aims of the Policy

We have already noticed that the policy had its origins in the spectacular levels of unemployment prevailing in some localities in the 1930's. Figure 24 shows that the different levels of unemployment are still important.

Ordinary macro-economic policies are not designed to deal with such problems. The reflation of demand necessary to bring full employment to the regions of high unemployment would be such as to cause severe inflation in the areas already fully employed. For this reason special policies need to be

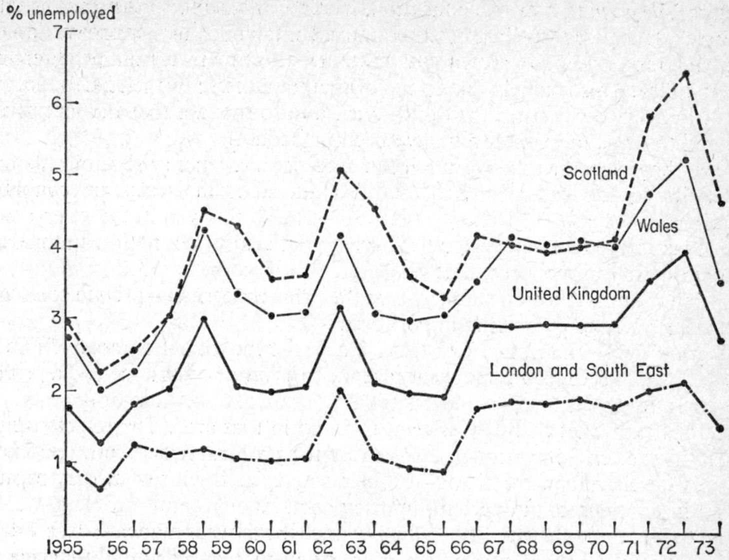

(*Source: Department of Employment*)

Fig. 24. United Kingdom unemployment by region (1955–73)

developed to reduce the unemployment. But the objects of the policy are rather broader than this. This higher level of unemployment implies a waste of resources for the whole economy. If it could be eliminated the whole country would benefit. Furthermore the opportunities available to those who happen to live in the Development Areas are often much more limited than in other areas: children do not stay at school so long, the social services have difficulty in attracting staff, there is a greater percentage of slum-dwellings, and so on. The aim of the policy has grown to take all these factors into account, and to secure greater balance between regions, but there are those who believe that it is wasteful to intervene and that we would be better served by leaving the problem to market forces. In that case as industry crowded into the London area and the South-East the pressure on resources would increase, resulting in higher wages, higher rents, and greater congestion eventually forcing industry back to the regions. But the point is that under the *laissez-faire* conditions of the inter-war period the reversal of the trend did not occur. The Government was therefore bound to take actions to prevent the regional imbalance becoming too severe—even if it accepted the view that in the long run rising costs would force industry back to the regions.

(11) Assessment of the Policy

Figure 24 shows the extent to which unemployment in the Development Areas has moved nearer to the national average in the last twenty years. The gap closed during the early 1950's, widened towards the end of the decade and has been a problem ever since. That differences still exist is suggested by

Figure 25, showing housing, education, income, and health statistics. The fact remains that the South-East of the country, containing a higher proportion of growing industries, has grown and continues to grow faster than the rest of the country. This is partly due to the dismally weak use of the IDC policy to force industry away from the South-East, and to the fact that the incentives offered to firms to move away have been inadequate.

But those incentives have not been ungenerous. There are limits to the subsidies society can afford to establish industries in clearly uneconomic location.

However, the fact that regional differences still exist does not mean that the intention was misconceived. It has gradually become clear that industrial location cannot be seen just in terms of the firms concerned—private costs are not necessarily of overriding importance.

Private Costs and Social Costs. As far as the individual company is concerned its aim is to secure sufficient revenue to cover its costs and yield a profit. If it believes this is better achieved in the London area because of the importance of the market then it will want to build in that area. The reluctance to move may often be irrational, inspired by the problem firms think they may find in the Development Areas—problems associated with what they regard as an inexperienced and perhaps undisciplined labour force—problems which seem to be overcome with little difficulty once the move is made.

The bases of the Government's policy were twofold: first that many industries are foot-loose and not tied to particular locations. With the improvement of transport facilities and the declining dependence on basic raw materials this is almost certainly true; second and more important is the belief that *social costs* as well as *private costs* must be taken into account. Some of the 'disbenefits' of industrial activity are discussed in Chapter Two. The important points to note here are that the social costs in the form of congestion and pollution in the South-East, and in the form of unemployment, lost production, and low morale in the Development Areas, may be greater than the extra private costs involved in moving industry away from the South-East. If this is so there is clearly a strong case for encouraging industry to areas of high unemployment. And indeed there are few who would argue against such a policy in general terms.

The difficulty is to achieve the right balance of industry in the Development Areas. If industry is to be induced into the region for employment reasons it is important, first that it should be profitable and secondly that it should create jobs in the fairly short run. Frequently the former requirement is fulfilled but not the latter. The system of grants introduced in the 1966 Industrial Development Act gave assistance to all industry irrespective of its profitability, its contribution to the solution of the unemployment problem, its contribution to the Balance of Payments or any other criterion. According to some critics the general availability of grants resulted in the movement of capital-intensive industry to the regions, with relatively little impact on the employment situation. But surely there is no point in creating jobs for the sake of them. While the economist recognizes the problem of regional unemployment he does not necessarily subscribe to the idea of maintaining labour-intensive industry just to solve it. And the future of the areas depends on their ability to attract industries which can survive unaided in the long run.

It is too early yet to assess the impact of the Conservative changes of

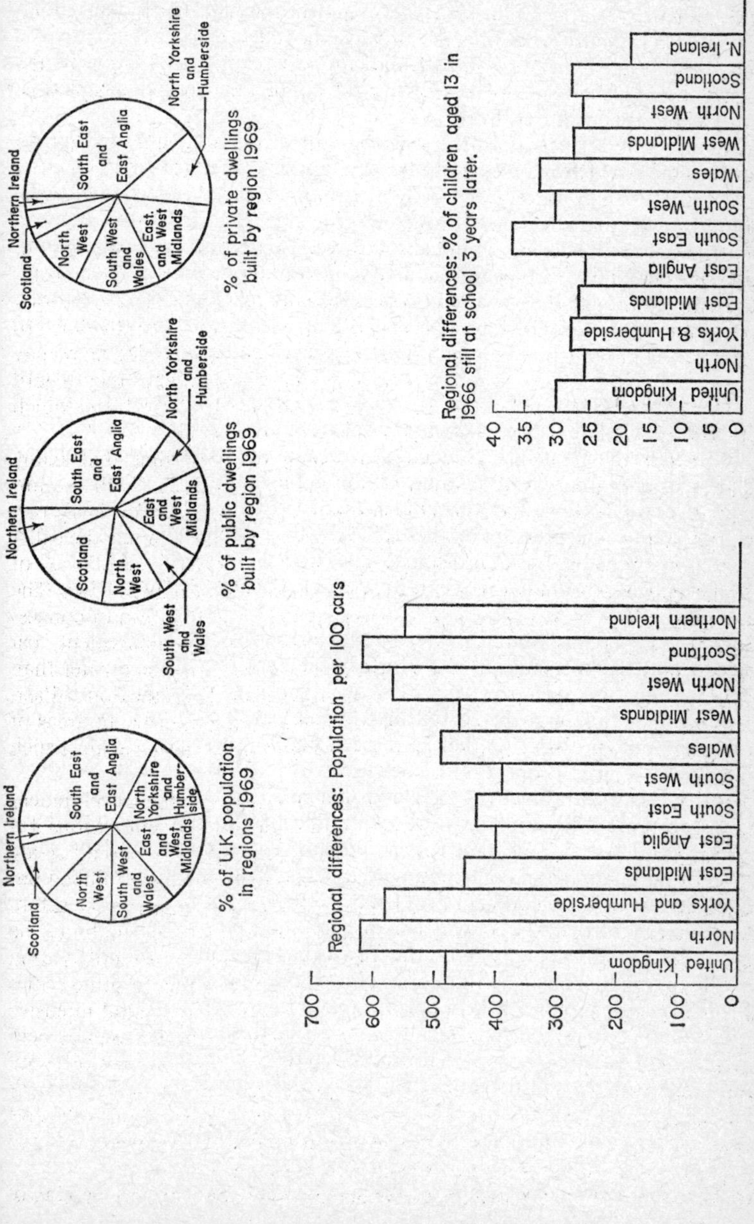

(*Source: Regional Abstract of Statistics*)

Fig. 25. Regional social statistics

October 1970, but they do have the merit of relating assistance to efficiency, even though they do have the obvious demerit of seeming to care less about the regions, and will almost certainly emphasize regional inequalities. If the Government is sincere about the regional unemployment problem then it could perhaps use the Industrial Development Certificate System more vigorously to keep firms out of areas already enjoying a high level of employment. But this does not overcome the difficulty of creating jobs—rather than industry in the Development Areas where the conflict between efficiency and employment remains unresolved.

Further possibilities to assist the regions occur through the use of Government contracts which may be placed in the regions where other things are equal. But these can normally be only a temporary expedient when what is required is a permanent policy, attracting growing industries to the regions, and at the same time keeping population there. This probably requires comprehensive planning of a type that United Kingdom Governments have as yet not attempted though the Regional Economic Planning Councils represent an important initiative in this respect (see page 205). Meanwhile, the possible use of new towns in reducing regional differences merits attention.

(12) The New Towns

Concern at the imbalance in economic activity in the 1930's was not associated only with the areas of high unemployment. An equally serious problem was that of the great overcrowding of the conurbations of London, Birmingham, and Glasgow. *The New Towns Act* of 1946 represents an important attempt to reduce the pressure on these cities by the establishment of purpose-built, self-contained towns at a distance from them. This aspect of the policy was especially important in the South-East with the heavy pressure on housing in London.

Such towns as Basildon, Crawley, and Harlow in the South-East and Runcorn and Skelmersdale in the North-West may therefore be regarded largely as lungs for overcrowded cities, an attempt to deal tidily with the overspill population. But the significance of the New Towns is greater than the housing they provide. As they have been developed solely since the war they contain a large proportion of new growth industries. We have noted earlier that the great problem of the Development Areas is that they contain a high proportion of declining or low growth industry. So new towns in those areas are fulfilling an important role as growth centres countering the emigration of population and contributing to a better economic balance overall, and to the regional development problem.

But this role of the New Towns has only recently received any emphasis. The bulk of capital expenditure on the Towns has been in the South-East to meet the overspill problems of London. Now if the New Towns are to play a full role in regional policy it is important that a higher proportion of expenditure should go to establishing such towns outside the South-East. Figure 26 shows that of twenty-seven new towns fewer than half are in or close to Development Areas, a distribution that reflects the original overspill function of the towns.

The case for giving future priority in New Town developments to the regions is a strong one.

(i) The New Towns have shown themselves to be growth centres, attracting new foot-loose industries, providing a wide range of employment, and exercising a favourable influence on the surrounding areas.

(ii) The emigration of workers elsewhere is halted.

Among the most recent and important developments is the proposal for a major New Town (or city) in Central Lancashire as a counter magnet to Manchester and Liverpool. While it would initially require vigorous assistance from the Government to ensure a sufficient movement of industry to the area it would eventually provide an important growth centre and perhaps reverse the migration of labour from which the region still suffers. The possibility of similar initiatives elsewhere should be considered as a possible solution to the regional problems.

But while there are clear advantages for the regions in such a policy the problem of the South-East still grows—transport and housing difficulties have

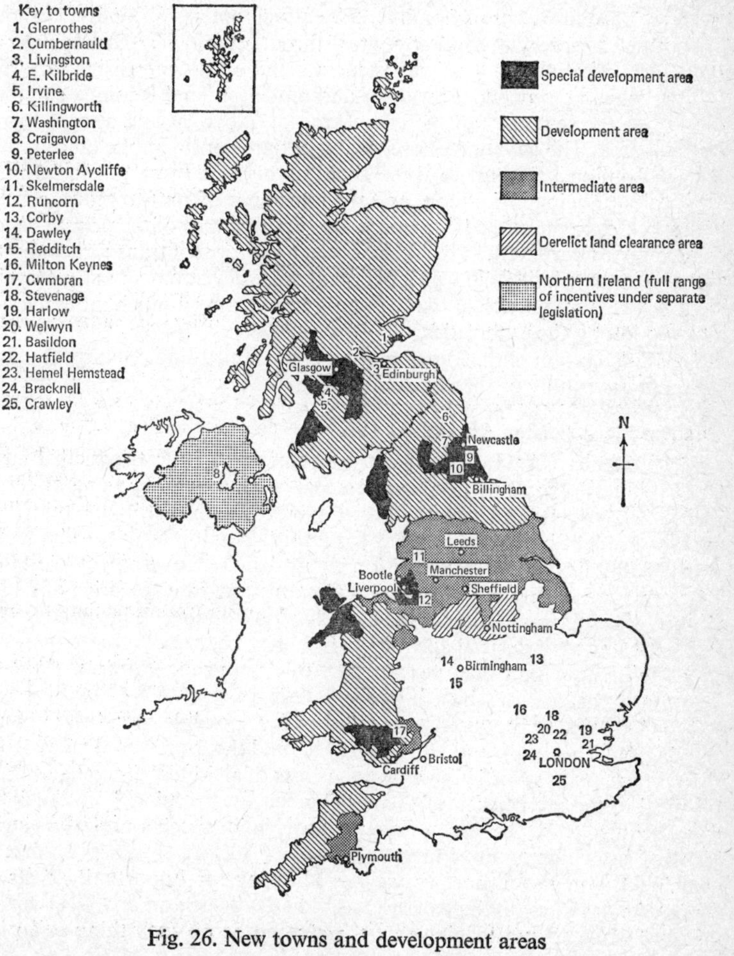

Fig. 26. New towns and development areas

increased in recent years despite the successful growth of the New Towns. If future New Towns are to be located away from the South-East other arrangements have to be made for the growing population of the latter region, and the present intention is the expansion of a series of towns such as Peterborough and Swindon, 75–100 miles away from the City. But it must be emphasized that this is essentially a London problem rather than a South-East problem and the answer must ultimately lie in reducing the overwhelming attraction of London as a source of employment.

(13) Office Location

In 1963 the congestion of central London and the commuting difficulties that result from it led the Government to establish the *Location of Offices Bureau* to encourage the movement of offices away from central London. It is perhaps a sad comment that at the same time as the Location of Offices Bureau seeks to move firms out of London, office development in London is allowed to continue apace, with modest control through the *Office Development Act 1965*. The Government itself has made a stand on decentralizing, operating Motor Vehicle Licencing at Swansea and moving Inland Revenue Computer Centres to the regions. But there is a kind of 'office inertia' attached to the London area. The advantages of moving out are considerable, office rents in central London being up to three times as high as those outside. But the economies of being in London, and the reluctance of staff to move, combine in most cases to offset the lower rents. It is another case of the private benefits being more important than the social costs in the form of transport congestion and also in the relatively low proportion of office development in the Development Areas, and a problem that can only be eased by a much more vigorous intervention by the authorities.

The investigation of the location of a possible third London airport made a pertinent case study of the issues involved.

(14) The Third London Airport

Air transport is one of the great conveniences of the twentieth century. Unfortunately aeroplanes need airports and of course no one wants an airport in his back garden. The growth of air travel was such that by the mid-1960's the Government began to lay plans for a third London airport to be built at Stansted. Public outcry at the decision persuaded the Government to establish a Commission of Enquiry, the Roskill Commission, into the siting of such an airport. A brief examination of the Commission's findings is included for here is a problem of industrial location which has been the subject of greater scientific investigation than perhaps any other, a prime example of the currently fashionable cost—benefit analysis.

The Commission produced a short-list of four possible sites, three inland at Cublington, Thurleigh, and Nuthampstead, and the fourth on the Essex coast at Foulness, and proceeded to assess the costs of all kinds, present and future, involved in the use of each of them. (The benefits accruing from the airport were assumed to be the same wherever it was built.) Such a procedure strictly involves attaching a monetary value to all the inconveniences that are associated with the airport as well as allowing for opportunity costs and straightforward accounting costs. On the basis of such an analysis the Commission, while acknowledging that there could be no such thing as an ideal site for the airport, recommended that it should be built at Cublington, thereby provoking a further powerful rural lobby in favour of Foulness.

The main question is whether the techniques of cost-benefit analysis are suitable for the determination of such problems. While it might be possible to assess in money terms whether a power-station should be oil-fired or coal-fired the location of a major airport seems to involve too many subjective judgements to be amenable to such analysis. No one can know the value placed by the community on open spaces or on easy access to an airport. In the event the social considerations were given less emphasis than the economic benefits by the Commission. While accepting that there were clear environmental advantages attached to Foulness and obvious disadvantages within Cublington the Commission found that the economic advantages of an inland site were overwhelming. Cublington would cost £100 million less than Foulness and would be far more accessible to passengers and freight, not only from the London and South-East area but also from the Midlands (the increasing importance of air freight in the export trade makes this a significant point). Not only would Foulness therefore draw considerably less traffic than Cublington (the reason for the airlines and the British Airports Authority favouring the latter) but the pressure on other airports such as London and Birmingham would rise and in total probably cause more inconvenience than Cublington from the point of view of 'noise pollution'.

Against these economic advantages are set the environmental losses stressed by Professor Colin Buchanan in his minority report—the loss of agricultural land, the destruction of ancient buildings, and the demolition of homes. Once again a well-organized, highly articulate lobby exerted pressure to ensure that the Government rejected the recommendation of the Commission and chose Foulness instead, holding that the environmental considerations outweighed the economic. At the moment the plans have been shelved—probably permanently. Existing airports are to be used to accommodate extra traffic.

(15) Regional Planning

Finally in this chapter let us take note of the *Regional Economic Planning Councils* established in 1964–5, whose members (chosen by the Government) have the task of studying the economies of their regions (eight in England and one each in Scotland, Wales, and Northern Ireland), drawing up strategies for the future and making appropriate recommendations to the Government. The establishment of the Councils may be regarded as an important landmark on the journey towards a more fully planned economy. But the role of the Councils is only advisory. While they have produced fascinating studies of their regions they have no power to implement their recommendations and have no direct link with the electorate. However, they do draw attention to the problems of regional development and perhaps their greatest days will come with the reform of Local Government.

(16) Summary of Chapter Thirteen

(1) Left to themselves firms tend to locate in what they regard as the profitable areas.

(2) In the nineteenth century this led to a heavy concentration of industry on the coalfields.

(3) In the 1930's structural and regional unemployment combined with

cyclical unemployment to throw 60 per cent of workers out of work in some areas.

(4) Since 1934 the Government have tried to encourage industry back to the areas, initially to alleviate the heavy unemployment but more recently for social reasons as well.

(5) It is possible that New Towns, established to absorb the 'overspill' population of large cities could be used more vigorously as growth centres in the regions.

(6) The overcrowding of the South-East will remain until the attraction of London as an employment centre is reduced.

(7) The Roskill Commission inquiring into the location of the third London airport provides a detailed example of the conflict between social and economic considerations in location decisions.

(8) Regional imbalance is likely to remain a problem until Local and Regional Government are reformed, perhaps giving more power to the Regional Economic Planning Councils.

(17) Suggested Further Reading

Labour Party, *Regional Planning Policy*, London, 1970.

LUTTRELL, W. F., *Factory Location and Industrial Movement*, National Institute of Economic and Social Research, London, 1962.

Regional Studies (Department of Economic Affairs), HMSO.

RICHARDSON, H. W., *Elements of Regional Economics*, Penguin, London, 1970.

Exercises Set 13

1. What are the main determinants of industrial location?
2. In what ways have the influences on industrial location changed since 1900?
3. To what extent has Government policy for the regions sacrificed efficiency for employment?
4. 'The Development Areas should not be seen merely as areas of high unemployment.' In what other ways are they underdeveloped?
5. 'Market forces would solve the regional problem. There is no need for the Government to interfere.' (Right-wing economist.) Comment.
6. What contribution could new towns make to regional development?
7. Distinguish between private costs and social costs. What role should they each play in deciding on the location of new industrial developments?
8. 'The regional problem should be seen in terms of the mobility of labour rather than the location of industry.' Comment.
9. 'The average level of unemployment is 1·5 per cent but in Lancashire it is 8 per cent. We must reduce Bank Rate and taxation.' Comment.
10. 'Regional unemployment is the necessary concomitant of economic growth.' Discuss.

CHAPTER FOURTEEN

INDUSTRIAL RELATIONS

(1) Introduction

Nothing has caused more dispute in recent years than attempts by both the Labour and Conservative Governments to reform the Trade Unions, or more accurately to reform the system of industrial relations in the United Kingdom. Charges and counter-charges have filled the air, the Labour Government was forced to withdraw its proposals in the face of Trade Union opposition, official and unofficial demonstrations against the Conservative proposals were widespread and the ministers responsible for the legislation had to be given special protection.

While the very need for reform was questioned by some commentators most felt that change had to come from within the Trade Union movement, and was bound to be a very gradual process. Against this it could be argued that progress has been minimal over the post-war period and that in view of increasing labour problems and militancy in some sectors the Government was bound to try to induce change and to instil a greater sense of responsibility. But before examining the various proposals for reform we must look at the background developments since the war.

(2) The Growth of Trade Unions

Table 66. Trade Union Membership (1961–72)

Year	Number of unions at end of year	Membership at end of year Males 000's	Females 000's	Total 000's
1961	646	7,905	1,992	9,897
1962	626	7,860	2,027	9,887
1963	607	7,859	2,075	9,934
1964	598	7,936	2,143	10,079
1965	583	7,973	2,208	10,181
1966	574	7,890	2,221	10,111
1967	555	7,724	2,246	9,970
1968	533	7,713	2,321	10,034
1969	508	7,841	2,460	10,302
1970	496	8,323	2,718	11,041
1971	489	8,366	2,742	11,168
1972	466	8,426	2,889	11,315

Source: Employment and Productivity.

At the end of 1972 Trade Union membership stood at 11,315,000 compared with 9,887,000 a decade earlier and compared with a total working population of approximately 25,000,000. The membership was distributed between 466 different unions of which the twenty-four largest accounted for 78 per cent of members, while at the other end of the scale 232 unions with membership of

; than 1,000 accounted for less than 1 per cent total members. Table 66 shows that while membership has grown very slowly in recent years the process of amalgamation of Trade Unions has made ground, the total in 1959 being 608. For example 1969 saw a reduction of twenty-five in the number of Unions and the 1968 total was itself twenty-one down on the previous year.

These global figures disguise changes in the balance between Unions. Some have been growing rapidly; partly because the economic sectors in which most of their members work have been expanding, and partly because of an aggressive approach to amalgamations, while others, in declining industries, have experienced heavy reductions in membership. Among the expanding Unions the Transport and General Workers gained almost a quarter of a million members between 1960 and 1969 and now has almost 1,500,000 members; the Society of Graphical and Allied Trades, an amalgamation of the National Union of Printing, Bookbinding, and Paper Workers and the National Society of Operative Printers and Assistants had a membership of 283,000 in 1969 compared with the combined 1960 membership of its parents of 193,000. On the other hand the National Union of Miners experienced an almost 50 per cent drop in membership from 639,000 to 344,000.

An important recent development has been the growth of White Collar unionism, symbolized especially by the growth of Mr. Clive Jenkins' Association of Scientific, Technical, and Managerial Staffs, whose membership in 1970 stood at about 220,000. The growth of such unions reflects popular awareness of the benefits of organization to the working force, and is likely to continue as employers react to economic squeezes by shedding administrative employees.

(3) The Structure of Trade Unions

As amalgamations and take-over bids are continuously altering the structure of Trade Unions the traditional boundaries between them are becoming blurred. The process is accelerated by changing technology rendering traditional crafts and techniques obsolete. Still, it is worth reminding ourselves of the traditional divisions because the basic framework is still discernible and many of the present difficulties of the Unions are derived from that framework.

(*a*) *Craft Unions* are the oldest of the existing types and seek to cover all workers with a particular skill. Membership was originally very closely controlled frequently being associated with the successful completion of an apprenticeship.

More recently some dilution has occurred as non-skilled grades have been allowed in to take advantage of economies of scale, turning the Unions into *occupational unions*, with much wider boundaries than the original craft union.

(*b*) *Industrial Unions* try to cover all workers in a particular industry whatever their skill or trade. While this has the attraction of being a logical approach to organization it does not eliminate differences between working groups—the interests of skilled men within an industrial union do not usually coincide with those of the unskilled. There is a danger that industrial unions will be little more than federations of groups of workers with little in common.

(*c*) *General Unions*. The federal aspect is even more obvious with the gigantic general unions, membership of which is open to workers of any industry.

In practice it is difficult to find unions that are confined to one craft or to one industry. If craft unions still exist it is only in very specialized activities; in general they have preferred to extend their scope by enrolling members in related trades as is indicated by names such as the Society of Graphical and Allied Trades, and the Society of Goldsmiths, Jewellers, and Kindred Trades. In other areas amalgamations of two or more craft unions may occur as with the merger between the electricians and plumbers.

Nor are there any industrial unions enrolling all employees in a particular industry and none outside. The National Union of Mineworkers is usually quoted as the best example but many grades of non-colliery workers in that industry are in other unions. Nor has the National Union of Railwaymen been able to win over many of the more skilled workers in the industry from other unions. Among white-collar workers the National Union of Teachers may be regarded as an attempt at an industrial union, though again there are several other organizations catering for groups whose objectives are different from those of the NUT.

(4) The Need for Reorganization

Further investigation would reveal many more subtle differences between unions, many instances where unions are in conflict over the enrolment of a group of workers because their frontiers overlap, many enclaves of perhaps semi-skilled workers holding out against attempted take-overs by larger unions. We have noted already (Table 66) that the process of rationalization is under way, and the complexity of negotiations between employers and unions resulting from the multiplicity of unions makes such change a matter of urgency. But just as the take-over of one firm by another may be resisted for personal or political reasons even though it makes good economic sense, so does the process of Trade Union amalgamation have to overcome such obstacles even though almost everyone agrees that some restructuring is necessary. It is one of the aims of the Industrial Relations Bill (1971) to facilitate such change though hostility to other parts of that Act make co-operation over this a remote possibility.

Proposals for reform may perhaps be seen in terms of economies and dis-economies of scale. Many of the smaller unions cannot afford to provide a full range of services to their members. As the organization of capital in the guise of management is improved unions must be able to meet the challenge; for example by the careful and scientific presentation of wage claims based on a proper appraisal of the economic and accounting facts relating to the industry. This cannot be achieved without employing quite expensive specialists.

If such a careful approach should be unsuccessful then a union needs to be able to offer some support to workers on strike. The smaller unions can afford neither the experts nor the strike pay, especially in view of the increasing demands on their resources for training, education, and liaison with Government and other authorities. At the other end of the scale the gigantic general unions which can afford all kinds of research facilities—and strike pay—suffer from some of the difficulties of communication and management experienced by large commercial organizations.

One widely suggested solution is the creation of more industrial unions, which it is claimed would have the following benefits:

(*a*) Union organization would correspond more closely with the organization of employers through their Trade Associations which are almost always organized by industry.

(*b*) The interests of all workers in an industry could be more effectively channelled through one union than through half a dozen or more.

(*c*) It would be in the national interest since the bargaining process would be more rational, and inter-union rivalry would be eliminated.

This really only amounts to a cry for superficial tidiness which could not be expected to affect the underlying reality of labour relations, for the difficulties of moving towards industrial unionism by the amalgamation of small unions and the dismantling and reconstruction of the giants are almost insurmountable for several reasons.

(*a*) What is an industry? In theory it might be possible to create Trade Unions to correspond with the divisions of the Standard Industrial Classification (whereby industries are grouped together to facilitate the collation of official statistics), but many of the classifications are so broad that parallel unions would amount to general unions. Perhaps another set of definitions could be used? For such industries as agriculture and teaching this might just be possible (but does teaching include university dons as well as primary-school teachers?). How does one define the motor industry? Does it include the production of sparking-plugs, rubber tyres, or leather for interiors? Furthermore the structure of industry is constantly changing, established industries declining, new ones emerging, so that the 'Minister of Trade Union Organization' would need to conduct a quinquennial review to maintain order.

(*b*) Even if these problems could be overcome and everyone be drafted to the appropriate union the very differences in interests and outlook which are responsible for the present diversity of union structures would still exist—in fact there would probably be more splinter groups than before. Inter-union rivalry would become intra-union rivalry.

(*c*) The whole point of Trade Unions is that they are voluntary organizations. Under a system of industrial unions the only choice would be to join or to stay out.

(*d*) The present system allows a worker to maintain loyalty to his union even if he does change employers, an important consideration, and one that would be lost under industrial unions.

(*e*) Finally, there is no more reason for imposing a system of industrial unions than there is for insisting that each firm should confine itself to a particular industry, and that subsidiaries acquired in the process of diversification should be sold back to their 'proper' owners. In fact the general unions have grown in response to the demands of the working force, just as industrial amalgamation is partly a response to the shareholders' demands for protection.

While these considerations do not deny the need for change they do effectively close one avenue. The route for union reform lies in the continuation of the gradual process of the 1960's. Union leaders are acutely aware of benefits that may come from amalgamations but those amalgamations must be based firmly on mutual interests and common problems. As industrial conditions change so will the structure of Trade Unions.

(5) The Role of the Unions

Whatever the structure of Trade Unions their functions and objectives are broadly the same. Sidney and Beatrice Webb defined a Trade Union as an 'association of wage-earners for the purpose of improving their working lives', and this must still be their broad objective. In its evidence to the Royal Commission on Trade Unions and Employers Associations, the Trades Union Congress distinguished several different aspects of the broad aim, which may be summarized as:

(*a*) *Improved terms of employment*, not only in terms of higher wages, but shorter hours, longer holidays, improvements in the facilities available to workers—toilets and washing facilities, canteens, medical units for example. To ensure security and continuity of employment for their members is also a function of the Unions, and so they will protect workers against wrongful dismissal or discrimination by an employer.

(*b*) *Broader economic aims*. The micro-economic aims above will be more easily reached if the Government can maintain full employment, and the TUC has been absolutely consistent in its advocacy of an expansionary economic policy, arguing that the very restrictions imposed by successive Governments to reduce our difficulties, are the cause of those difficulties, and that greater prosperity will not develop until policies are changed. Nor should greater prosperity be an aim in itself—the distribution of that prosperity is of major concern to the Unions, especially in view of the very unequal distribution of wealth in the country. Again it is not simply the prosperity of workers that is important: the improvement of the social security system and of social services commands high priority among trade unionists.

(*c*) *Political Aims*. The objectives above obviously do not fit into watertight economic boxes, but there are some aims of the Unions that are more clearly political than others. The cause of *industrial democracy*, with greater worker participation in the decision-making process, is carried mainly by the Trade Unions. The idea of 'them' and 'us', those who give the orders and those who obey them, is very gradually giving way to more civilized procedures. After all an industry is just as dependent on a supply of labour as a supply of capital. Many trade-unionists also demand greater public control of industry if not always public-ownership. And it is apparent from the membership of Royal Commissions, Courts of Inquiry, and the Boards of Public Bodies that increasing attention is given to the voice of Trade Union leadership.

While few would argue that all these are not legitimate objectives for the Unions to pursue an increasing number take exception to the way in which the objectives are interpreted and the methods used by some unionists to achieve them.

(6) Trade Associations

Parallel to the Trade Unions are associations of employers, technically Trade Unions themselves. These Trade Associations provide for their members many of the services that Unions provide for their members especially in the field of research and information.

They are frequently responsible for the negotiations with the Unions over wages and other matters. But as local and plant bargaining supersedes national bargaining this function becomes less important, and the Trade Associations become little more than general spokesmen and public relations officers. Increasingly the Confederation of British Industry, the employers' equivalent of the Trades Union Congress, takes over this role.

(7) Wages

The most obvious function of a Trade Union is to secure higher wages for its members, and it is the level of wages and wage awards that is responsible for much public hostility towards the Unions. Wage payments may be divided into two broad categories:

(*a*) *Time rates*, where the worker is paid by the hour. Such systems have the great merit of simplicity, both for employers and employees, but carry the danger that they become merely attendance money, and do not offer stronger or more able employees the incentives they need. Consequently it is usually necessary to establish several time rates or to relate rates to certain amounts of work, representing to the employer a fair return for his outlay.

(*b*) *Piece rates*, where a worker is paid according to the work he does. The more units he completes the more he is paid. There is thus an incentive for him to work hard and fast but there is a danger that quality will suffer. So piece rates are suitable only for easily measurable jobs where quality does not depend on the worker. Piece rates also involve difficulties of assessment and work—measurement to ensure that those with the most difficult jobs receive the highest rates—the disputes that this can cause constitute a good reason for not introducing piece rates. If they are to be used team rates, where payment is related to the output of a group of workers may be preferable.

Piece rates may be either flat rates so that payment is the same for every unit produced; progressive where higher rates are paid for output above a certain level, or where the higher rate is paid for all pieces once that level is reached; or regressive where the rates payable per unit fall as output rises. One of the difficulties is to divide the benefits of the extra output that piece rates usually cause, between employers and workers, and the disagreements that this may occasion account for the slow growth of this method of payment in this country.

The Level of Wages. While it may be possible in theory to pay labour the value of its marginal product, in practice wages are determined by the interaction of a variety of forces whose relative strength varies from one industry to another. Table 67 presents average earnings in various activities in 1973.

What factors account for these differences and the much wider ones that are concealed by the averages? Why do some employees secure substantial pay rises while others have difficulty in increasing their pay at all. A variety of influences are at work to determine the rates in any particular industry:

(*a*) Earnings may be expected broadly to reflect the value of the product of the employee, though there are glaring exceptions mainly in the public sector. In the private sector an employer will be prepared to pay for high productivity.

(*b*) The established pattern depends partly on the relative militancy of unions in the past. In the case of well-organized labour with aggressive leadership prepared to employ all the methods open to unions, wages will tend to be high. But if labour is loosely organized, and not at all militant, wages will be low. Only in the last couple of years have the traditionally 'responsible' sectors of the labour force caught on to this and resorted to industrial action.

(*c*) Some workers really do have benefits other than their money income and

Table 67. Average Weekly Earnings and Hourly Rates in the United Kingdom (October 1973)

	Men (21 years and over) £	Women (18 years and over) £
Weekly earnings		
All manual workers	40·92	21·16
Food, Drink, and Tobacco	40·24	22·68
Chemicals	41·31	21·47
Vehicles	45·74	26·18
Textiles	36·75	19·89
Public Administration	31·32	23·37
Hourly earnings		
Food, Drink, and Tobacco	85p	59p
Chemicals	96p	56p
Vehicles	106p	69p
Textiles	81p	53p
Public Administration	71p	58p

Source: Employment and Productivity Gazette.

in the past they have been prepared to take this into account in their wage negotiations. Thus the low rents of farmworkers, the long holidays of schoolteachers, the job satisfaction itself especially in the public sector, security of employment, clothing allowances, free travel, the opportunity to buy at a discount, all contribute towards the differences between various groups. But differences between monetary rewards especially between the public and private sectors have recently led to these other benefits being discounted in negotiations by the Unions.

(*d*) Control over entry to a particular occupation is often important in achieving and maintaining high earnings especially in the professions. A large part of the earnings of solicitors and accountants amounts to a scarcity rent contrived by limiting entry to the professions.

(*e*) Spectacular increases in pay may be secured as a result of the abandonment of *restrictive practices* in the course of *productivity bargaining* (see page 214).

(*f*) There are still wide differences between the pay of men and women in the same jobs, though under the Equal Pay Act of 1970 such discrimination should have been ended by the end of 1975, but many industries may not have reached the target.

(*g*) Wage-drift often accounts for differences within an occupation. The Union negotiates a national minimum rate and by local bargaining, some groups are able to secure increases above this. Or the drift may take the form of nominally upgrading workers, or of the payment of 'perks' of various kinds.

These and many other influences are at work in determining wage levels and rises. It is the traditional British practice for the process to be left to the Unions and employers concerned with only minimal interference from the Government except where they have specifically established machinery for the conduct of negotiations—Wages Councils for example.

Only rarely have attempts been made to introduce a formal incomes policy and even then they have been extensions of deflationary policy. The emphasis has never been on the need to establish a minimum national wage or a more equitable distribution of income. In this respect incomes policies under the Conservatives in 1957 (the Council on Prices Productivity and Incomes: the 'three wise men') and in 1962 (the National Incomes Commission) and under Labour from 1965 to 1969 (National Board for Prices and Incomes) may be regarded as negative in intent rather than positive. The reason for this is the conflict between micro- and macro-economic aims with the latter taking precedence over the former, as priority is given to the control of inflation. (A full discussion of the incomes policy is in Chapter Four.)

(8) Restrictive Practices and Productivity Bargaining

An important development in recent years has been the growth of productivity bargaining, beginning with the Fawley Agreements in 1960, when the elimination of restrictive practices by labour led to higher productivity and wages at the Esso oil refinery near Southampton. Productivity bargaining may be regarded as an extension of orthodox wage bargaining (which is concerned mainly with countering inflation, parity with similar workers, or sharing higher profits), to relate increases in pay more closely to rises in productivity. Such a process normally involves the removal of restrictive practices of various kinds in exchange for substantial pay rises. Restrictive practices frequently originate as defence mechanisms against low rates of pay, and are as often the result of weak management as of militant labour. They might include:

(*a*) Excessive overtime working, deliberately contrived to force up average earnings.

(*b*) The unnecessary use of craftsmen's mates, perhaps rendered redundant by changing methods but retained as a matter of prestige.

(*c*) Rigid demarcation lines between members of different unions.

(*d*) The overmanning of machines to preserve jobs when labour-saving techniques are introduced.

The effect of such practices is to reduce the productivity of labour and of capital. International comparisons, such as those given in Table 51, suggest that productivity of labour in the United Kingdom is considerably lower than elsewhere, and while the discrepancy is not attributable only to labour the elimination of restrictive practices can make an important contribution to narrowing the gap. It is the object of productivity bargaining to exploit the possibilities not merely by buying off restrictive practices but also by creating greater flexibility in the use of labour, and a more responsible approach—a general change of atmosphere.

There should be benefits for all sides: workers enjoy high wage rates and shorter hours of work, greater security, and a better working situation; the company benefits from the greater flexibility and their share of the proceeds of higher productivity; the community benefits from the more rational allocation of labour and perhaps price reductions or at least more modest price increases.

Against these benefits, productivity bargaining requires intensive and protracted efforts from management and unions, and the greater flexibility required imposes on workers who may have to switch jobs or change to shift-work. The increase in earnings achieved through such bargaining may actually have an inflationary effect by spilling over to other firms in the same area or industry being forced to grant 'comparability' increases without the same concessions on productivity.

The spread of productivity agreements has been one of the most constructive developments in industrial relations in recent years, though they have been confined mainly to capital-intensive industries where the benefits are likely to be smaller than in labour-intensive industry.

A less desirable development on the other hand has been the recent upsurge in the number of strikes.

(9) Strikes and Industrial Action

The most powerful weapon available to the Trade Union is the strike. Table 68 shows the number of stoppages beginning each year, the numbers involved, and the days lost.

Table 68. Stoppages in Years (1952–73)

Year	Number of stoppages beginning in year	Number of workers involved 000's	Aggregate number of working days lost beginning in year 000's
1952	1,714	303	1,769
1953	1,746	1,329	2,157
1954	1,989	402	2,441
1955	2,419	599	3,741
1956	2,648	464	2,036
1957	2,859	1,275	8,398
1958	2,629	456	3,461
1959	2,093	522	5,257
1960	2,832	698	3,001
1961	2,686	673	2,998
1962	2,449	4,297	5,757
1963	2,068	455	1,731
1964	2,524	700	2,011
1965	2,354	673	2,906
1966	1,937	414	2,372
1967	2,116	552	2,765
1968	2,378	2,074	4,672
1969	3,116	1,426	6,799
1970	3,888	1,784	10,970
1971	2,228	1,171	13,551
1972	2,497	1,722	23,909
1973	2,873	1,513	7,145

Source: Employment and Productivity.

The trend is unmistakably upwards since 1966 and the reaction to the Industrial Relations Bill suggests that the trend will be maintained, though strikes in protest against the Bill are not included since they are not regarded as arising from an industrial dispute. The majority of strikes are of short duration and involve relatively few workers, and nearly all of them are unofficial or unconstitutional, in that they are in breach of an agreement with an employer or in breach of Union rules. A debate rages about our position in the international league table of strikes, figures being available to support all sides depending upon whether one counts the number of working days lost or the number of strikes or the number of workers directly involved.

Whichever of these indices is used there is no mistaking the increasing industrial unrest that is indicated by the figures for the United Kingdom, and although some industries suffer much more than others the causes of disputes are often the same.

Table 69 shows the causes of strikes occurring in a typical year. Frequently a strike will have more than one cause but here it is allocated under the main one.

Table 69. Causes of Strikes

Wage disputes	1,155
Hours of work	23
Demarcation disputes	57
Disputes over employment or discharge of workers, and personnel questions	511
Working arrangements, rules, and discipline	362
Trade Union status	83
Sympathetic action	37
	2,228

Source: Employment and Productivity

While over half of the disputes arise from wage negotiations other areas of conflict are also important. The fact that so many disputes are allowed to develop into strikes is indicative of the underlying fragility of industrial relations in the United Kingdom, but all the causes listed in the table have existed for many years. Why is the strike weapon invoked more frequently now?

(*a*) The most obvious reason for striking rather than prolonging negotiations is that it works. While most trade-unionists would prefer to negotiate a settlement, the best results may often be secured by striking. This is especially so as management cannot afford a prolonged stoppage owing to the expensive waste of capital and the permanent loss of markets. Moreover, because of the interdependence of various sectors of the economy the effects of a strike soon spread elsewhere and the pressure on employers to settle is all the greater.

(*b*) Possibilities of a negotiated settlement may have been exhausted, especially during an inflationary period when the only acceptable rises are very large.

(*c*) A strike is the only way of bringing public attention to the needs of a particular group of low-paid workers.

(*d*) The increasing welfare payments available to a striker's family, and the income tax rebates payable to the striker himself make a strike a less fearful prospect. Moderates are accordingly less disposed to oppose a strike call.

(*e*) Many feel that there has been a change in the balance of power between

Unions and management, the Unions and their members not only realizing the great strength they possess, but being prepared to use it.

(*f*) A minority of strikes may be politically motivated and others may simply reflect a more irresponsible attitude by various groups of workers.

The effects of strikes are widespread.

(*a*) While a strike is in progress it is not only the output of the participants that is lost but those engaged in processes before and after that that is temporarily stopped. The longer the dispute continues the greater the disruption caused to other parts of the economy, the greater the number of workers that have to be stood off, and the greater the overall loss of production.

(*b*) Perhaps the worst effect of one successful strike is to inspire the next one, either from the same group of workers or another group. One reason for the prolonged Postal Strike of 1971 was the successful outcome to similar action by Local Authority workers. In 1970 the National Union of Teachers was quite open about the lesson to be learnt from more militant industrial sectors.

(*c*) Employers claim that strikes cause not only loss of output but permanent loss of markets. Lord Stokes was emphatic about the damage done to British Leyland profits in 1970 by the chaos resulting from unofficial strikes in the Midlands. The more competitive the markets and the more successful the strike in securing an inflationary rise the greater the damage to markets.

(*d*) The incidence of unofficial strikes often for apparently trivial reasons is completely unpredictable and the disruption caused is correspondingly greater.

The Transport and General Workers Union has calculated that on average each worker loses approximately one-quarter of a working day each year through strike action. Many more days are lost through illness. Such a comparison is, however, irrelevant since a day lost through sickness does not have the same impact as a day lost through strike action. If one man is away from his position on the production line through illness he does not bring the job to a halt and there are no repercussions on the jobs and earnings of men in other industries. Moreover illness among workers in a particular factory will normally spread over the working year in a fairly predictable way and can be catered for accordingly, but days lost through strikes occur at random, and are concentrated in particular areas of the economy.

While the strike is not the only weapon available to the Unions (working to rule, non-co-operation, go-slow being the others and having the same object as the strike) it is the most powerful. But it is something that needs to be used with care: too frequent resort to strike action has led to a hardening of public opinion against the Unions and to a growing belief that almost anything is preferable to capitulation to a strike—public resistance and solidarity during the Electricity Workers work to rule in 1970 and the Postal Strike of 1971 undoubtedly developed out of the frustration of constantly being inconvenienced by strikes. These developments in public opinion have been paralleled by the recent proposals for the reform of industrial relations.

(10) Reform of Industrial Relations

The role of Trade Unions in an industrial society has not been a matter of conscious planning, but has been allowed to develop in response to changing industrial circumstances. The need for a general inquiry into Trade Unions and Trade Associations was increasingly apparent in the early 1960's and was perhaps crystallized by the case of Rookes *v.* Barnard which seemed to imply that to threaten to strike was to threaten an illegal act, contrary to what had previously been understood of the Trades Disputes Act of 1906. As a result, the immunity of Trade Unions was restored by the Trade Disputes Act 1965, and at the same time a full investigation of Trade Unions was planned.

(*a*) *The Royal Commission.* In 1965 a *Royal Commission on Trade Unions and Trade Associations* was appointed under the chairmanship of Lord Donovan. The Donovan Report was published in 1966 and came down heavily in favour of a continuation of the voluntary system of industrial relations rather than the establishment of any legalistic framework of controls and compulsion. The Royal Commission proposed the establishment of the *Commission on Industrial Relations* to supervise industrial relations—and its role was to be essentially one of investigation and advice: it was to have no power of compulsion, a victory for the views of Mr. George Woodcock, an influential member of the Royal Commission, and late chairman of the CIR.

Conservative Party thinking meanwhile was announced in a policy statement, 'Fair Deal at Work', most aspects of which were to be embodied in the Industrial Relations Bill of 1971.

(*b*) *In Place of Strife.* In January 1969 the Labour Government's White Paper *In Place of Strife* drew attention to the weaknesses of the system, the lack of effective bargaining procedures in many industries, the premium it put upon militancy, and so on. It proposed the introduction of various restrictions—a cooling-off period to delay strikes, a secret ballot before certain strikes could go ahead, and even fines on individual workers in some circumstances. The Bill to which the White Paper was to lead was to be the basis of a new era for industrial relations but such was Trade Union opposition to the proposals that they were dropped—except for establishment of the Commission on Industrial Relations in its advisory role.

(*c*) *The Industrial Relations Act.* Upon re-election, one of the earliest initiatives of the Conservatives was to set in motion the reform of industrial relations amid violent opposition from all parts of the labour movement. The immediate need for the Industrial Relations Act was the increasing number of strikes. Almost everyone agreed that they constituted a serious problem: they did not however agree that legislation was the best way of reducing strikes. The Government itself recognized that the promotion of 'freely and responsibly conducted collective bargaining' was the best way to improve industrial relations. But they insisted that the jungle had become so overgrown with abuse and malpractices that a legal framework was necessary to channel energy in the right directions. The main proposals of the Act (clearly based on the American system) included:

(i) The establishment of a code of good industrial relations practice to guide both sides of industry.

(ii) The establishment of the freedom of a worker to join or not to join a registered Trade Union (i.e. the ending of the closed shop).

(iii) Safeguards against unfair dismissal.

(iv) Arrangements for the establishment of an *agency shop*, and arrangement whereby a registered Trade Union represents all employees and is financially supported by them; conscientious objectors may subscribe to a charity instead. This is not so rigid as a pre-entry closed shop.

(v) The presumption that any written collective agreement concluded after the Bill came into force shall be legally binding (like all other contracts) unless it contains a statement to the contrary. It is likely that most agreements will include such a clause and will be binding in honour only.

(vi) The creation of a sytem of Industrial Tribunals and a National Industrial Relations Court to handle disputes over the Bill. The extension of the functions of the Commission for Industrial Relations. The creation of a new Chief Registrar of Trade Unions and Trade Associations to supervise the registrations and rules of those bodies.

(vii) Power for the Government to apply to the National Industrial Relations Court for an order delaying industrial action for sixty days if such action would cause a national emergency.

(viii) Power for the Government to apply to the NIRC for an order for a ballot to be held where industrial action would lead to a national emergency or where there is doubt that it is supported by a majority of employees.

(*d*) *Repeal:* for three years industrial relations were conducted rather unhappily within the framework of the Act. It was repealed in 1974, but the following points emerge from its brief life:

(i) Both sides of industry are in favour of the continuation of the closed shop system since it facilitates bargaining, ensures that all workers contribute towards the Union, and simplifies recruitment for employers. The Government saw the closed shop as an unjustifiable restriction on individual freedom.

(ii) Where Unions and employers have been trying for many years without success to establish acceptable negotiating machinery, it is unlikely that any of the statutory bodies are likely to be immediately successful in tackling the problem.

(iii) Both *In Place of Strife* and the Act made provision for secret ballots in certain circumstances, and this seems a reasonable safeguard against possible intimidation of workers voting on a show of hands, but is strongly opposed as unwarrantable interference by the Unions.

(iv) Similarly the cooling-off period is common to both sets of proposals. There is though no evidence that the imposition of such delays facilitates the resolution of disputes. American experience suggests that cooling-off periods are used by both sides to prepare for a war of attrition—management stockpiling output, workers accumulating savings and reducing financial commitments. Consequently strikes tend to be very prolonged.

(v) There were no provisions in the Act for financial assistance to encourage the amalgamation and natural growth of Unions, which was an important feature of Labour proposals.

(vi) Any Government wishing to 'reform the Trade Unions' finds itself in an almost impossible position: the growth of strikes seems to indicate the weakness of Union control over their members and the proposals are designed to improve that control. But the Unions regard this as interference in their internal affairs and are determined that reform must come from within and may refuse to co-operate in implementing the proposed changes. Part of the difficulty is that the legislation is seen by the Unions as yet another negative attempt to deal with Britain's economic problems, an excuse for the lack of constructive policies in other directions.

(vii) The problem of industrial relations like many other economic problems is more likely to be resolved when the economy is steadily expanding than when it is shackled by restrictions.

(11) Summary of Chapter Fourteen

(1) Trade Unions have a total membership of about ten million, shared between over five hundred unions, and united in the Trades Union Congress.

(2) The old structure of Trade Unions is changing but still apparent. Changes are occurring in response to changes in the industrial environment, but the call for industrial unions is an ill-considered one.

(3) The main functions of the Unions—the furtherance of the interests of their members—remains unaltered as they take an increasingly important part in public affairs.

(4) Wage claims still occupy the bulk of their time and cause much acrimony.

(5) Recent emphasis on relating wage increases to productivity has led to important productivity bargains to eliminate restrictive practices.

(6) Against this desirable change there has been a rapid increase in the number of strikes—evidence of fragile relations between employers and workers.

(7) The reaction to the increasing strikes was embodied in the Industrial Relations Act.

(12) Suggested Further Reading

In Place of Strife (Cmnd 3888), HMSO, 1969.

FLANDERS, A., *Collective Bargaining: Prescription for Change*, Faber & Faber, London, 1968.

Royal Commission of Trade Unions and Employers' Associations, HMSO, 1968.

Exercises Set 14

1. What are the advantages and disadvantages of paying workers on piece-rate systems?

2. 'The introduction of equal pay for women will result in lower wages for men.' Is there any economic basis for this statement?

3. In what ways have the traditional boundaries between Trade Unions been changing in recent years?

4. 'British Trade Unions would be more effective if organized on an industrial basis.' Comment.

5. What is meant by the phrase 'restrictive labour practices'? In what ways are they to the benefit of labour?

6. 'Trade Unions are too weak rather than too strong.' To what extent do you agree with this statement?

7. Why did successive Governments find it necessary to propose the reform of industrial relations in the United Kingdom?

8 'The Industrial Relations Act 1971 created more problems than it solved.' Why?

9. How do you account for the increase in the number of strikes in recent years?

10. 'Each factor of production should earn the value of its marginal product.' Why does practice differ from the theory?

Index